ANNUAL EGYPTOLOGICAL BIBLIOGRAPHY
BIBLIOGRAPHIE ÉGYPTOLOGIQUE ANNUELLE

INTERNATIONAL ASSOCIATION OF EGYPTOLOGISTS
ASSOCIATION INTERNATIONALE DES ÉGYPTOLOGUES

ANNUAL EGYPTOLOGICAL BIBLIOGRAPHY

BIBLIOGRAPHIE ÉGYPTOLOGIQUE ANNUELLE

1972

COMPILED BY/COMPOSÉE PAR

JAC. J. JANSSEN

WITH THE COLLABORATION OF/AVEC LA COLLABORATION DE

INGE HOFMANN

LEIDEN
E. J. BRILL
1976

The editor acknowledges the financial contributions for collecting the material for this volume kindly given by the following institutions :

Ægyptologisk Institut, Københavns Universitet,
Centre d'Études Orientales, Genève,
Deutsches Archäologisches Institut, Berlin-Cairo,
Durham University, Durham,
Egypt Exploration Society, London,
The Griffith Institute, Oxford,
Heidelberger Akademie der Wissenschaften, Heidelberg,
The Metropolitan Museum of Art, New York,
Museum of Fine Arts, Boston, Mass.,
Oosters Genootschap in Nederland, Leiden,
The Oriental Institute, The University of Chicago, Chicago, Ill.,
Schweizerisches Institut für Ägyptische Bauforschung und Altertums-kunde, Cairo,
University of Liverpool, Liverpool,
The University Museum, The University of Pennsylvania, Philadel-phia, Pa.
Uppsala Universitet, Uppsala

Adres van de redacteur / Address of the editor
Adresse du rédacteur / Anschrift des Schriftleiters :

Dr. Jac. J. JANSSEN

Nederlands Instituut voor het Nabije Oosten

Noordeindsplein 4-6
LEIDEN

ISBN 90 04 04522 8

TABLE OF CONTENTS

LIST OF ABBREVIATIONS

1) *periodicals*, Festschriften *and serials* :

Aegyptus : Aegyptus. Rivista Italiana di Egittologia e di Papirologia, Milano 52 (1972); rev. *Sefarad* 34 (1974), 185-186 ([Benito] Ce[lada]).
Address : Università Cattolica (Scuola di Papirologia), Largo A. Gemelli 1, 20123 Milano, Italia.

AJA : American Journal of Archaeology, [New York] 76 (1972).
Address : General Secretary, Archaeological Institute of America, 260 West Broadway, New York, N.Y. 10013, U.S.A.

Antiquity : Antiquity. A Quarterly Review of Archaeology, [Cambridge] 46 (1972).
Address : Heffers Printers Ltd, 104 Hills Road, Cambridge, CB2 1LW, Great Britain.

Archaeology : Archaeology. A Magazine Dealing with the Antiquity of the World, [New York] 25 (1972).
Address : Archaeology, 260 West Broadway, New York, N.Y. 10013, U.S.A.

BASOR : Bulletin of the American Schools of Oriental Research Number 205 (February, 1972), 206 (April, 1972), 207 (October, 1972) and 208 (December, 1972).
Address : American Schools of Oriental Research, Publications Office, 126 Inman Str., Cambridge, Massachusetts 02139, U.S.A.

BIFAO : Bulletin de l'Institut français d'Archéologie orientale, Le Caire 71 (1972) and 72 (1972).
Address : Imprimerie de l'Institut français d'Archéologie orientale, 37 Rue el-Cheikh Aly Youssef (ex-rue Mounira), Le Caire, Égypte (R.A.U.).

BiOr : Bibliotheca Orientalis, Leiden 29 (1972).
Address : Noordeindsplein 4-6, Leiden, Nederland.

BSFE : Bulletin de la Société française d'Égyptologie. Réunions trimestrielles. Communications archéologiques No 63 (Mars 1972); No 64 (Juin 1972); No 65 (Octobre 1972).
Address : Mme. F. Le Corsu, Cabinet d'Égyptologie, Collège de France, 11 Place Marcelin-Berthelot, Paris 5ᵉ, France.

CdE : Chronique d'Égypte. Bulletin périodique de la Fondation égyptologique Reine Élisabeth, Bruxelles XLVII, Nos 93-94 (1972); rev. *Sefarad* 33 (1973), 398-400 ([B.] Ce [lada]).
Address : Fondation égyptologique «Reine Elisabeth», Musées Royaux d'Art et d'Histoire, Parc du Cinquantenaire, B 1040 - Bruxelles, Belgique.

Древний Восток и античный мир : Древний Восток и античный мир. Сборник статей посвященных профессору Всеволоду Игоревичу Авдиеву. Москва, Издательство Московского университета, 1972 (15 × 22cm; 256 p., frontispiece). Pr. руб. 1, коп. 46

Enchoria : Enchoria. Zeitschrift für Demotistik und Koptologie. Herausgegeben von E. Lüddeckens, H.-J. Thissen, K.-Th. Zauzich, in Kommission bei Otto Harrasso-

witz, Wiesbaden 2 (1972); rev. *BiOr* 30 (1973), 244-245 (Richard Holton Pierce).
Address: Otto Harrassowitz, Taunusstrasse 5, Postfach 349, 6200 Wiesbaden, Bundesrepublik Deutschland.

Ex Orbe Religionum: Ex Orbe Religionum. Studio Geo Widengren XXIV Mense Apr. MCMLXXII quo die lustra tredecim feliciter explevit oblata ab collegis, discipulis, amicis, collegae magistro amico congratulantibus. Pars Prior, Lugduni Batavorum, E. J. Brill, 1972 (15.5 × 24 cm.; 479 p., 12 pl., frontispiece).

Forschungen und Berichte: Forschungen und Berichte. Archäologische Beiträge, Berlin 14 (1972). At head of title: Staatliche Museen zu Berlin.
Address: Staatliche Museen zu Berlin, Bodestr. 1-3, 102 Berlin.

GM: Göttinger Miszellen. Beiträge zur ägyptologischen Diskussion, Göttingen Hefte 1, 2, 3 (1972).
Address: Seminar für Ägyptologie der Universität, 34 Göttingen, Prinzenstrasse 21, Bundesrepublik Deutschland.

JAOS: Journal of the American Oriental Society, New Haven, Connecticut 92 (1972).
Address: American Oriental Society, 329 Sterling Memorial Library, Yale Station, New Haven, Connecticut 06250, U.S.A.

JARCE: Journal of the American Research Center in Egypt, Princeton, New Jersey 9 (1972).
Address: J.J. Augustin Publisher, Locust Valley, New York 11560, U.S.A.

JEA: The Journal of Egyptian Archaeology, London 58 (1972); rev. *Sefarad* 33 (1973), 404-411 ([B.] Ce [lada]).
Address: Honorary Treasurer of the Egypt Exploration Society, 2-3 Doughty Mews, London WCIN 2PG, Great Britain.

JEOL: Jaarbericht van het Voorasiatisch-Egyptisch Genootschap Ex Oriente Lux, Leiden VII, No. 22 (1971-1972), 1972; rev. *Sefarad* 33 (1973), 205-206 ([B.] Ce [lada]).
Address: Noordeindsplein 4-6, Leiden, Nederland.

JNES: Journal of Near Eastern Studies, Chicago, Illinois 31 (1972); rev. (fasc. 1-2) *Sefarad* 32 (1972), 418-420 ([B.] Ce [lada]); (fasc. 3-4) *Sefarad* 33 (1973), 412-416 ([B.] Ce [lada]).
Address: University of Chicago Press, 5801 Ellis Avenue, Chicago, Illinois 60637, U.S.A.

Kêmi: Kêmi. Revue de philologie et d'archéologie égyptiennes et coptes, Paris 21 (1971).
Address: Librairie Orientaliste Paul Geuthner, 12 rue Vavin, Paris 6ᵉ, France.

Man, Settlement and Urbanism: Man, Settlement and Urbanism. Proceedings of the Research Seminar in Archaeology and Related Subjects held at the Institute of Archaeology, London University. Edited by Peter J. Ucko, Ruth Tringham and G. W. Dimbleby, London, Duckworth, 1972 (16.1 × 25.4 cm.; XXVIII + 979 p., 8 pl., numerous fig., including maps and plans); rev. *Antiquity* 47 (1973), 269-278 (Gordon R. Willey); *Man* 8 (1973), 484 (Charles C. Kolb).   Pr. £18

MDAIK: Mitteilungen des Deutschen Archäologischen Instituts Abteilung Kairo, Wiesbaden 28 (1972); rev. (Heft 1) *Sefarad* 33 (1973), 416-419 ([B.] Ce [lada]).
Address: Verlag Philipp von Zabern, P.O.B. 4065, Mainz/Rhein, Bundesrepublik Deutschland.

Miscellanea Wilbouriana 1: Miscellanea Wilbouriana 1, Brooklyn, N.Y., The Brooklyn Museum, 1972 (23.4 × 30.6 cm.; VIII + 160 p., 2 plans, 16 fig., 71 ill. (10 in colour), frontispiece in colour); rev. *AJA* 78 (1974), 81-82 (Hans Goedicke); *CdE* XLVIII, No. 96 (1973), 297-300 (Michel Malaise); *JARCE* 11 (1974), 96-98 (David Lorton). Pr. bound $ 28

MNL: Meroitic Newsletter. Bulletin d'Informations meroitiques, [Paris-Montreal] No 9 (June 1972), No 10 (Juillet 1972), No 11 (Décembre 1972).
Address: Jean Leclant, 77 rue Georges Lardennois, F-75019 Paris, France.

Mundus: Mundus. A Quarterly Review of German Research Contributions on Asia, Africa and Latin America. Arts and Science, Stuttgart.
Address: Wissenschaftliche Verlagsgesellschaft mbH, Postfach 40, 7000 Stuttgart 1, Bundesrepublik Deutschland.

Muséon: Le Muséon. Revue d'études orientales, Louvain 85 (1972).
Address: Le Muséon. Imprimerie Orientaliste, B.P. 41, 3000 Louvain, Belgique.

Newsletter ARCE: Newsletter of the American Research Center in Egypt, Princeton, N.J. Nos 80 (January 1972), 81 (April 1972), 82 (July 1972), 83 (October 1972).
Address: 20 Nassau Street, Princeton, N.J. 08540, U.S.A.

OLZ: Orientalistische Literaturzeitung, Berlin 67 (1972).
Address: Akademie-Verlag GmbH, Leipzigerstraße 3-4, 108 Berlin.

Oriens Antiquus: Oriens Antiquus. Rivista del Centro per le Antichità e la Storia dell' Arte del Vicino Oriente, Roma 11 (1972).
Address: Centro per le Antichità e la Storia dell' Arte del Vicino Oriente, Via Caroncini 27, 00197 Roma, Italia.

Orientalia: Orientalia, Commentarii trimestres a facultate studiorum orientis antiqui pontificii instituti biblici in lucem editi in urbe, [Roma] Nova Series 41 (1972).
Address: Pontificium Institutum Biblicum, Piazza del Pilotta 35, I-00187 Roma, Italia.

RdE: Revue d'Égyptologie, Paris 24 (1972) = Mélanges dédiés à Michel Malinine.
Address: Librairie C. Klincksieck, 11 rue de Lille, Paris 7ᵉ, France.

Rivista: Rivista degli Studi Orientali, Roma 47 (1972).
Address: Dott. Giovanni Bardi editore, Salita de crescenzi 16, Roma, Italia.

Spiegel Historiael: Spiegel Historiael. 150 jaar Egyptologie, Bussum Jaargang 7, Nummer 9 (September 1972), 451-512, with colour ill. on cover and ill., maps and fig. in the various articles.

ВДИ: Вестник Древней Истории, Москва 1 (119)- 4 (122), 1972; rev. *GM* Heft 4 (1973), 45-49 (Reinhard Grieshammer).
Address: Москва В-36, ул. Дмитрия Ульнова. Д. 19, Комн. 237, Институт всеобщей Истории, АН СССР.

WZKM: Wiener Zeitschrift für die Kunde des Morgenlandes, Wien 63/64 (1972).
Address: Selbstverlag der Wiener Zeitschrift für die Kunde des Morgenlandes, Universitätsstraße 7/V, A-1010 Wien 1, Österreich.

ZÄS: Zeitschrift für ägyptische Sprache und Altertumskunde, Berlin 98,2 (1972) and 99,1 (1972) = Gedenkschrift für Siegfried Morenz. Teil Ia; rev. (98,2) *Sefarad* 33 (1973), 427-429 ([B.] Ce [ada]) and (99,1) *Sefarad* 34 (1974), 440-446 ([B.] Ce [ada]).
Address: Akademie-Verlag GmbH, Leipzigerstraße 3-4, 108 Berlin.

ZAW : Zeitschrift für die alttestamentliche Wissenschaft, Berlin.
   Address : Walter de Gruyter & Co., Postfach 110240, 1000 Berlin 11.

ZDMG : Zeitschrift der Deutschen Morgenländischen Gesellschaft, Wiesbaden 122 (1972).
   Address : Franz Steiner Verlag GmbH, Bahnhofstrasse 39, Postfach 743, 62 Wiesbaden, Bundesrepublik Deutschland.

2) *other abbreviations* :

AEB :	*Annual Egyptological Bibliography*/*Bibliographie égyptologique annuelle*.	m :	metre(s).
		p. :	page(s).
		pl. :	plate(s).
		publ. :	publication(s).
cfr :	*confer*, compare	pr. :	price.
cm :	centimetre(s)	rev. :	review *or* summary.
col. :	column	⟼ :	above a numeral, this
etc. :	*et cetera*		hieroglyph indicates a
fig. :	figure(s).		monograph.
ill. :	illustration(s).		
km :	kilometre(s).		

ALPHABETICAL LIST OF AUTHORS AND TITLES

72001 ABAD, M., Le Musée Champollion de Figeac, *Archeologia*, Paris No 52 (novembre 1972), 77, with 3 ill.

In the Musée Champollion de Figeac a section is devoted to Champollion, containing some items relating to him personally.
L. M. J. Zonhoven

ABDALLAH, A. B., see our number 72301.

72002 ACKROYD, Peter R., Père Roland de Vaux, *Palestine Exploration Quarterly*, London 104 (1972), 75-76.

Obituary article. Compare our number 71654.

72003 AHARONI, Y., Beersheba, *Bible et Terre Sainte*, Paris 141 (Mai 1972), 8-16, with a plan, 1 fig. and 19 ill. (3 on cover).

General article on the excavations at Beersheba by the University of Tel Aviv. Several Egyptian objects have been discovered, among which bronze statuettes of a goddess and a sphinx (ill. on cover) and a bone amulet shaped as the Horus falcon (ill. 13).

72004 AHITUV, S., Did Ramesses II Conquer Dibon?, *Israel Exploration Journal*, Jerusalem 22 (1972), 141-142.

Against Kitchen (compare our number 64274) the author argues that *tbn*, mentioned in the inscription on the east wall of the court of Ramses II in the Luxor temple, is not Dibon, while other places there occurring, *bwtrt* excepted, are also not to be located in Moab.

72005 AHITUV, S., The 𓈗𓏲𓏒 measure, *JEA* 58 (1972), 302.

The quantity of the *mni* measure can be determined by the price of honey in Egypt in the time of Ramesses IX, and was equal to 30 *hnw* (i.e. c. 15 litres).
E. Uphill

72006 AHITUV, Shmuel, ‏לדיהויה של פיתום‎, *in* : ‏המקרא ותולדות ישראל‎ / Bible and Jewish History. Studies in Bible and Jewish History Dedicated to the Memory of Jacob Liver, Tel-Aviv, Tel-Aviv University, Faculty of Humanities, 1971, 157-160, with an English summary on p. XVIII.

"The Location of Pithom".
The author argues that Pithom is not be located at Tell el-Ratâba, as Gardiner proposed, but at Tell el-Maskhûta. Apart

from other arguments such as an inscription from the latter place mentioning a *pr-'Itm*, whereas no such building is known from the former, the author points out that Herodotus states Pithom to be an Arabian town, while the silver bowls recently found there (cfr Rabinowitz, *JNES* 15, 1956, 1-15) were dedicated to an Arabian goddess.

ALAND, Kurt, see our number 72495.

72007 ALDRED, Cyril, Akhenaten. Pharaoh of Egypt — a new study, London, Sphere Books Ltd, [1972] (13.2 × 19.8 cm; 222 p., 37 ill. on 24 pl., 16 colour ill. on 8 pl., colour ill. on cover). Series : Abacus.   Pr. 75 p.

Paperback edition of our number 68013.

72008 ALEEM, A. A., Fishing Industry in Ancient Egypt, *Proceedings of the Royal Society of Edinburgh*. Section B (Biology), Edinburgh 73 (1971-1972), 1972, 333-343, with 6 fig. and 1 pl.

General article about fishing gear and methods in ancient Egypt. The author briefly mentions harpoon and spear, hooks and lines, various types of nets, etc. (with drawings). There follow notes on fishing boats and fisheries economy, and remarks on the evolution of fish-catching techniques during Egyptian history.

72009 el-ALFI, Mostafa, Recherches sur quelques scarabées de Ramsès II, *JEA* 58 (1972), 176-181, with 6 fig. and 1 pl.

A comparison between motifs and texts on scarabs and monumental art. The Mnevis bull cult is shown on a scarab in Cairo CCG 36437 in similar style to such stelae as Cairo No. Prov. 2/2/21/1, depicting the king offering incense to the bull of Rē'-Atum. Similarly scarab Fraser 302 is placed alongside a relief at Abu Simbel to demonstrate the depiction of the royal name monogram as a female figure, and other scarabs mentioning the royal statues, or war scenes and religious rites.   *E. Uphill*

72010 ALI, Ahmed M., Meroitic Settlement of the Butana (Central Sudan), *Man, Settlement and Urbanism* 639-646, with 2 maps and 1 plan.

The author studies the Meroitic occupation of the Butana, of which Musawwarat became the religious and Naga the administrative centres. All settlements in the plain and on the sandstone plateau, except for these two, consist of a single-chambered temple and a *hafir*, an earth embarkment for storing large quantities of water from the summer rainfall.

From the sharp difference between the skill as reflected by the temple buildings and their reliefs and that of the poor funerary structures, as well as from from the absence of domestic buildings in the area (except at Naga) the author concludes that the population consisted of nomads. Temples, and probably *hafirs*, were built by the kings, who by this means controlled the area.

72011 ALLAM, S., De l'adoption en Égypte pharaonique, *Oriens Antiquus* 11 (1972), 277-295.

After pointing out that various texts incorrectly have been connected with adoption the author discusses the contents of Pap. Ashmolean 1945.96 (the so-called Adoption Papyrus), Pap. Louvre E 7832, the Nitocris Adoption Stela and the Pap. dém. Louvre E 10935. The first one contains according to Allam an *adoptio mortis causa*, the second an imitative *adrogatio* (the adopted person being an adult); the adoption of the God's Wives of Amon is an *adoptio inter vivos*, while the last text in fact does not contain an adoption at all.

72012 ALLEN, James P., The Function of *jw*, *Newsletter ARCE* No. 83 (October 1972), 24.

Abstract of a paper.
As an explanation for the radical change in the role of *iw* between Middle and Late Egyptian is suggested its basic role as a sentence-predicator. *L. M. J. Zonhoven*

72013 ALTENMÜLLER, Brigitte, Re und Herischef als "*nb dšr.w*", *GM* Heft 2 (1972), 9-13.

The epithet *b3 imy dšrw.f*, originally an attribute of Re as god of the setting sun, was eventually re-interpreted as a reference to blood, and applied to Herishef *nb dšrw*, in whose Heracleopolitan cult the blood of slaughtered cattle played an important role. Herishef's attribute *k3 '3t* (*CT* V, 257e) is explained in *BD* 175 as a blister which developed when Re crowned Osiris with the burning-hot atef-crown; when lanced, the secretion formed Herishef's sacred lake at Heracleopolis. *Dieter Mueller*

72014 ALTENMÜLLER, Hartwig, Die Bedeutung der "Gotteshalle des Anubis" "im Begräbnisritual, *JEOL* VII/No. 22 (1971-1972), 1972, 307-317, with 1 fig.

The author discusses Grdseloff's suggestion that the "text of purification" and the "place of embalmment" are to be identified with the "god's hall (*sh-ntr*) of Anubis", and this hall with the valley temple of the pyramids. In the hall, the outer appearance of which cannot be derived from the determinative, the dead was purified. Inscriptions to the burial scenes from the New Kingdom suggest that it was situated near the entrance of the temple complex, and from the pictures it appears to be a building with a ḫkr-frieze, The author argues that the hall of Anubis has to be sought in the valley temple, near the entrance.

72015 ALTENMÜLLER, Hartwig, Bemerkungen zur frühen und späten Bauphase des Djoserbezirkes in Saqqara, *MDAIK* 28 (1972), 1-12.

The striking similarity between the original design of Djoser's tomb and the so-called southern mastaba suggests a correspondence between the two. After recent investigations of the early dynastic cemetery at Abydos have shown that each royal burial was supplemented by a separate tomb for the ka-statue, a similar relationship may be assumed for the two main structures of Djoser's funerary precinct; from the Fourth Dynasty onward, the statue was moved to the pyramid, but entombed in a separate chamber.

During the second phase of construction, Djoser's tomb was converted into a pyramid, and the precinct extended toward the north. The vast space between the pyramid and the northern enclosure wall contains an elevated platform with a square indentation in the center. Since both Djoser's pyramid and the funerary complex of Userkaf are oriented toward this platform, it may be assumed that it once served as a base for an obelisk. This would make the extension the oldest sun-temple known so far.   *Dieter Mueller*

72016 ALTENMÜLLER, Hartwig, Die Texte zum Begräbnisritual in den Pyramiden des Alten Reiches, Wiesbaden, Otto Harrassowitz, 1972 (21.9 × 30.9 cm; XII + 296 p., 1 folded pl.) = Ägyptologische Abhandlungen, Band 24; rev. *Mundus* 9 (1973), 99-100 (Waltraud Guglielmi); *Orientalia* 43 (1974), 426-429 (Dieter Mueller).   Pr. DM 63

Die Texte der Pyramiden wurden in Einzelabschnitten, in Phasen niedergeschrieben. Bei Unas und Sesostrisanch (Mastaba Lischt) bestimmte Verfasser drei längere Abschnitts- (mit Spruch-)folgen und die "Frühe Fassung" der Sprüche. Letztgenannte Sprüche dienten zum Opfer- und zum Begräbnisritual, besonders die dramatischen Texte und die mythologischen Rezitationstexte. In den Hymnen wird das Ritualgeschehen dem Gott berichtet.

Die Bildfassung des Begräbnisrituals ist in den Privatgräbern des Mittleren und Neuen Reiches belegt. Altenmüller stellte eine Kongruenz her zwischen den Pyramidentexten und diesen

Bildern, namentlich der "Späten Gruppe" aus unserer Nummer 63467. Seine Analyse ergab drei Phasen : Riten während der Beisetzung der Mumie, Riten mit der Statue und Schutzriten. Mit den Hauptgöttern Re, Horus, Thot und Seth sind vier Priester identisch. Die "Frühe Fassung" (Unas) geht wohl auf die Zeit des Sahure zurück, darin verwertetes Textgut vielleicht auf die erste Dynastie. *M. Heerma van Voss*

AMBROSINO, C., see our number 72406.

72017 AMIET, Pierre, Les ivoires achéménides de Suse, *Syria*, Paris 49 (1972), 167-191 and 319-337, with 4 pl. and 71 ill. and fig.

In this study of a group of Achaemenid ivories from Susa, preserved in the Louvre Museum, the author distinguishes a series in Egyptian or mixed Egyptian-Persian style (p. 319-324). Most of them are small fragments. Among them we mention : the head of a statuette (Pl. VI, 6; Louvre Sb 9452), in Saite style; a plaquette representing a servant with an animal upon his shoulders (Pl. VI, 5; Louvre Sb 3722); a Nubian bearing a vessel (Pl. VI, 7; Louvre Sb 3723); a feather-crowned cartouche with some hieroglyphs, probably purely decorative (fig. 35).

72018 ANGEL, J. Lawrence, Biological Relations of Egyptian and Eastern Mediterranean Populations during Pre-dynastic and Dynastic Times, *Journal of Human Evolution*, London and New York 1 (1972), 307-313, with 4 tables.

The author studies the spread of *falciparum* malaria from Greece and Italy, crossing the flow of genes from Africa northward, and the influences of it on the Egyptian population. Reprinted in : Population Biology of the Ancient Egyptians. Edited by D. R. Brothwell [and] B. A. Chiarelli, London and New York, Academic Press, 1973.

72019 Anonymous, Department of Egyptian Antiquities. Acquisitions, January to June 1970, *The British Museum Quarterly*, London 36 (1971-1972), 63-64.

Five small objects are listed.

72020 Anonymous, Profesor Antonio García y Bellido (1903-1972), *Ampurias*, Barcelona 33-34 (1971-72), 433-441, with a portrait.

Obituary notice, followed by a bibliography.

72021 Anonymous, "It will be thy counsel that causeth the work to be accomplished", *The Freight Forwarder*, Richmond, Surrey 23, No. 1 (March 1972), 15-18, with 2 ill. (one on cover).

Article about the insurance and shipment of the objects intended for the Tutankhamon exhibition in the British Museum.

The Freight Forwarder is published by the Institute of Freight Forwarders Ltd, Suffield House, 9 Paradise Road, Richmond, Surrey, Great Britain.

72022 Anonymous, Jahresbericht des Deutschen Archäologischen Instituts für 1970. Abteilung Kairo, *Archäologischer Anzeiger*, Berlin (1971), 1971/72, XIX-XXI.

Survey of the activities of the DAIK and its members, particularly the excavations at Aswân and Qurna.

72023 Anonymous, Les journées internationales d'études méroitiques de Berlin-Est. 6-12 Septembre 1971, *MNL* No 11 (Décembre 1972), 30-31.

Report on the Meroitic Congres at Berlin in 1971.
For the lectures and the discussions see now Fritz Hintze, Sudan im Altertum. 1. Internationale Tagung für meroitische Forschungen in Berlin 1971, Berlin, Akademie-Verlag, 1973 (= Meroitica 1).

72024 Anonymous, Gamal Mehrez, 1918-1972, *Newsletter ARCE* No. 81 (April 1972), 3.

Obituary notice.

72025 Anonymous, [Le Comte Jacques Pirenne], *BSFE* No 65 (Octobre 1972), 9.

Obituary notice. See our number 72814.

72026 Anonymous, [Siegfried Schott], *BSFE* No 63 (Mars 1972), 5.

Obituary notice. See our number 71652.

72027 Anonymous, Siegfried Schott. 20. August 1897 - 29. Oktober 1971, *Informationsblatt der deutschsprachigen Ägyptologie*, Berlin Heft 3 (Januar 1972), 3.

Obituary notice. See our number 71652.

72028 Anonymous, La table ronde du CNRS, Paris, 29 Juin - 1er Juillet 1972, sur les "Aspects semantiques du Méroitique", *MNL* No 11 (Décembre 1972), 32-33.

Brief report on a conference at Paris concerning semantic aspects of the Meroitic language.

72029 Anonymous, Timna : Inscription de Ramsès III, *Revue Biblique*, Paris 79 (1972), 601-602.

Short description of an inscription of Ramses III.

72030 ANUS, Pierre [et] Ramadan SAʿAD, Habitations de prêtres dans le temple d'Amon de Karnak, *Kêmi* 21 (1971), 217-238, with 3 pl., 4 ill., 3 plans (2 folding) and 13 fig. (4 folding).

Cet article décrit la partie Est des fouilles à l'angle Sud du Lac sacré. Six maisons rectangulaires contiguës sans mur mitoyen se suivent le long de l'enceinte "de Thoutmosis III". Elles ont subi un incendie et des remaniements. L'alignement se continuait au nord de la zone fouillée. Le gros œuvre en briques crues s'accompagnait d'éléments de grès, de bois et de mortier au plâtre.
La IIᵉ maison pourra être restaurée; elle appartenait au Père divin Ameneminet, voisin du Prophète d'Amon Ankhefen-khonsou. La relative exiguïté, le style précieux des objets, correspondraient à des "logements de fonction" pour la durée de service des prêtres. Une stèle et un linteau y rappellent des dévotions personnelles. Des fragments de stèles nomment Aménophis III et Ramsès IV, mais la plupart des documents trouvés remontent aux IXᵉ et VIIIᵉ siècles av. J.-C.

J. Custers

ANUS, Pierre, see also our number 72405.

72031 Archäologisches Lexikon zur Bibel. Herausgegeben von Abraham Negev. Deutsche Bearbeitung Joachim Rehork, München-Wien-Zürich, Kunstverlag Edition Praeger, [1972] (14.3 × 21.9 cm; 344 p., 106 ill., 3 fig., 9 plans, maps on endpapers).

We did not see the original French edition published by Robert Maillard. Several lemmata deal with subjects from pharaonic Egypt. We mention, for example, under the A: Abydos, Ächtungstexte, Ägypten, Amarnabriefe, (Tell el-) Amarna. In other lemmata references to Egypt as well.

72032 ARMELAGOS, George J., James H. MIELKE, Kipling H. OWEN, Dennis P. van GERVEN, John R. DEWEY, Paul Emil MAHLER, Bone Growth and Development in Prehistoric Populations from Sudanese Nubia, *Journal of Human Evolution*, London and New York 1 (1972), 89-119, with 20 fig., 2 maps, 9 tables and 3 ill. on 2 pl.

Skelettmaterial von Angehörigen der meroitischen Kultur, der X-Gruppe und der christlichen Kultur wird untersucht hinsichtlich der Knochenentwicklung und der altersbedingten Veränderungen der inneren Struktur der Femora.
Wieder abgedruckt in: Population Biology of the Ancient Egyptians. Edited by D. R. Brothwell [and] B. A. Chiarelli, London and New York, Academic Press, 1973.

Inge Hofmann

72033 ARNOLD, Dieter, Bericht über die vom Deutschen Archäologischen Institut Kairo im *Mnṯw-ḥtp*-Tempel und in El-Târif unternommenen Arbeiten, *MDAIK* 28 (1972), 13-31, with 5 plans (1 folding), 3 fig. and 16 pl.

The contination of the clearing operations in the temple of Mentuhotep at Deir el-Bahari has led to the discovery of two new chambers filled with wooden models of ships and houses. The excavation of the royal tomb at Saff el-Dawâba, presumed to be that of Inyotef III, revealed the remains of a big courtyard by numerous secondary tombs and ending in a colonnaded façade, behind which lie three tomb chambers. Sondage work at Abu Majit east of the Saff el-Dawâba has led to the discovery of two small tombs of the XIth Dynasty.

Dieter Mueller

72034 ARNOLD, Dieter, Neue Funde aus dem Mentuhotep-Tempel von Deir el-Bahari, *Antike Welt*, Küsnacht-Zürich 3, Heft 3 (1972), 26-30, with 7 ill.

Survey of the recent work by the DAIK in the Mentuhotep temple, mentioning: study of its reliefs; the find of three deposits, among which an unexplained faience object shaped like a plant-sceptre, bundles of linen cloth, small bronze figures and faience vessels with their stands; and, in the corridor, two rooms filled with 500 small wooden figures of moderate quality, remains of models stolen before the New Kingdom.

72035 ARNOLD, Dorothea, Weiteres zur Keramik von el-Târif. Saff el Dawâba 1970/71, *MDAIK* 28 (1972), 33-46, with 7 fig., 4 pl. and 1 colour pl.

The pottery from the XIth Dynasty tomb at Saff el-Dawâba, though obviously related to that from the Asasif, is clearly far less advanced than the latter, which can be dated to the reign of Mentuhotep-Nebhepetre. None of the typical beer-and-water jugs have been found there, and the origin of these vessels remains problematical.   *Dieter Mueller*

72036 ASSELBERGHS, Henri, Beschouwingen over Religie, Cultuur en Kunst in Egypte, III: De nauw verwante wortels van Religie en Kunst, *JEOL* VII / No. 22 (1971-72), 1972, 247-254, with 9 ill. on 3 pl.

"L'étroite affinité originelle de la religion et de l'art".
L'Égyptien s'exprime dans l'art, dès le Néolithique, par des formes réelles, agréables à voir et pour ainsi dire enjouées. Il y manifeste sa recherche d'un monde métaphysique ordonné. Les circonstances l'ont amené à un style mesuré, unissant

l'esprit du Delta et celui de la Vallée, respectivement concret et abstrait. L'architecture funéraire aboutit ainsi aux grandioses complexes des pyramides. L'émulation la fécondera encore pendant l'histoire, sans jamais aplanir la dualité complémentaire. La tradition plastique africaine culmine dans la fine statuette abydénienne de *heb-sed* en ivoire (Brit. Museum). Par la suite, la découverte de l'espace et du temps produira une conception nouvelle de la statuaire, construisant l'œuvre suivant des aspects pris à angle droit. Elle est issue du bas-relief aux hiéroglyphes. La sélection réitérée des éléments rénovera, en épurant leur caractère, non seulement l'art, mais la religion et l'État. Un monde intérieur permanent tisse ces trois phénomènes en une culture; l'effort de style y restera une pulsation essentielle.

J. Custers

72037 ASSMANN, Jan, Die "Häresie" des Echnaton : Aspekte der Amarna-Religion, *Saeculum*, Freiburg/München 23 (1972), 109-126.

The author discusses in his inaugural lecture the problem whether indeed, as is at present communis opinio, Akhnaton merely elevated the old sun-religion to a position of uniqueness, without introducing anything essentially new.

Assmann first sketches the traditional sun-religion from representations and hymns, pointing out the conflicting tendencies : multiplication of divine figures as against subordination of various divinities under a supreme god. The hymns identify life on earth with the process of the sun-course, attempting to connect the conflicting tendencies by "temporization of essence", that is, by placing the unity in primordial times.

Against these concepts the Amarna "heresy" (in fact more exclusive, i.e., orthodox, than the traditional religion) teaches that there is only one god, Aton, more the light- than the sun-god. The parousia of the god in light is an all-changing concept : the god does not speak anymore in the texts; earth is not anymore equalized in the cult with the sky, but contrasted to it as the object of the sun's rule. No more allusions to primordial times; multitude is liquidated; Creator and creation are almost identical, the latter merely existing in the sight of the former. In the king all forms of personal relations between god and human beings are monopolized; for him alone Aton is a personal god.

In the last section the author mentions the later "personal piety" as the successor of Akhnaton's piety, and the recurrence to the dialectical concepts of unity and multitude. By the Amarna "heresy" the traditional religion has not been reformed but it became more self-conscious.

72038 ASSMANN, Jan, Die Inschrift auf dem äußeren Sarkophag-deckel des Merenptah, *MDAIK* 28 (1972), 47-73, with 1 folding pl.

The lid of the outer coffin of Merenptah in his tomb in the Valley of the Kings bears an inscription of unusual length. It is accompanied by a representation of the king surrounded by various gods, and strikingly resembles a stela. The text itself consists of twenty-six lines with a unique hymn of the goddess Neith to the dead king. The monument is reproduced in a drawing; the inscriptions are transcribed and translated. Copious notes on the text and its interpretation conclude the article.   *Dieter Mueller*

72039 ASSMANN, Jan, Neith spricht als Mutter und Sarg (Inter-pretation und metrische Analyse der Sargdeckelinschrift des Merenptah), *MDAIK* 28 (1972), 115-139.

Continuation of our preceding No. The author describes the structure of the text and connects its subdivisions with various funerary rites.   *Dieter Mueller*

72040 ASSMANN, Jan, Palast oder Tempel? Überlegungen zur Architektur und Topographie von Amarna, *JNES* 31 (1972), 143-155.

The writer disagrees with the arguments set forth in *JNES* 29, 151-166 (our No. 70540), in favour of the great central stone structure at Amarna having been a vast temple, possibly the *pr itn* often mentioned in the inscriptions. He would rather see it as the setting for a novel kind of worship in which the common people venerated a Triad of God, King and Queen, while the Kiosque that the royal family visits had the function of the traditional barque station.   *E. Uphill*

ASSMANN, Jan, see also our number 72537.

72041 ASTOUR, Michael C., Some Recent Works on Ancient Syria and the Sea Peoples, *JAOS* 92 (1972), 447-459.

A review article of our numbers 68185, 68186 and 69052.

ATHANASIUS of Qûs, see our number 72059.

ATIYA, Aziz Suryal, see our number 72291.

72042 ATZLER, Michael, Ein ägyptisches Reliefbruchstück des Königs Alexander IV., *Antike Kunst*, Bern 15 (1972), 120-121, with 1 ill. on pl.

Publication of a relief fragment of unknown provenance in a private collection. The piece is inscribed with hieroglyphs, among which the name of Alexander IV, the son of Alexander the Great and Roxane, in a cartouche. The author lists other occurrences of his name.

72043 ATZLER, M., Einige Bemerkungen zu ▯ und ⊗ im Alten Reich, *CdE* XLVII, Nos 93-94 (1972), 17-44.

L'auteur cherche à établir le sens exact des mots *nìwt* et *hwwt*, traduits généralement par ville et domaine. Par une demonstration toute au conditionnel, il vaut prouver que le premier désignerait toute concentration d'habitants (la notion de "ville" étant inconnue à l'Égypte) et que le second exprimerait un statut particulier de la terre (y compris des lieux habités). Il s'agirait de fondations royales à destination non obligatoirement funéraire relevant d'une administration centrale appelée *hww.t* *'3.t*.   *Ph. Derchain*

72044 ATZLER, M., Randglossen zur ägyptischen Vorgeschichte, *JEOL* VIII / No. 22 (1971-1972), 1972, 228-246.

The author argues that the alleged contrast between agriculturists and nomads in the Egyptian Prehistoric Period has never existed; there are no indications whatever for nomadism in the neolithic cultures.

First the climate and its fluctuations and the landscape in the Nile valley and the surrounding desert areas are described. Everywhere possibilities for fishing, hunting, cattle-breeding and agriculture appear to have been present.

Then the neolithic sites and the results of their excavations are discussed, and once more no indications for nomadism are found, neither in Upper- nor in Lower-Egypt.

In the last pages the author adduces arguments for the refutation of Ricke's theory that the panelled facade as seen in the *srh* was Upper-Egyptian and reflected a wood-and-mat construction, and that this architectural feature would indicate a nomadic way of life.

ATZLER, Michael, see also our number 72765.

72045 AVNER, U., Nahal Roded, *Israel Exploration Journal*, Jerusalem 22 (1972), 158, with 1 ill. on a pl.

Mention of the discovery of an inscription containing prenomen and nomen of Ramses III on the rock cliff of Nahal Roded (Wadi Radadi).

72046 BACON, Edward, Tutankhamun's Treasures, *The Illustrated London News*, London 260/6885 (April 1972), 39-47, with 17 ill. (11 in colour) and colour ill. on cover.

General article about the Tutankhamon exhibition in London. The article is preceded by an interview of Sir John Wolfenden, director and principal librarian of the British Museum, by Nicolas Wright.

72047 BADAWY, Alexander, A Monumental Gateway for a Temple of King Sety I. An Ancient Model Restored, *Miscellanea Wilbouriana 1*, 1-20, with 2 plans, 11 fig. and 13 ill. [including frontispiece in colour].

Study of a model (mentioned by Breasted, *Ancient Records* III, 99-101) representing the approach to a sanctuary erected or projected for erection by Seti I (Brooklyn acc. No. 49.183), measuring 28 to 87.5 to 112 cm. The inscriptions on three sides of the block describe the pieces lost from the superstructure, of which only the sockets are left, thus enabling a reconstruction. These pieces are : pylons, flagstaffs (for which no sockets are available), obelisks, four sphinxes and two standing statues. A particularity of the model is the staircase in front of the temple.
Badawy describes the principles according to which he reconstructed the model, discusses its scale, and studies its purpose, which was probably connected with the foundation ritual. The author also gives copies of the texts with translations, interpreting the scenes as related to the sun's journey through the upper and lower skies. The model may represent a temple built at Heliopolis or at Tell el-Yahûdîya, where it has been found.
Compare our number 72599.

72048 BAINES, John, R. T. Rundle Clark's Papers on the Iconography of Osiris, *JEA* 58 (1972), 286-295.

These consist of a set of notes aimed at relating representational forms of the god to cult actions or stages in the myths, and would have included a typology of these forms. There is also a notebook begun in Oct. 1967, dealing with Osiris in the Coffin Texts and containing about forty pages of notes. Chapter subjects include such items as : The Nature of the God, Osiris as funerary deity in the *Pyramid Texts*, the rites of Khoiak and the New Year, the Lamentations and Relations with other cultures. A brief bibliography lists Rundle Clark's five published Egyptological works.   *E. Uphill*

72049 BAINES, John, Further remarks on statuettes of Atum, *JEA* 58 (1972), 303-306.

Consisting of a number of corrections and additions to the earlier article (our No. 70031) refuting among other things the author's previous statement (p. 140) that only Atum is shown as old, Hornung's study on the ageing sun-god being cited.
          E. Uphill

72050 BAKRY, Ḥassan S. K., Akhenaten at Hēliopolis, *CdE* XLVII, Nos. 93-94 (1972), 55-67, with 4 ill., 3 fig. and 1 plan.

L'auteur donne quelques indications sur des trouvailles occasionnelles faites depuis une quinzaine d'années dans l'actuelle Héliopolis ('Ain Chams), notemment une stèle de style amarnien, un fragment de relief ayant conservé la main d'Akhenaton, ainsi que quelques blocs (dont une "talatat") provenant de l'ancienne muraille fatimide du Caire. En annexe, il dresse l'inventaire sommaire de trouvailles faites depuis 1957 sur un chantier cairote, dont une grande jarre au nom de Siptah (à ajouter à la liste des monuments de ce roi réunis par Vandier, notre No 71586). *Ph. Derchain*

72051 BAKRY, Hassan S. K., A Family of High-Priests of Alexandria and Memphis, *MDAIK* 28 (1972), 75-77, with 1 fig. and 2 pl.

Publication of a limestone torso discovered in 1946 in the district of Ghorbal and now in the Graeco-Roman Museum at Alexandria (No. 27806). It represents the highpriest Padibast, who held office in the main temples of Memphis and Alexandria, and was apparently related to the Psherenptah whose statues were discovered by E. Breccia in 1905/06 in the Serapeum at Alexandria. *Dieter Mueller*

72052 BAQUÉS ESTAPÉ, Lorenzo, Catálogo inventario de las piezas egipcias del Museo Episcopal de Vic, *Ampurias*, Barcelona 33-34 (1971-72), 209-250, with 10 ill.

Catalogue of 46 Egyptian objects preserved in the collection of the Episcopal Museum at Vich (Catalonia).
After an introduction describing the origin of the collection the author deals with each of the objects, providing the technical data, a description and some observations. The objects are: a number of small figures of divinities, mostly in bronze; 8 scarabs, among which a heart scarab; some amulets, shawabtis and statuettes; animal figures; fragments of mummy cartonnage and a mummy mask; a copy of the *Book of the Dead* from the XXIst or XXIInd Dynasty; an anthropoid sarcophagus from a chantress of Amon, dated to the period of the XXVIth to XXXth Dynasties. The last piece, which may be the most important, is extensively discussed (p. 240-249).
Some non-Egyptian objects of the collection are briefly mentioned.

72053 BARB, Alphonse A., Magica Varia, *Syria*, Paris 49 (1972), 343-370, with 1 fig., 8 ill. and 2 pl.

Although beyond the scope of the *AEB*, the article is mentioned since it contains important remarks on the roles of the ibis and the scarab in Graeco-Roman magic.

72054 BARGUET, Paul, L'Am-Douat et les funérailles royales, *RdE* 24 (1972), 7-11, with 3 fig.

S'efforçant de relier la symbolique abstruse du livre de l'Am-Douat à une réalité cultuelle, l'auteur suggère que les différentes étapes de la course nocturne du soleil peuvent être mises en parallèle avec les phases des funérailles royales, telles qu'on peut les reconstituer d'après les monuments et les textes. Il établit ainsi, entre autre, une équivalence entre le symbole du double lion Aker entourant l'ovale où repose le cadavre du Soleil-Osiris et les sphynx qui montent la garde par paires aux portes du temple de la vallée de Khéphren, entre le serpent de la 12e heure et la tombe, la renaissance dans le ventre de Nout et le dépôt de la momie dans le sarcophage (voir à ce sujet Schott, *RdE* 17 [1965], 81-87 = notre No 65477), etc.

Ph. Derchain

72055 BARGUET, Paul, L'œuvre de Champollion, *Archeologia*, Paris No 52 (novembre 1972), 30-36, with 11 ill.

Survey of the scientific work of Champollion, particularly during his journey to Egypt.

72056 BARNS, John W. B., Some Readings and Interpretations in Sundry Egyptian Texts, *JEA* 58 (1972), 159-166, with 2 fig.

In *Inscriptions du Ouadi Hammamat*, No. 191, the writer would read *irt ḥw* as "making a strike" not "a great rain-storm", which fits the context much better. He also gives a continuous translation of Kagemni, 1, 3-12, differing from Gardiner in some respects, and discusses points in Sinuhe, P. Westcar, Gebel Barkal Stela, the Taking of Joppa, Doomed Prince, Wenamun and Setne.   *E. Uphill*

72057 BARTA, Winfried, Der Epilog der Götterlehre von Memphis, *MDAIK* 28 (1972), 79-84.

The words in the middle of l. 61 of the Memphite Theology are to be read *šnwt nṯryt is st wrt* "the divine granary is the Great Throne", identifying Ptah-Tatenen (the divine granary) with the Mother Goddess (the Great Throne) in his temple at Memphis.   *Dieter Mueller*

BARTA, Winfried, see also our number 72687.

BARTSON, Lester J., see our number 72295.

72058 BASS, George F., A History of Seafaring Based on Underwater Archaeology, London, Thames and Hudson, 1972 (21.5 × 27 cm; 320 p., 137 fig. including maps and plans, 369 ill. [150 in colour]); rev. *Antiquity* 47 (1973), 165 (Joan du Plat Taylor).   Pr. £ 6

The first chapter, on the earliest seafarers in the Mediterranean and the Near East (by the editor himself) contains short sections on ships and seafaring in ancient Egypt (see p. 15-16 and 18-21). There are also representations of wall scenes and objects from Egypt on the plates and in drawing.

A Dutch edition (Geschiedenis van de Scheepvaart) has appeared in 1973 (series : De Boer Maritieme Handboeken).

72059 BAUER, Gertrud, Athanasius von Qūs. Qilādat at-taḥrīr fī 'ilm at-tafsīr. Eine koptische Grammatik in arabischer Sprache aus dem 13./14. Jahrhundert, Freiburg im Breisgau, Klaus Schwarz Verlag, 1972 (14.8 × 21 cm; 349 + 92 p.) = Islamkundliche Untersuchungen 7.

The first part of this study deals with Coptic grammaticians from the 13th and 14th century A.D. in general, with life and works of bishop Athanasius of Qûs, whom the author dates to the second half of the 13th or to the 14th century, with the manuscripts of his well known grammar, its language, contents and characteristics, and its grammatical terminology.

The second part consists of the Arabic and Coptic text of the Qilâdat, both in its Bohairic and its Sahidic version. The former is given on the left, the corresponding part of the latter on the right hand page. They are followed by the German translation. The last part contains three glossaries : one to Arabic grammatical terms and some particularities of the vocabulary, one to Coptic words not occurring in Crum's *Coptic Dictionary*, and one to Greek words.

Bibliography on p. 344-349.

72060 BAUMEISTER, Theofried, Martyr Invictus. Der Martyrer als Sinnbild der Erlösung in der Legende und im Kult der frühen koptischen Kirche. Zur Kontinuität des ägyptischen Denkens, Münster, Verlag Regensburg, 1972 (15 × 23 cm; 220 p.) = Forschungen zur Volkskunde begründet von Georg Schreiber herausgegegeben von Bernhard Kötting und Alois Schröer, 46; rev. *Orientalia* 43 (1974), 147-148 (H. Quecke); *Rivista* 48 (1973/74), 271-276 (Tito Orlandi).   Pr. DM 50

This study of the function of the martyr in the Coptic church discusses in chapter 2 the problem raised by Morenz (see our number 2991) to what extent Coptic martyr legends are influenced by the ancient Egyptian belief concerning the death, particularly the conception of the integrity of the body. The author sketches the cult of the dead in Pharaonic, Graeco-Roman and Christian Egypt, the development from this cult to the worship of martyrs, and the presence of ancient Egyptian concepts in the latter, stressing that there is more adaptation of Christian-Jewish belief to Egyptian ideas than simple continuity of these ideas.

The other chapters deal with the character of Coptic martyr legends in general and the Greek influence.

Indexes on p. 207-219.

72061 BELL, Lanny, The New Egyptian Mummy Room of the University Museum, *Newsletter ARCE* No. 80 (January 1972), 32.

Abstract of a paper.

The new Egyptian mummy room of the University Museum Philadelphia exhibits private burials as though *in situ*, provided with the relevant objects.   *L. M. J. Zonhoven*

72062 BELL, Lanny, Progress in the Tombs of the Ramesside High Priests at Luxor : 1972, *Newsletter ARCE* No. 83 (October 1972), 24-25.

Abstract of a paper.

A report of the activities in Tomb No. 35 (Bekenkhons I) and No. 157 (Nebwenenef) at Thebes.   *L. M. J. Zonhoven*

72063 BELL, Lanny, The Tombs of the High Priests at Dira Abu el-Naga, *Newsletter ARCE* No. 82 (July 1972), 7-8.

On the Dra' Abû el-Naga' project of the University Museum, Philadelphia, which was primarily concerned with the High Priests Bekenhons (No. 35) and Nebwenenef (No. 157), in whose tomb was discovered a new cross-word stela.

The tomb of the Viceroy of Kush Anhotep (No. 300) was opened and Tomb No. 286 (Niay) was identified as the probable source of a wall-fragment now in the Louvre Museum.
                    L. M. J. Zonhoven

BELMANE, A., see our number 72602.

72064 BENOIT, Pierre, Le R.P. de Vaux n'est plus, *Archeologia*, Paris No 44 (janvier-février 1972), 88, with portrait.

Obituary notice. Compare our number 71654.

72065 BERGER, Catherine, Internationale Tagung für meroitistische Forschungen. 6. bis 12. September 1971 in Berlin, *Orientalia* 41 (1972), 81-82.

72066 BERGMAN, J., Decem illis diebus. Zum Sinn der Enthaltsamkeit bei den Mysterienweihen im Isisbuch des Apuleius, *Ex Orbe Religionum* 332-346.

The ten days of abstinence preceding the initiation of Lucius into the Isiac mysteries (Apul. *Metam.* XI, 23,2; 28,5; 30,1) are related to the gestation period of ten months attested in some Greek and Egyptian texts, and explain the initiation as a process of rebirth.   *Dieter Mueller*

72067 BERGMAN, Jan, Zum « Mythus vom Staat » im Alten Ägypten, *in* : *The Myth of the State*. Based on Papers read at the Symposium on the Myth of the State held at Åbo on the 6th-8th September, 1971. Edited by Haralds Biezais, Stockholm, Almquist & Wiksell, [1972] (= Scripta Instituti Donneriani Aboensis 6), 80-102, with 1 fig.

The author briefly describes the central position of Maat in the political thinking of the ancient Egyptians.   *Dieter Mueller*

72068 BERLEV, O. D., Table d'offrandes appartenant à un habitant de la ville de la pyramide de Sésostris II, *RdE* 24 (1972), 12-16, with 1 pl.

Publication de la table d'offrandes Moscou, Musée des Beaux Arts Pouchkine I. 1 a 5339 (= Coll. Golénischeff 4093) appartenant au chef trésorier *'nḫw rn*, connu également par le P. Kahun XIII, 12, et datée par là de la fin du règne d'Amménemès III. Le texte, limité à la formule d'offrande classique est brièvement commenté. Photographie de l'objet.

Ph. Derchain

72069 BERLEV, O.D., Египтология, *in* : *Азиатский музей* — Ленинградское отделение Института востоковедения АН СССР, Москва, Издательство "Наука", 1972, 500-515.

« Egyptology ».

A short history of egyptology at the Asiatic Museum, the Leningrad department of the Institute of Oriental Research. With biographical sketches and bibliographical notices of the following russian egyptologists : O. E. Lemm, I. M. Alekseeva, P. V. Jernstedt, B. A. Turaev, V. V. Struve, M. A. Korostovtsev, Y. Y. Perepelkin, I. G. Livchitz, N. S. Piotrovskiy, V. I. Evgenova, Kh. A. Kink, O. D. Berlev and I. V. Vinogradov. Cf. our number 72210.   *J. F. Borghouts*

72070 BERLEV, O. D., Трудовое население Египта в эпоху Среднего царства, Москва, Издательство Наука. Главная редакция восточной литературы, 1972 (15 × 22 cm ; 363 p., 296 fig.). At head of title : Академия наук СССР. Институт востоковедения ; rev. *GM* Heft 2 (1972), 61-62 (Reinhard Grieshammer); *Oriens Antiquus* 13 (1974), 60-63 (Alessandro Roccati).

Pr. руб 2, коп. 12

"The working-class population in Egypt during the Middle Kingdom".

In seven chapters, the following terms referring to social classes are discussed with the prosopography of their representatives : the "slaves", *ḥmw.w-nsw.t* (p. 7-27), the *ḥmw.w* (28-44), *ḥm.wt* (45-72), the *'ẖm.w* (74-95), *mrjj.t* (96-146), *b3kw.w* (147-171) and *ḏı* (172-262). In a long appendix, illustrative material concerning their activities (mainly drawn from tomb reliefs and paintings) is discussed (263-316). Indexes and bibliography on p. 317-335.   *J. F. Borghouts*

72071 BERLEV, O. D., Не замеченный до сих пор финикизм в отчете венамуна о поездке в библ, *in* : *Письменные памятники и проблемы истории культуры Народов Востока.* уш годичная научная сессия ло ив ан (автоаннотации и краткие сообщения), [Moscow], издательство "Наука", 1972, 73-74.

"A Hitherto Unnoticed Phoenician Element in the Report of Wenamun on his Journey to Byblos".
An analysis of the name of the Prince of Byblos, rendered as *Ṯkr-Bʿr* by Wenamun (1, 16-17 and 1, 29). The meaning of the name is clear ("Baʿal-has-remembered") but one rather expects **Ḏkr-Bʿr*. However, in Phoenician the voiceless /s/ was used (= Eg. *ṯ*), not the voiced /z/ (= Eg. *ḏ*). The local variant of the name was correctly noted by Wenamun; the transliteration should therefore rather be Sakar-Baʿal than Zakar-Baʿal.
                                                          J. F. Borghouts

72072 BERNAND, André, De Koptos à Kosseir, Leiden, E. J. Brill, 1972 (21.7 × 27.5 cm; XVIII + 285 p., 91 pl., 1 loose map); rev. *BiOr* 31 (1974), 78-79 (John F. Oates); *CdE* XLVII, Nᵒˢ 93-94 (1972), 325-328 (Jean Bingen); *Studia Papyrologica* 12 (1973), 59-60 (J. Pegueroles).

The author studies the Greek and Latin inscriptions in the area of the Wâdi Hammâmat, between Koptos and el-Quseir.
In the Introduction earlier editions of the inscriptions are listed, classical authors on Pan quoted (with translations), and the contents of the inscriptions in general discussed : chronology, the role of the Roman army, the names occurring, etc.
The material itself is divided into three chapters. Chapter I deals with the valley at the entrance of the Wâdi Hammâmat, chapter II with the Paneion of the Wâdi, chapter III with that of el-Bweib, SE of el-Laqeita. The two first chapters begin with descriptions by various travellers, the third by a description of the Paneion discovered by the author. There follow full discussions of each of the 185 inscriptions.
Although the material is outside the scope of the *AEB* the texts are of interest to egyptologists, e.g. because of the prosopographical evidence and the later history of Min (= Pan).
Tables of concordance on p. 253-258, extensive indexes p. 261-272. The plates bear clear photographs of most of the inscriptions.

72073 BERNAND, André, Le Paneion d'El-Kanaïs: les inscriptions grecques, Leiden, E. J. Brill, 1972 (22 × 27.5 cm; XXII + 180 p., 1 map, 2 plans, 55 pl.).

This volume is sequel to our preceding number, being the second devoted to Pan of the Desert.

After a preface discussing i.a. the name el Kanâyis — the place is also indicated as Redesîya, Wâdi ʿAbbâd and Wâdi Miâh — the introduction lists earlier publications of the Greek inscriptions, discusses the discovery of the temple by Cailliaud and its descriptions by Belzoni, Golénishev, Weigall and Gauthier, and deals with position, nature, date and importance of the texts.

The main part of the book consists of the publication of 90 texts, of which 31 here for the first time. Each is given in transcription with translation and comments.

Extensive indexes on p. 159-172, including tables of concordance to earlier publications.

72074 BERRY, A. C. and R. J. BERRY, Origins and Relationships of the Ancient Egyptians. Based on a Study of Non-metrical Variations in the Skull, *Journal of Human Evolution*, London and New York 1 (1972), 199-208, with 3 fig. and 2 tables.

The authors summarize the results of earlier studies (see our number 67070) and state that comparison showed the early Egyptian "type" to be much more like a North Indian series than ones of Semitic, Negroid or North European origins.

Reprinted in: Population Biology of the Ancient Egyptians. Edited by D. R. Brothwell [and] B. A. Chiarelli, London and New York, Academic Press, 1973.

BIDOLI †, Dino, see our number 72357.

72075 BIERBRIER, Morris L., The length of the reign of Sethos I, *JEA* 58 (1972), 303.

The Munich statue of Bakenchons I gives him 70 years service as a priest, yet Roma-Roy was inducted as High Priest of Amun by Ramesses II. Hence assuming no pluralism his 4 years as a *wʿb* must have been spent under the previous king, which added to the 11 years spent as a youth under Sethos means a reign for this pharaoh of at least 15 years.   *E. Uphill*

72076 BIERBRIER, M. L., A Second High Priest Ramessesnakht?, *JEA* 58 (1972), 195-199, with 1 fig.

A Theban graffito, No. 1860a, refers to a year 8 in which the tomb of the high priest Ramessesnakht was closed. This can be either dated to the reigns of Ramesses VI, VII, or VIII, if there was a chief workman Amennakht living then, or else to those of Ramesses X or XI, thereby postulating a second high priest of this name.   *E. Uphill*

72077   BIETAK, Manfred, Die österreichische Feldforschungstätigkeit im Distrikt Sayala (V.A.R.). Mit einer Bibliographie, *Anzeiger. Österreichische Akademie der Wissenschaften.* Philosophisch-historische Klasse, Wien 108 (1971), 1972, 234-247.

Die österreichische Expedition arbeitete 1. in der Ausgrabung von archäologischen Objekten, 2. im Studium und in der Bergung der menschlichen Skelette, 3. in der Aufnahme aller Felsbilder in der Konzession. Aus der A-Kultur (Naqada II bis Frühdynastik) stammt eine Abrisiedlung mit einer Felsmalereihöhle. Eine kralartige Siedlung mit Überresten von runden zeltartigen Hütten ist in die früheste C-Gruppe zu datieren. Einige Pan-Gräber-Friedhöfe und ein Lagerplatz dieser Kultur wurden gefunden. Besonders interessant waren die Funde aus spätrömischer Zeit, die außer großen Friedhöfen auch 19 Tavernen und wahrscheinlich ein kleines Bordell zeitigten. Aus christlicher Zeit stammen eine Einsiedelei, eine befestigte Siedlung mit einer dreischiffigen Kirche mit Freskenschmuck an den Wänden sowie christliche Gräberfelder. Eine Bibliographie über die österreichische Feldforschung in Sayala ist angefügt.   *Inge Hofmann*

72078   BIETAK, Manfred, Theben-West (Luqsor). Vorbericht über die ersten vier Grabungskampagnen (1969-1971), Wien, Hermann Böhlaus Nachf., 1972 (15.5 × 23.8 cm; 38 p., 25 pl., 5 plans [2 folded] and 4 fig. [2 folded]) = Österreichische Akademie der Wissenschaften. Philosophisch-historische Klasse. Sitzungsberichte 278,4; rev. *BiOr* 31 (1974), 70-71 (Gun Björkman).   Pr. ÖS 120

The introduction describes the site in ʿAsâsîf along the causeways of Montuhotep and Tuthmosis III and the organization of the campaigns, while chapter 2 offers topographical and stratigraphical informations.
Chapter 3 discusses the results. Five layers are distinguished. Layer E of the causeway of Montuhotep; layer D containing two Middle Kingdom tombs, reoccupied first in the XVIIth to early XVIIIth Dynasties and again in the Late Period; layer C dates from the time of Tuthmosis III. To layer B belongs the area of the Ramesside temple discovered by Winlock and Lansing. The Austrians found a foundation deposit of Ramses IV and hieratic inscriptions recording the progress of the work. The material of the temple i.a. consists of blocks from an annex of the Ramesseum, itself built from earlier

blocks. The temple was decorated, according to some cartouches, by Ramses V and VI.

Layer A contains tombs of the Late and the Ptolemaic Periods. Their ground plan was either that of a temple or that of a house, while one enormous tomb (no X) was found belonging to an Ankh-Hor from the time of Apries. A special section is devoted to tomb VII in which several funerary objects were found, among which sarcophagi from the XXVth Dynasty. One of the owners was a Nubian woman called *Ḥryrw*.

72079   BILBO, Queenie M., The Story of Egypt and Sudan, Cincinnati, Ohio, McCormick - Mathers Publishing Company, Inc., [1972] (16.2 × 23.2 cm; [IV+] 188 p., 11 maps in colours, 79 ill., 3 fig., frontispiece, colour ill. on cover).

This is a book for children on the entire history of Egypt and the Sudan down to modern times. Land and people of Egypt are discussed in four units, the Sudan in a fifth, each unit ending with questions and tasks.

72080   BINGEN, Jean, Rapport des Directeurs, *CdE* XLVII, N°s 93-94 (1972), 5-8.

72081   BIRKENFELD, Helmut, Das Ibistaphion unter der Nekropolis von Nordsakkara, *Armant*, Köln Heft 9 (1972), 28-39.

The first part of the article contains a short report of the excavation of the Cemetery of the Sacred Ibises at Saqqâra, while in the second part the author evaluates the question whether the Ibis Cemetery is to be connected with the cult of Imhotep and to what extent the Toth-cult at Tûna el-Gebel is comparable with it.   *L. M. J. Zonhoven*

BJÖRKMAN, Gun, see our number 72528.

72082   BLEEKER, C. J., Thoth in den altägyptischen Hymnen, *Ex Orbe Religionum* 3-15.

The author investigates the hymns to Thoth in order to discover the personal relations of men to him. After sketching the figure of Thoth and the nature of the poetic texts he lists his material, seven short hymns and two other texts, a Demotic letter (compare our number 58315) and an ostracon as well as *BD*, spells 18, 20 and 182.

Bleeker demonstrates from quotations that Thoth was venerated as the Moon-God, as an ibis and a baboon, as the god granting writing and law, the Lord of Maat, etc. He was really loved and trusted since he took care of men. His functions in the Sun-Bark and in the process of Osiris are not mentioned. The tendency of the hymns is praise of the gracious god who rewards his followers, particularly the scribes.

72083 BLERSCH, Hartmut Gustav, Das aspektivische Denken in der altägyptischen Medizin, *Sudhoffs Archiv*, Wiesbaden 56 (1972), 1-21.

Blersch findet in dem Begriff der Aspektive, der sich in der ägyptischen Kunstgeschichte anstelle von Heinrich Schäfers "geradvorstellig" eingebürgert hat, den Schlüssel zum Verständnis auch der ägyptischen Medizin, indem dieser Begriff eine ägyptische Denkweise trifft. Das Phänomen von Synonyma wie *jb* und *ḥꜣtj*, oder, für den "Leib", *ḏt*, *ꜥt* (*nbt*), *ḥꜥw*, *jwf* und *ḥt* wollte bisher jeder einleuchtenden Deutung wiederstehen; Blersch erklärt das Nebeneinander als Ausdruck verschiedener Aspekte desselben Gegenstandes. "Das oberflächennahe, aspektivische Sehen der ägyptischen Ärzte konnte sehr genau einzelne Ansichten und Erscheinungsformen der Dinge erfassen, doch verhüllte es den Blick auf die Funktionen und auf einheitliche innere Zusammenhänge, also auf die Innenseite der Dinge" (S. 19). *Hellmut Brunner*

72084 BLIQUEZ, Lawrence J., A New Bronze Harpocrates (?) in the De Young Museum in San Francisco, *AJA* 76 (1972), 189-192, with 4 ill. on a pl. and 2 fig.

Publication of a bronze statuette in Graeco-Roman style preserved in the De Young Museum in San Francisco (no. 54666), with a difficult Greek inscription. The author argues that the nude figure represents Harpocates, although of the usual characteristics only the sidelock is present, and that it was originally produced in Egypt.

72085 BLUMENTHAL, Elke, Die Erzählung des Papyrus d'Orbiney als Literaturwerk, *ZÄS* 99, 1 (1972), 1-17.

Das literarische Problem des *d'Orbiney* bildete das Thema der Probevorlesung der Verfasserin. Die Geschichte von den zwei Brüdern ist trotz den mythischen und folkloristischen Elementen primär eine neuägyptische, literarische Unterhaltungserzählung. Die Deutung muß von der Eigenart der Gattung ausgehen, im Anschluß an die Methoden der allgemeinen Literaturwissenschaft. *M. Heerma van Voss*

72086 BLUMENTHAL, Elke and Fritz HINTZE, Siegfried Morenz. 1914-1970, *ZÄS* 99,1 (1972), I-III, with a portrait.

Obituary notice. Compare our numbers 70619 and 72313.

BÖHLIG, Alexander, see our numbers 72367, 72390 and 72391.

72087 BOGOSLOVSKY, E., Конусы наместника египетской Эфиопии Май-Масе в Эрмитаже, *Сообщения Государственного*

Эрмитажа, Ленинград 35 (1972), 62-66, with 4 ill. and an English summary on p. 91.

"Cones of Mai-Masi, Viceroy of Egyptian Ethiopia".
The inscriptions on the cones Nos 2258 and 18066 of the Hermitage were made by the use of a different stamp than in the case of cone No. 18065. The cones are reproduced and discussed for the first time. Mai-Masi, an older contemporary of Amenhotep III, ruled over Egyptian Ethiopia for over a quarter of a century.   *E. S. Bogoslovsky*

72088 BOGOSLOVSKY, Eug. [E.S.], Памятники и документы из Дэр-эль-Мэдина, хранящиеся в музеях СССР. Введение [and] выпуск I, *ВДИ* 1 (119), 1972, 79-103, with 2 pl. and an English summary on p. 103; выпуск II, *ВДИ* 2 (120), 1972, 62-93, with 3 ill., 5 pl. and an English summary on p. 93; выпуск III, *ВДИ* 3 (121), 1972, 64-105, with 6 ill., 2 pl. and an English summary on p. 104-105; выпуск IV, *ВДИ* 4 (122), 1972, 65-89, with 1 ill., 4 pl. and an English summary on p. 88-89.

"Monuments and Documents from Deir el-Medîna in the Museums of the USSR. Introduction and Part I-IV".
In these four articles, which are followed by two more and one with indexes and addenda and corrigenda in the numbers 1 to 3 (= 123-125), 1973, of the same periodical, the author discusses all monuments from Deir el-Medîna preserved in the museums of the USSR at Leningrad, Moscow, Voronesh and Odessa. The extensive treatment of the objects presents a wealth of information about the necropolis workmen, their gods, tombs, family relations, etc. The pieces are carefully described, the texts translated with comments, palaeography and date and genealogy of the persons mentioned discussed. Part I deals with the stelae Hermitage Museum Nos 3937 and 8728, the former of a Setau of the XVIIIth Dynasty, the latter, badly damaged, of Amenmose son of Pshedu, bearing part of a hymn to Amon-Re (cfr. Bakir, *ASAE* 42, 1943, 83-91). Part II first discusses the stelae Nos 156 and 157 of the Museum of Fine Arts at Voronesh, the former, with a representation of Thueris of the Dumpalm, belonging to the scribe Ramose (whose monuments are discussed), the latter to Nebamente. The second part deals with two Qadesht-stelae from the Pushkin Museum, Moscow (Nos 5613 and 5614). Part III begins with the publication of a shawabti in the Odessa Archaeological Museum (No 52909), of a *Pn-n-mr-n-ʿbw* (for a list of the monuments of this workman, see p. 66-67). Then follow the shawabti with its sarcophagus of Sennedjem in the Puskhin Museum (No 1662), and two shawabti boxes

of his sons Khonsu and Kha'bekhnet (Nos 1918 and 1920), all three from Theban Tomb 1.

Part IV deals with : a plank of a shawabti box (Pushkin Museum No 4882) from the tomb of Irinufer (Theban Tomb 290); a pyramidion (Hermitage No 19491) from the tomb of Turobay (327), and two wings of the door of a naos (Pushkin Museum No I.1a. 4867 a-b) of Amenwahsu.

For a more extensive summary see Grieshammer, *GM* Heft 1 (1972), 36-40.

BONNET, Charles, see our number 72338.

72089 BORCHHARDT, Jürgen, Homerische Helme. Helmformen der Ägäis in ihren Beziehungen zu orientalischen und europäischen Helmen in der Bronze- und frühen Eisenzeit, Mainz am Rhein, Philipp von Zabern, 1972 (20.8 × 27 cm; X + 162 p., 6 maps, 12 fig., 45 pl., 6 folding tables); at head of title : Römisch-germanisches Zentralmuseum Mainz; rev. *AJA* 78 (1974), 93-95 (Jane C. Waldbaum). Pr. DM 120

The book is of interest to egyptologists since it deals in a short section with the helmets of the New Kingdom (p. 88-89). No actual objects are known, but helmets occur in the representations of the Battle of Qadesh and the Battle against the Sea Peoples and those in the tomb of Ramses III.

On p. 109-118 there is a discussion of various types of helmets worn by the Shardana and of the headdress of the Philistines and related peoples.

72090 BORGHOUTS, J. F., Egyptische Magie, *De Ibis*, Amsterdam 3 (1973), 5-8, 33-39, 66-72, 100-104, with 7 fig.

General article about various aspects of magic in Egypt. Continued in vol. 4 (1973), 16-24, 61-64 and 84-88.

72091 BORGHOUTS, J. F., A Special Use of the Emphatic *sdm.f* in Late Egyptian, *BiOr* 29 (1972), 271-276.

The author discusses the construction : independent pronoun or *in/m* + noun — emphatic *sdm.f* with suffix subject, enumerating several examples, but also adding a series in which the *sdm.f-* form lacks the *i*-augment. Both constructions appear from the context to demand future translation. In the former series no stress on the adverbial part is probable; in some cases there is no following adverbial extension at all. The future meaning may be caused by the interrelation between the proleptic element and its verbal endorser, while in the second construction the verb-form may, at least in some instances, be the prospective independent *sdm.f.* That in the former series the adverbial predicate (with a modern linguistic term : the comment) precedes the emphatic *sḏm.f* is a construction not without parallels. It may be explained by the character of the independent pronoun which has to precede in order to fulfill its role as comment-pointer.

72092 BORGOGNINI-TARLI, S. M. and G. PAOLI, Biochemical and Immunological Investigations on Early Egyptian Remains, *Journal of Human Evolution*, London and New York 1 (1972), 281-287, with 1 table.

Presentation of the results of an investigation of 50 right femura from skeletons of the Dynastic Period, which were typed for ABO by the Haemagglutinin-inhibition test. The investigation was supported by biochemical analyses. See also our number 72540.
Reprinted in: Population Biology of the Ancient Egyptians. Edited by D. R. Brothwell [and] B. A. Chiarelli, London and New York, Academic Press, 1973.

72093 BOSTICCO, Sergio, Museo Archeologico di Firenze. Le stele egiziane di epoca tarda, [Roma, Istituto Poligrafico dello Stato. Libreria dello Stato, 1972] (18.3 × 26 cm; 81 p., 64 pl.). At head of title: Ministerio della Pubblica Istruzione. Direzione Generale delle Antichità e Belle Arti / Cataloghi dei Musei e Gallerie d'Italia; rev. *CdE* XLIX, No. 97 (1974), 96-97 (Herman de Meulenaere).

Sequel to our number 65073.
The volume contains photographs and descriptions of 62 stelae and fragments thereof, dating from the ages between the XXIst Dynasty and the Roman Period. Apart from data concerning measures, material, date and provenance the author offers a transcription of the texts, notes on epigraphy and technique of each single piece as well as a bibliography being added.
Most stelae belong to private persons, though in some instances anonymous (nos 28 and 46-48). Nos 14 and 28 record the acquisition of a tomb; nos 49-50 and 62 are anepigraph votive stelae; nos 51-57 Horuscippi; and nos 58-60 dedicated to various gods, the latter two with Greek inscriptions.
Concordance of museum numbers on p. 70; indexes p. 75-80.

72094 BOTHMER, Bernard V., A Bust of Ny-user-Ra from Byblos, in Beirut, Lebanon, *Kêmi* 21 (1971), 11-16, with 8 ill. on 2 pl.

Le buste en granit rose B 7395 au Musée de Beirouth, trouvé à Byblos par Dunand, ne fut peut-être pas achevé et a souffert du temps. L'auteur en rapproche la statue de Néouserrè Caire CG 38, de même matière. Les traits du visage et le bon travail du torse évoqueraient le même atelier, tout comme les proportions du *némès*, aux retombées rayées parallèles vers l'intérieur, et l'indication de la tête seule de son uraeus. L'épaule gauche un peu haute trahit une attitude inhabituelle, ce dont la Cachette de Karnak montre un précédent sous le même règne. Le nom de Néouserré apparaissait déjà à Byblos. Trouver à l'étranger une statue royale de la Ve dynastie requerrait la présence d'un sanctuaire important, et Hathor n'y est pas encore attestée à l'époque.   *J. Custers*

72095 BOTHMER, Bernard V., The Head That Grew a Face. Notes on a Fine Forgery, *Miscellanea Wilbouriana 1*, 25-31, with 12 ill.

In 1956 a small Egyptian head with remains of the back pillar attached to it was seen with a Cairo dealer. The face was destroyed, but in 1966 the head turned up in Germany with a new face. In 1971 it was bought for a token price by the Brooklyn Museum (acc. no. 71.10.2), since as a really good forgery it deserves a place in a museum collection.
In its original state the head shows some features which caused its dating to the 4th century B.C., possibly the XXXIst Dynasty or the early Greek Period. It represents a link between realism of the Persian Period and the naturalistic tendencies of the Ptolemaic Period.

72096 BOTHMER, Bernard, The Iconography of Ny-user-ra, *Newsletter ARCE* No. 80 (January 1972), 32.

Abstract of a paper.
The bust found by Dunand at Byblos represents a king of the Vth Dynasty, most likely Ny-user-ra. See our number 72094.
                                          L. M. J. Zonhoven

72097 BOULOS, Ayad Ayad, The Topography of Elephantine according to the Aramaic Papyri, *in* : *Medieval and Middle Eastern Studies* in Honour of Aziz Suryal Atiya. Edited by Sami A. Hanna, Leiden, E. J. Brill. 1972, 23-37, with 5 plans.

The author discussed the topography of the surroundings of the Yahu temple on Elephantine, comparing the views of various scholars. He argues that in the Aramaic text "above" means the south and "below" the north, drawing a revised plan on account of this conception.

72098 du BOURGUET, Pierre, A propos de l'origine du relatif $\overset{\sim}{\supset}_\backslash\backslash$ *nty*, *RdE* 24 (1972), 17-19.

L'auteur conteste le bien fondé de l'étymologie du relatif *nty* telle qu'elle a été proposée autrefois par Gardiner (*Egyptian*

Grammar, §199) et reproduite par Lefebvre (*Grammaire* §752), pour qui il s'agit d'un nisbé dérivé du féminin de l'adjectif nisbé issu lui-même de la préposition *n*. Il n'apporte toutefois pas de solution au problème ni ne renvoie à Edel, *Altäg. Gramm.*, §345 chez qui l'on trouvera l'explication complémentaire.

Ph. Derchain

72099 du BOURGUET, Pierre, Les nouvelles salles coptes, *La Revue du Louvre et des Musées de France*, Paris 22 (1972), 423-424, with 2 ill.

Short description of the rearranged Coptic rooms in the Louvre Museum.

72100 BOURKE, J. B., Trauma and Degenerative Diseases in Ancient Egypt and Nubia, *Journal of Human Evolution*, London and New York 1 (1972), 225-232, with 4 fig. and 2 pl.

Die Analyse von Knochenüberresten sowie der Edwin Smith-Papyrus zeigen, daß die Behandlung von Knochenbrüchen auch komplizierter Art bekannt war. Die Abnutzungskrankheiten im alten Ägypten und Nubien waren im wesentlichen dieselben, an denen wir heute leiden.
Reprinted in Population Biology of the Ancient Egyptians. Edited by D. R. Brothwell [and] B. A. Chiarelli, London and New York, Academic Press, 1973. *Inge Hofmann*

BOURLARD-COLLIN, Simone, see our number 72525.

72101 BOWEN, James, A History of Western Education. Volume One. The Ancient World : Orient and Mediterranean. 2000 B.C. — A.D. 1054, London, Methuen & Co. Ltd, [1972] (15.7 × 23.4 cm; XX + 395 p., 6 maps, 16 pl.).

Although mainly dealing with education in the classical antiquity the book contains a chapter on ancient Egypt (p. 22-42; notes on p. 348-350). After some general sections on prehistory, the temple, and reckoning and writing, the author deals with the Old and Middle Kingdoms, called the proto-literate period. He then discusses what he calls "the high culture of Egypt 1800-525 B.C.", with sections on the temple, literacy and learning, the training of the scribe, and the House of Life. There follows a section on Egypt's relations with the Near East and the invention of the alphabet.
The author seems not to know Brunner's Altägyptische Erziehung (our number 57071), which is referred to neither in the notes nor in the bibliography (p. 376-378).

72102 BRANDON †, S. G. F., The Proleptic Aspect of the Iconography of the Egyptian "Judgment of the Dead", *Ex Orbe Religionum* 16-25.

The author argues that the Judgment of the Dead was performed as a ritual, of which illustrations have survived in the vignettes accompanying *BD* Chapter 125.   *Dieter Mueller*

BREJNIK, Antoine and Claire, see our number 72296.

72103 BRENTJES, Burchard, Das Pferd im Alten Orient, *Säugetier-kundliche Mitteilungen*, München 20 (1972), 325-353, with 14 fig. and 37 ill.

Horse and chariot were introduced in Egypt towards the end of the Hyksos Period. Two-wheeled chariots are known from the XVIIth Dynasty onwards, and originated from Asia according to archaeological and textual evidence. Egyptian representations of chariots and an original at the Florence Museum lead to the conclusion that up to the 13th century B.C. small horses prevailed, but since the 14th century B.C. slender, high-legged horses are dominant in representations of Egyptian armies. From the XVIIIth Dynasty onwards there appear depictions of the horse as a riding animal, probably used as such without saddle and reins. As a riding animal it must have been used not only by private persons, but also by the army (the goddess of war, Astarte, was also a goddess of horsemen). There is no evidence for other functions of the horse (e.g. animal of burden) in ancient Egypt.   *L. M. J. Zonhoven*

72104 BRENTJES, Burchard, Zur Entwicklung des Menschenbildes im Alten Orient, *Das Altertum*, Berlin 18 (1972), 197-217, with 17 ill. and 1 fig.

The author investigates the representation of man in the ancient Orient from the Marxist point of view, this area especially being important since its cultures emerged from the primitive society via the "military democracy" to the fully developed class society.
He deals with the representation of man in the primitive society with its emphasized collectivity and concrete, non-individual character of representation, and next with that of the beginning period of the high cultures, when the class society is already apparent with its suppression of the productive people by the upper class (temple, king).
In the last section, on the Ancient Oriental class society, Egypt is frequently mentioned. The opposition of the classes led to the decline of the state order. The pyramids, the statues, and representations in the Old Kingdom reflect the self-

consciousness of the ruling class, but artistic representations of the productive class, although in the service of the ruling class, occur. The Middle Kingdom royal portraits show sensitive and thoughtful kings, the humanization being result of the inner social crisis. This humanization became prominent in the Amarna art.

The insolvable class conflict led to the representation of character, of feelings, the opposing lower class thus contributing to the perfection of human representation in art.

L. M. J. Zonhoven

72105 BRENTJES, Burchard, Zur ökonomischen Funktion des Rindes in den Kulturen des Alten Orients (I), *Klio*, Berlin 54 (1972), 9-43, with 14 ill. and 1 fig.

In this survey of the economic function of oxen in the Ancient Orient there are references to Egypt on p. 21 (two late representations of riding an ox), p. 31-33 (ox-saddles), and p. 37-38 (the ox as a beast of burden).

72106 BRESCIANI, E., Ancora su Papremi : proposte per una nuova etimologia e una nuova localizzazione, *Studi classici e orientali*, Pisa 21 (1972), 299-303.

Against Altenmüller (compare our number 65016), who explained the name Papremis as P^2-n-p^2-$rm.wy$, "the (place of) the two fishes", and identified it with Letopolis, the author argues that the name means $P^2(-m)$-p^2-$rm(t)$, "the (place of) the man" (= Androupolis), as its Aramaic name *PPRM* indicates. She also adduces arguments that it is to be sought in the Eastern Delta, in the Gynaicopolitan nome, on the place of the modern Kherbîta.

72107 BRESCIANI, Edda, Annotazioni demotiche ai ΠΕΡΣΑΙ ΤΗΣ ΕΠΙΓΟΝΗΣ, *La Parola del Passato*, Napoli 27 (1927), 123-128.

The author argues that in some instances the Greek translation of the Demotic expression *Wjnn ms n Kmj* (lit. Ionian born in Egypt) is Πέρσης τῆς ἐπιγονῆς, the Demotic indicating by *Wjnn* that the man is a soldier. In a few instances one finds *Mtj* [*ms n*] *Kmj* (Μῆδος τῆς ἐπιγονῆς), indicating a person descending from the military colony of the Persian Period.

72108 BRESCIANI, E., L'expédition franco-toscane en Égypte et en Nubie (1828-1829) et les antiquités égyptiennes d'Italie, *BSFE* No 64 (Juin 1972), 5-29, with 7 ill.

The author deals with Rosellini's share in the expedition to Egypt in 1828-1829 led by him and Champollion. She particularly discusses the objects discovered by Rosellini, most of which came to the Egyptian Museum at Florence, though a few are now in other collections. At the end a discussion of Rosellini's reconstruction of the satirical papyrus at Turin.

72109 BRESCIANI, E., Una mandibola di cammello con testo demotico di epoca augustea, *RdE* 24 (1972), 25-30, with 1 pl.

L'objet mentionné dans le titre porte une liste de noms de bénéficiaires de rations d'eau datée de l'an 38 d'Auguste, et doit provenir d'une station de ravitaillement sur la route d'Oxyr-rhynque à la petite Oasis. L'article contient une photographie, la traduction, la transcription du document et un commentaire philologique.   *Ph. Derchain*

72110 BRESCIANI, E. - E. DELLA VALLE - M. P. GIANGERI - G. GIANNESSI - S. PERNIGOTTI, Ostraka demotici da Ossirinco, *Studi classici e orientali*, Pisa 21 (1972), 321-387, with 18 pl.

Continuation of our number 71092.
Publication of 28 Demotic ostraca from the collection in Pisa, mostly containing accounts of various kinds. Of every text there is given a photograph, a description, and a translation with comments. Index of names on p. 379-387.

BRILL, Robert H., see our number 72600.

72111 BRINKMAN, J. A., Foreign Relations of Babylonia from 1600 to 625 B.C. : The Documentary Evidence. Summary [Chrono-logies in Old World Archaeology. Archaeological Seminar at Columbia University 1970-1971], *AJA* 76 (1972), 271-281, with 1 table.

Extensive summary of a paper, of which section 3 deals with the period 1460-1340 B.C., called "the Egyptian Phase". The author discusses the gold trade of Babylon with Egypt and their relations during the Amarna Period.

BRODRICK, A. Houghton, see our number 72128.

72112 van den BROEK, R., The Myth of the Phoenix according to Classical and Early Christian Traditions, Leiden, E. J. Brill, 1972 (15.6 × 23.9 cm; XII + 487 p., 40 pl., 2 folding maps, coloured frontispiece) = Études préliminaires aux religions orientales dans l'empire romain publiées par M. J. Vermaseren, 24; rev. *AJA* 77 (1973), 462 (Morton Smith). Pr. bound fl. 182.

Although mainly outside the scope of the AEB the first part of this study contains a chapter on the Egyptian *benu* and its relation to the classical phoenix (p. 13-32), and another on a

Coptic text on the phoenix (33-47). The latter, part of the *Sermon to Maria*, is here published after a ms. recently acquired by the Utrecht University Library from the estate of Carl Schmidt. On p. 44-47 one finds the Coptic text with translation and some notes.

In the chapter on the *bnw* the author deals with its various features and relations to divinities and the *bnbn*. The *bnw* is one of the forms in which Atum-Re manifested himself, and a symbol of creation. Although there are strong parallels, the author attempts to demonstrate that the classical myth of the phoenix did not develop directly from the Egyptian conceptions (see also p. 397-399). That the word «phoenix» has been derived from *bnw* is highly improbable (see also p. 61-66).

Pl. 1-3 depict the *bnw*; for comments and bibliography see p. 425-427.

72113 BRUNNER, Hellmut, *Dbt* "Werkzeugkasten", *JARCE* 9 (1971-1972), 137.

A reply to Goedicke's contention that *dbt* denotes a sawbuck (see our No. 68235); the meaning "box" or "chest" is confirmed by a hieratic inscription (No. 46) on one of the chests from the tomb of Tutankhamun.   *Dieter Mueller*

72114 BRUNNER-TRAUT, Emma, Ancient Egyptian Literature : the Beginnings of World Literature, *Universitas* [English Edition], Stuttgart 14 (1971-1972), 329-338.

Survey of Egyptian literature, its genres and its most important works, with translations of parts of them.

72115 BRUNNER-TRAUT, Emma, [Letter to the Editor], *Israel Exploration Journal*, Jerusalem 22 (1972), 192.

Critical remarks to our number 70448.

72116 BRUNNER-TRAUT, Emma, The Origin of the Concept of Immortality of the Soul in Ancient Egypt, *Universitas* [English Edition], Stuttgart 14 (1971-1972), 47-55.

English version of our number 66097.

BRUNON, Jean and Raoul, see our number 72525.

72117 BRYCE, Glendon E., Another Wisdom-"Book" in Proverbs, *Journal of Biblical Literature*, Missoula, Montana 91 (1972), 145-157.

The author compares *Prov.* 25, 2-27 with the *Instruction of Sehetepibre*, of which as yet only a condensed version in the form of a panegyric has been published (occurring, e.g., on Cairo stela 20538) and with the book *Kemyt*. Although there is no direct relation between the Egyptian and the biblical texts all three have a similar "Sitz im Leben" since they are "loyalist texts".

72118 BUHL, Marie-Louise, Kult og idraetslege i Den gamle Orient, in: For sportens skyld, [København], Nationalmuseet, 1972, 7-13.

"Cult and athletic games in the ancient orient".
The article appears in the catalogue of a special exhibition "For the Sake of Sport" held at the National Museum. The Egyptian material includes two ill. and one fig.

                                                          Torben Holm-Rasmussen

BURNEY, Ethel W., see our number 72564.

72119 [BURRI, Carla], Bollettino d'informazioni. Sezione archeologica. Istituto Italiano di Cultura del Cairo, Cairo No. 26 (Novembre 1971 - Febbraio 1972), 19 p.

Sequel to our number 71106.
The present number of the Bollettino i.a. contains surveys of the American campaign at Malkata, the Austrian excavations at 'Asâsîf, the French missions at Tanis and South Saqqâra, and various activities of the Service des Antiquités.

72120 [BURRI, Carla], Bollettino d'informazioni. Sezione archeologica. Istituto Italiano di Cultura del Cairo, Cairo [No. 27] (Marzo-Giugno 1972), 15 p.

Sequel to our preceding number.
In this number particularly the French campaigns at North Karnak, Deir el-Medîna and Wâdi Natrûn, and various activities of the Centre Franco-Égyptien and the Centre de Documentation.

72121 BURRI, Carla M., Bollettino d'informazioni. Sezione archeologica. Istituto Italiano di Cultura del Cairo, Cairo [No. 28] (Agosto-Ottobre 1972), 14 p.

Sequel to our preceding number.
We mention a survey of the mission by the University of Rome at 'Asâsîf, and the Belgian excavations in the same area.

72122 BURTON, Anne, Diodorus Siculus. Book I. A Commentary, Leiden, E.J. Brill. 1972 (15.5 × 24 cm; XXVIII + 301 p., frontispiece) = Études préliminaires aux religions orientales dans l'empire romain publiées par M.J. Vermaseren, 29; rev. BiOr 30 (1973), 481-484 (Michel Malaise); CdE XLVIII,

No. 95 (1973), 199-200 (Michel Muszynski); *JEA* 60 (1974), 287-290 (Alan B. Lloyd).   Pr. bound fl. 74

After a chapter on the sources of Diodorus Siculus' βιβλιοθήκη ίστορική, Book I, the author offers extensive comments on all its chapters, throughout referring to material from ancient Egypt and to recent studies on the subjects. The volume does not contain either the text of Diodorus or a translation.
Indexes on p. 291-301.

72123 BYSTRIKOVA, M. G., Коптская коллекция в Эрмитаже и ее изучение, *ВДИ* 3 (121), 1972, 233-238.

"The Coptic collection in the Hermitage and its studies".
Survey of the collection, followed by a full bibliography (p. 237-238).

72124 CALLAWAY, Joseph A. and Kermit SCHOONOVER, The Early Bronze Age Citadel at Ai (Et-Tell), *BASOR* No. 207 (October, 1972), 41-53, with 5 ill. and 3 plans.

The Early Bronze III A citadel at Ai, built c. 2700 B.C. bears evidence of strong Egyptian influence, as other rebuilt parts of the city do.   *L. M. J. Zonhoven*

72125 CAMINOS, Ricardo A., Another Hieratic Manuscript from the Library of Pwerem Son of Ḳiḳi (Pap. B.M. 10288), *JEA* 58 (1972), 205-224, with 6 folding pl.

This papyrus is a neglected relation of two other fine Ptolemaic papyri, has never previously been published and is a small hieratic document with magico-mythological texts, coming from the tomb-library of Pwerem and one Pkherkhons, possibly his brother. It may have formed part of the Salt collection acquired in 1821. It consists of two sheets 24.5 cm. by 12.3 cm. clumsily mounted but with neat legible writing. The grammar is Middle Egyptian tinged with Late Egyptianisms, as is the orthography, and there are two new words in it, the name of a serpent-demon and a place name. A translation and extensive grammatical notes are given.   *E. Uphill*

72126 CARBONELL, Ch. O., Jacques-Joseph et Jean-François Champollion. La naissance d'un génie, *BSFE* No. 65 (Octobre 1972), 25-42, with 2 ill.

Extensive discussion of the relations between the brothers Champollion and the influence the elder brother has had on the studies of the younger.

72127 CARDON, Patrick D., A Problem concerning the New "Green Head" in West Berlin, *Newsletter ARCE* No. 80 (January 1972), 33.

Abstract of a paper.
The "Green Head" in West Berlin has to be dated to the early Ptolemaic Period, contrary to Kaiser's opinion (cfr our number 66325). *L. M. J. Zonhoven*

72128 CARRINGTON, Richard, Animals in Egypt, *in*: *Animals in Archaeology*. Edited by A. Houghton Brodrick, London, Barrie and Jenkins, [1972], 69-89, with 6 ill. and 4 colour pl.

General survey of the subject, dealing with stock-breeding and hunting, animals as pets, the horse, some invertebrates as the beetle and the bee, and with animals in art. Notes and a select bibliography on p. 170-171.

72129 CARROLL, Diane Lee, Wire Drawing in Antiquity, *AJA* 76 (1972), 321-323, with 17 ill. on 2 pl.

Article about wire drawing in Antiquity in general, in which the author summarizes her study on the technique applied in Egypt (see our number 70107).

72130 CARTER, Theresa Howard, The Johns Hopkins University Reconnaissance Expedition to the Arab-Iranian Gulf, *BASOR* No. 207 (October, 1972), 6-40, with 30 ill. and 2 maps.

In the Barbar Temple III, on the Bahrein Islands, a foundation deposit has been discovered containing Protodynastic alabaster jars of Egyptian origin. *L. M. J. Zonhoven*

72131 de CENIVAL, Françoise, Un acte de renonciation consécutif à une partage de revenus liturgiques memphites (P. Louvre E 3266), *BIFAO* 71 (1972), 11-65, with 12 pl.

Publication of the very long (19 cols) Demotic papyrus Louvre E 3266, from the year 8 of Ptolemy V Epiphanes (197 B.C.). The text contains a deed of renunciation (*sḫ n wj*) by the chancellor of the god Imhotep on behalf of his half-sister Shemti, concerning various properties and revenues which came from their mother. In the list of properties some quarters of Memphis are mentioned; several of the words indicating funerary revenues are *hapax legomena*.
The author offers a transliteration and a translation of the text, with commentary.

72132 de CENIVAL, Françoise, Les associations religieuses en Égypte d'après les documents démotiques, 2 vols, Le Caire, Publications de l'Institut français d'Archéologie orientale du Caire, 1972

(20.3 × 27.5 cm; [Vol. I :] X + 270 p.; [Vol. II :] [VI p.] + 17 folding pl.) = Bibliothèque d'étude 46.

Subject of this thesis is a group of nine demotic papyri in Berlin, Cairo, Hamburg, Lille, and Prague (P. Berlin 3115; P. Cairo 30605, 30606, 30619, 31178, 31179; P. Hamburg I; P. Lille 29; P. Prague). Seven of these papyri are reproduced in the plate volume; for P. Hamburg I and the papyrus in Prague, the reader is referred to W. Erichsen's publication of these documents (see our Nos 59198 and 61214).

All nine documents are statutes of Egyptian cult guilds, drawn up in the Faiyûm area between 223 and 107 B.C.; only P. Berlin 3115 comes from Djeme. Although the cult guilds known so far from their statutes have counterparts in Greek institutions of a similar character, and flourished in the Ptolemaic Period, the practice of forming such associations must be older, since P. dem. Louvre E 7840[bis] attests to the existence of such a guild (6-nt) under Amasis. The statutes are invariably agreed upon unanimously by the members, and are valid for a period of twelve months; P. Berlin 3115 provides an example of a founding charter amended several times in the following two years. They define the authority of the elected officials, establish the rights and obligations of each member, assess the membership dues, regulate their collection, and fix the penalties for violations of the code. The duties include regular attendance at festivals and burials, provide for assistance to members and their families, and impose a rigid discipline.

The study of these statutes is divided into two main sections. The first consists of a transcription and translation of each document, followed by an extensive and painstaking commentary (p. 3-135). In the second half, the various problems raised by the text of the statutes are examined in detail. In this connection, one whole chapter is devoted to the officials and their functions; it includes an exhaustive discussion of the titles *mr šn, mr mš', wr, rwḏ, mḥ-2, 'š ('jš), ḫl-'3j, '3 n 6-nt, '3.w, ts*, and *sḥn*. Other chapters deal with legal and technical details. The membership lists and accounts attached to the statutes (including, in addition to the documents listed above, P. Cairo 30618 A and B) are reproduced on pl. IX-XVII, and transcribed and translated in an appendix to Vol. I (215-236). Four indexes and a bibliography round off this important contribution. *Dieter Mueller*

72133 de CENIVAL, Françoise, Une vente d'esclaves de l'époque d'Artaxerxes III (P. Inv. Sorbonne Nos 1276 et 1277), *RdE* 24 (1972), 31-39, with 2 pl.

Les deux papyrus mentionnés dans le titres, fragmentaires, sont d'un contenu identique relatif à la vente d'un esclave. Transcrits parallèlement, ils se complètent l'un l'autre. Il se peut que l'on ait affaire dans le second, soit à une simple copie du premier, soit à l'écrit corrélatif de renonciation, pourvu que l'on restitue dans une lacune du début la formule adéquate. La date des documents en fait le principal intérêt.   *Ph. Derchain*

72134 de CENIVAL, J. L., Sur la forme *sḏm.f* à redoublement ou *mrr.f*, *RdE* 24 (1972), 40-45.

Reprenant rapidement l'examen des emplois de la forme *sḏm.f* à redoublement, Cénival incline, à la suite de Polotski, à la considérer comme une forme nominale du verbe, fonctionnant la plupart du temps d'une manière analogue à l'infinitif. L'idée de continuité, de généralité ou d'habitude qui caractérise maintes fois cette forme serait une simple conséquence de la distribution des emplois sans impliquer pour autant la structure que Gardiner lui suppose à l'origine.   *Ph. Derchain*

72135 ČERNÝ, Jaroslav, Troisième série de questions adressées aux oracles, *BIFAO* 72 (1972), 46-69, with 11 pl.

The first series of questions addressed to the oracles and noted down on ostraca has appeared in *BIFAO* 35 (1935), 41-58, the second series in *BIFAO* 41 (1942), 13-24.
The present article, found among the papers of the author, has never been completed. It contains the numbers 38-95, all represented in facsimile on the plates. On pl. 25 four more texts are given (nos. 96-99), while the nos. 100-104 have been published previously by Sauneron (cfr our number 59538, the nos. 572-576).
Each text is transcribed and translated, with brief comments. A general discussion of the material is absent.

72136 CHADDICK, P. R. and F. Filce LEEK, Further Specimens of Stored Products Insects Found in Ancient Egyptian Tombs, *Journal of Stored Products Research*, Oxford 8 (1972), 83-86, with 2 tables.

Mention of insect remains found in 7 samples of bread from Egyptian tombs.

72137 Champollion et le 150ᵉ anniversaire du déchiffrement des hiéroglyphes. Musée du Caire, 2 Novembre 1972 (16 × 24.2 cm; 25 p., 2 pl.). At head of title : Organisation générale des antiquités égyptiennes.

Catalogue of an exhibition of books, manuscripts and other documents in the Cairo Museum in honour of Champollion. There is also an Arabic version.

72138 CHARLESWORTH, Dorothy, Tell el-Fara'in. Egypt. An Industrial Site in the Nile Delta, *Archaeology* 25 (1972), 44-47, with 1 plan, 1 map, 4 ill. and 1 fig.

Short discussion of the results of the excavations at Tell el-Fara'in; cfr our number 69573.
Industrial debris, pottery kilns and hearths demonstrate that the place (Buto) was an important industrial centre in the Graeco-Roman Period.

72139 CHASSINAT, É. et Fr. DAUMAS, Le temple de Dendara. Tome septième. Texte [et] Planches, Le Caire, Imprimerie de l'Institut français d'Archéologie orientale, 1972 (24.4 × 33.9 cm; [Texte] : VII + 223 p.; [Plates] : 100 pl. [numbered DXCII-DCXCI]. At head of title : Publications de l'Institut français d'Archéologie orientale du Caire.

Sequel to our number 65118.
The introduction discusses the modern approach to the reproduction of scenes and the necessity of overall pictures of complete walls, which is important for the order of rites and prescriptions.
The text volume continues with the inscriptions of the offering room (with notation T), the two adjacent ones U and V, the last of which is the room of the Eastern staircase, and the Eastern staircase itself (W). At the end there is an index to the titles of the scenes (p. 207-213).
The order in the plate volume corresponds with that of the text volume. The material on the plates is given in line drawing and in photograph, with diagrams of the disposition of the scenes on the walls.   *L. M. J. Zonhoven*

72140 CHEVRIER, Henri, Le troisième pylone de Karnak. Une aventure en archéologie, *Archéologia*, Paris No 51 (octobre 1972), 36-43, with 10 ill. (1 in colour).

The author describes the difficulties he had to oppose when rearranging the blocks from the interior of the Third Pylon of Karnak. He succeeded, however, in reconstructing the famous kiosk of Sesostris I, a sanctuary of Amenophis I, and a slightly younger unfinished (?) monument.   *L. M. J. Zonhoven*

CHIARELLI, B. A., see our numbers 72467 and 72577.

72141 CIBOIS, Philippe, Les erreurs de l'enregistrement sur ordinateur de REM 1001 à 1110. Repérage automatique des erreurs, *MNL* No 10 (Juillet 1972), 10-14.

Bei der Registratur der meroitischen Texte REM 1001-REM 1110 haben sich einige Fehler eingeschlichen, die zwar erst nach der Edition der Texte aber vor Fertigstellung des Indexes entdeckt wurden. Bei der Benutzung der Transliteration und Analyse der Texte (vgl. unsere Nummer 72286) muß daher der vorliegende Artikel herangezogen werden.   *Inge Hofmann*

72142 CIBOIS, P., J. LECLANT and M. de VIRVILLE, Le traitement sur ordinateur des inscriptions meroitiques, *Informatique et Sciences Humaines*, Paris 15 (Décembre 1972), 1-28, with 2 fig. and 1 table.

Die Studie beinhaltet die Aufnahme der etwa 900 bekannten meroitischen Texte, ihre Aufschlüsselung, Verarbeitung, Transkription und summarische Analyse. Es werden die verschiedenen Programme beschrieben, mit deren Hilfe das Meroitische aufbereitet und registriert wurde. Am Beispiel REM 1064 A und 1064 B wird aufgezeigt, wie der registrierte Text später aussieht (vgl. Stele S. 19 mit registriertem Text S. 23).

Inge Hofmann

72143 CLAYTON, P. A., Giovanni Belzoni, een pionier in de Egyptologie, *Spiegel Historiael* 468-471, with 9 ill.

"Giovanni Belzoni, a pioneer in Egyptology".
The author describes the life of Belzoni, his pioneer work in Egyptian archaeology and his importance for the Egyptian collection of the British Museum.   *L. M. J. Zonhoven*

72144 CLAYTON, Peter A., Royal Bronze Shawabti Figures, *JEA* 58 (1972), 167-175, with 1 fig., 1 table and 2 pl.

Only six royal bronze shawabtis were known before the discovery of the royal tombs at Tanis 1939, one being of Ramesses II and five of Ramesses III. A number of others were found in the tomb of Psusennes but were later stolen and dispersed throughout various collections. The Ramesses II figure in Berlin Museum now constitutes only the upper half with part of the sixth chapter of the *Book of the Dead* remaining, and must have been about 30 cm. high when complete, being probably once inlaid. It is a very early piece of hollow-casting which it is suggested may have come from a S.W. room in his tomb called M. All the Ramesses III figures are solid cast and about 12.5 cm. high, being inferior to the earlier work, with no insignia of royalty and having only a short inscription on the front. There are two types of Psusennes figures, workers and *reis*, both being solid cast and averaging about 8 cm. high, no less than 333 being catalogued. A table giving the results of microspectrographic analyses is appended, those of earlier date being shown to be almost pure copper.   *E. Uphill*

CLERC, Gisèle, see our number 72420.

72145 CLÈRE, J. J., Une statue naophore hathorique d'Époque
Saïte, *RdE* 24 (1972), 46-54, with 2 pl.

La statue en question, vue en 1964 pour la dernière fois chez un
antiquaire égyptien, appartient à un certain Ankhhor qui vivait
sous la XXVIᵉ Dynastie. On peut supposer qu'elle se dressait
dans le temple de Mefkat = Kom Abou Billouh. Elle porte
un texte biographique relatant l'activité du dédicant dans sa
ville et fournit sa titulature, qui ne permet toutefois pas
d'identifier autrement le personnage.   *Ph. Derchain*

72146 CLIFFORD, Richard J., The Cosmic Mountain in Canaan and
the Old Testament, Cambridge, Massachusetts, Harvard University Press, 1972 (13.7 × 21 cm; [XIV +]221 p.); rev. *Biblische
Zeitschrift* 18 (1974), 314-315 (Josef Scharbert); *BiOr* 31 (1974),
112-115 (Gerhard F. Hasel); *Journal of Biblical Literature* 92
(1973), 443-444 (David L. Petersen); *Revue Biblique* 80 (1973),
452 (B. Zuber).

In this study on the cosmic mountain, its meaning and function
in Canaan and the Old Testament a chapter is devoted to
ancient Egypt (p. 25-29), particularly dealing with the primeval
hill.

72147 COCHE-ZIVIE, Christiane, Nitocris, Rhodopis et la troisème
pyramide de Giza, *BIFAO* 72 (1972), 115-138.

After offering a translation of the passages about Nitocris,
Rhodopis and the daughter of Cheops by Herodotus and various
other classical authors Mme Coche attempts to interpret these
stories.
Elements of the story of Cheops' daughter may have been
derived from unknown Egyptian sources. Nitocris is the
Greek transcription of *Nt-ìḳrt*, a name occurring in the Turin
Royal Canon as that of a ruler of the VIth Dynasty, probably
to be connected with the prenomen *Mn-kȝ-Rˤ* elsewhere.
Confusion of her monument with the third pyramid is well
explicable. The features ascribed to Nitocris, blond hair and
pink cheeks, may originally have belonged to Rhodopis.
The historical Rhodopis was certainly a courtesan from Naucratis
called Doricha. Her relations with the Saite Dynasty were
reason to connect her with Gîza, where the dynasty restored
the third pyramid.
The two traditions, that of Nitocris and that of Rhodopis,
though deriving elements from each other, never have been
fused completely.

72148 COHEN, Chayim, Hebrew *tbh* : Proposed Etymologies, *Journal of the Ancient Near Eastern Society of Columbia University*, New York 4 (1972), 36-51.

The Hebrew word תבה is used both to indicate the ark of Noah and the receptacle for the child Moses. The author rejects the assumed Egyptian etymologies of the word (*dbȝt* or *dpt*). Its meaning is still obscure, but the double use has a parallel in the description of vessels in the Akkadian flood story and the story of Sargon's birth, doubtless because of the protective quality of divine origin which the "ark" and the receptacle both possessed.

72149 COLLON, Dominique, The Smiting God. A Study of a Bronze in the Pomerance Collection in New York, *Levant*, London 4 (1972), 111-134, with 9 fig. containing 73 drawings.

Study on account of a bronze statuette (15.1 cm. high) recently acquired by Mr Leon Pomerance, New York. The figure, wearing the Upper Egyptian crown, is standing on a lion, in his left hand a spear, his right hand raised above his head probably brandishing an axe or a mace (now lost). The badly corroded statuette was provided with a tenon protruding from the belly of the lion, hence fitted into a socket probably at the top of a staff or standard.
The author draws up a catalogue of bronze figures of the Smiting God (with full data and a drawing of each one) from various sites in the Near East and countries around the Mediterranean, all together over 75 instances, in numerous styles and techniques. The unifying feature is the tall head-dress, sometimes resembling the white crown, in other instances cylindrically or conically shaped, possibly as result of Hittite influence. No other examples standing on a lion are known, although the motif occurs in glyptic art. The smiting posture is of Egyptian origin. Outside Egypt it is connected with the Weather-god.
In this connection the author mentions the Reshef stelae from Egypt. At the end she sketches the history of the Smiting God down to the Roman Imperial Period.

72150 CONTI-FUHRMAN, Anna and Emma RABINO MASSA, Preliminary Note on the Ultrastructure of the Hair from an Egyptian Mummy Using the Scanning Electron Microscope, *Journal of Human Evolution*, London and New York 1 (1972), 487-488, with 1 pl.

Study of the ultrastructure of human hair may provide indications on the change which these structures underwent during time.

Reprinted in : Population Biology of the Ancient Egyptians. Edited by D. R. Brothwell [and] B. A. Chiarelli, London and New York, Academic Press, 1973.

CONTI, Anna, see also our number 72406.

72151 COOMBS, David, Treasures of Tutankhamun, *The Connoisseur*, London 180, No. 724 (June 1972), 159, with 1 ill.

Short report on the Tutankhamon exhibition at London in 1972.

72152 COONEY, John, Art of the Ancient World, *Apollo*, London 96, No. 130 (December 1972), 474-485, with 24 ill. (1 in colour).

The December issue of the periodical is devoted to the Nelson Gallery in Kansas City, which also possess a number of Egyptian works of art, e.g. : the Vth Dynasty statues of Re-wer and Methety, a head of Sesostris III, a fragment of the wall frescoes from the Tomb of Two Sculptors (Theban tomb no. 181) representing a banquetting scene, a XXVth Dynasty wooden statuette of a woman, a bronze statuette of an unknown king of the Late Period, and a porphyry torso representing the priest Archibeios (3rd century B.C.). Moreover there is in the collection one of the boy statues from the Isis shrine at Sheikh Ibada (Roman Period).

All objects are depicted and briefly discussed.

72153 COONEY, John D., Major Macdonald, a Victorian Romantic, *JEA* 58 (1972), 280-285, with 1 pl.

While working among the reserve collections of the Egyptian Department in the British Museum the writer stumbled across traces of a man, hitherto almost unknown in Egyptology, who had rendered considerable contributions to the subject. The life of this man, Major C. K. Macdonald, first excavator of Serabit el-Khadim and explorer of other places in Sinai, is here examined as far as is possible. Some account is also given of the interesting collection of antiquities assembled by this intrepid Major, and reference made to the important squeezes of inscriptions that he presented to the B.M., and at the end the suggestion made that he could be acclaimed "the first excavator in Egypt with any semblance of a scientific approach in his work".

Compare also *JEA* 59 (1973), 233.   *E. Uphill*

72154 COONEY, John D., Portraits from Roman Egypt, *The Bulletin of The Cleveland Museum of Art*, Cleveland, Ohio 59, Number 2 (February 1972), 50-55, with 4 ill. (one on cover).

In his introduction to the publication of three mummy portraits in the Cleveland Museum of Art the author makes remarks on the funerary masks of pharaonic Egypt.

72155 COONEY, John D., Two Royal Heads, *Newsletter ARCE* No. 80 (January 1972), 33.

Abstract of a paper.
On the dating of two heads in the Norbert Schimmel Collection and the Freer Gallery of Art.   *L. M. J. Zonhoven*

72156 COQUIN, René-Georges, La christianisation des temples de Karnak, *BIFAO* 72 (1972), 169-178, with 1 folded plan and 2 pl.

The author discusses the adaptation of the *Akh-Menu* to a Coptic church and some faint traces of Coptic paintings and an inscription in the building, as well as two inscriptions in the temple of Khonsu and traces of christianization in the temple of Opet.

72157 CORCORAN, Donald, A Collection of Egyptian Antiquities from the Twelfth Century B.C. to the Tenth Century A.D., New York - Vienne, [1972] (17 × 23.3 cm; 12 p., 9 pl.).

Catalogue of a collection sold by the art dealer Corcoran, containing i.a. three fragments of copies of the *Book of the Dead*, a cartonnage mummy mask formed from papyri with Demotic writing, and various Coptic papyri.

72158 Le CORSU, France, Index des tomes 1 à 20. Revue d'Égyptologie publiée par la Société française d'Égyptologie. Avec le concours du Centre National de la Recherche Scientifique, Paris, Éditions Klincksieck, 1972 (22 × 27 cm; 139 p.).

The volume contains very extensive indexes to vol. 1-20 of the *RdE*. After a list of articles and of reviews arranged after the author's name and a list of necrologies and bibliographies there follow indexes to: monuments, objects and documents; museums and collections; geographical names; divinities and their epithets; kings and members of the royal family; private names; titles and epithets of private persons; texts; Egyptian and other words; and a general index.

72159 CROZIER-BRELOT, Claude, Constitution d'un fichier de citations à l'aide d'un ordinateur. Application : Index des citations des Textes des Pyramides. Utilisation : Enquêtes sur la notion de *Sekhem* dans les T.P., *Annuaire. École Pratique des Hautes Études.* V^e section — sciences religieuses, Paris 69 (1971-1972), 443-445.

The author presents a brief survey of the method followed in her index to the Pyr. Texts (cfr our number 71135) and an example of its use as applied to the notion *sḫm*.

72160 CROZIER-BRELOT, Claude, Table de Concordances des Textes de Pyramides, 2 volumes, [Paris, 1972] (27 × 21 cm; 583 unnumbered p.).

Tables of concordances between the various versions of the *Pyramid Texts*, so far as present in Sethe's edition, as ordered and printed by the computer. The first part proceeds from the numbers of the paragraphs, the others from the versions in the pyramids of Unas, Tety, Pepy I, Merenre and Pepy II respectively.

72161 CROZIER-BRELOT, Claude, Textes des sarcophages. Index des citations, [Paris, 1972] (16 × 20.7 cm; X + 52 p.).

First edition of an index of quotations from the *Coffin Texts* (for the *Pyramid Texts*, cfr our number 71135).
In this volume are collected quotations from 19 publications (listed on p. VI-VII), arranged according to the publication of the *CT* by A. de Buck.

72162 CROZIER-BRELOT, Claude, Utilisation de l'ordinateur pour l'etablissement d'un index de citations. Application aux Textes des Pyramides, *BSFE* No 63 (Mars 1972), 33-43, with 2 tables.

Survey of the methods applied by the author in composing an index of quotations to the *Pyramid Texts*. Cfr our number 71135.

72163 CURTO, Silvio, Archaeological Outline from the Paleolithic to the Modern Arab State, *Journal of Human Evolution*, London and New York 1 (1972), 141-146, with 1 map.

Among the peoples of Antiquity, the ancient Egyptians have given us by far the largest and well-balanced evidence of texts and monuments as well as mummified human remains. Therefore historical and anthropological researches can be developed in this field through fruitful collaboration. The main components of said evidence are described; some original gaps and successive particular destructions should be kept in mind in order to avoid false generalizations and distortions in theory.
Reprinted in : Population Biology of the Ancient Egyptians. Edited by D. R. Brothwell [and] B. A. Chiarelli, London and New York, Academic Press, 1973.   *Author's own summary*

72164 CURTO, Silvio, Jean-François Champollion en Italie et en Égypte, *Archeologia*, Paris No 52 (novembre 1972), 20-29, with 8 ill. (1 in colour).

Description of the life and works of Champollion, particularly his travels through Italy and Egypt, for the general public.

72165 CURTO, Silvio, Jean-François Champollion et l'Italie, *BSFE* No. 65 (Octobre 1972), 13-24, with 2 ill.

Survey of Champollion's studies and honours in Italy, with particular attention to his work in the field of the history of writing.

72166 DANIEL, Laurent, Reconstitution d'une paroi du temple d'Aton à Karnak, *Kêmi* 21 (1971), 151-154, with 1 folding fig.

Chargé de dessiner des scènes amarniennes retirées du blocage du IXe pylône d'Amon, l'auteur n'a pas tardé à noter des raccords. L'appareil très régulier posait les assises de blocs alternativement en longueur et en largeur. D'épais joints de plâtre compensaient jadis les irrégularités de taille. Les scènes d'artisanat figuraient les ateliers de très grands bâtiments à enceinte, séparés par des avenues rectilignes à angle droit. Une figure, sur planche dépliante, représente l'un des 3 magasins réassemblés, dont la structure se ressemble. Les assises 11-13 du môle en voie de démontage ont permis de recomposer déjà une paroi de 18 × 4 m.   *J. Custers*

72167 DAUMAS, François, Champollion le Jeune déchiffre les hiéro-glyphes, *Archeologia*, Paris No 52 (novembre 1972), 10-19, with 13 ill. (1 in colour).

Vivid description of Champollion's decipherment for the general public.

DAUMAS, François, see also our number 72139.

72168 DAVIDE, D., Survey of the Skeletal and Mummy Remains of Ancient Egyptians Available in Research Collections, *Journal of Human Evolution*, London and New York 1 (1972), 155-159, with 4 tables.

Survey of the location of 475 mummified human remains and 8977 skeletons and isolated skulls from ancient Egypt in museums all over the world, a large part of which at Turin. Reprinted in : Population Biology of the Ancient Egyptians. Edited by D. R. Brothwell [and] B. A. Chiarelli, London and New York, Academic Press, 1973.

72169 DAVIES, W. V., The meaning of the group ⟨hieroglyphs⟩ in the inscription of *Ḥr-wr-r'* (Sinai, No. 90,8), *JEA* 58 (1972), 300.

Read here as *m r ḫȝt(y)* "at the door of the office".   *E. Uphill*

72170 DAVIS, Virginia Lee, Subdivisions of Egyptian and their Designations, *Newsletter ARCE* No. 83 (October 1972), 25.

Abstract of a paper.
Recent advances in Egyptian linguistics make the adequacy of the palaeographic and linguistic terms for the various subdivisions of Egyptian doubtful.   *L. M. J. Zonhoven*

DELLA VALLE, E., see our number 72110.

72171 DAVISSON, William I. and James E. HARPER, European Economic History. Volume I. The Ancient World, New York, Appleton-Century-Crofts Educational Division, Meredith Corp., 1972 (15.5 × 23.5 cm; XIV + 288 p., 10 maps and 4 fig.).

Subject of this textbook is a survey of the economic history of the ancient world. The first five chapters deal with the emergence of civilization in the great river valleys of Egypt and Mesopotamia. The pre-market economy of Egypt in the Bronze Age, described as a centralized system of re-distribution according to rank, is examined in some detail, though mainly on the basis of secondary literature (Frankfort, Gardiner, Kees, Wilson). Egypt is also mentioned in connection with the Iron-Age economy; the ninth chapter, a survey of the Hellenistic economy from Alexander the Great to the Roman conquest, includes a concise treatment of the economic system of Ptolemaic Egypt.   *Dieter Mueller*

72172 DAWSON, Warren R. and Eric P. UPHILL, Who was Who in Egyptology. A Biographical Index of Egyptologists; of Travellers, Explorers and Excavators in Egypt; of Collectors of and Dealers in Egyptian Antiquities; of Consuls, Officials, Authors, Benefactors, and others whose names occur in the Literature of Egyptology, from the year 1500 to the present day, but excluding persons now living. Second revised edition, London, The Egypt Exploration Society, [1972] (14 × 22 cm; XIV + 315 p., frontispiece); rev. *CdE* XLIX, No. 97 (1974), 80-85 (Baudouin van de Walle); *JARCE* 11 (1974), 108 (Hans Goedicke).   Pr. bound £ 7

Second, revised and much enlarged edition of our number 1736. The total of the entries has been increased from c. 750 to c. 1050, the new names mainly belonging either to people living between A.D. 1500 and 1700 or to scholars who have died between 1950 and 1968. Most of the entries were partly re-written, some are completely new. For the first time the major works of the principal figures have been mentioned. As in the first edition each entry ends with bibliographical references.

72173 DECKER, Wolfgang, "Sportlehrer" im alten Ägypten, *in* : *Perspektiven der Sportwissenschaft*, Schorndorff, Hofmann-Verlag, 1972 (= Jahrbuch der Deutschen Sporthochschule Köln, 1972), 29-37.

L'auteur réunit six documents égyptiens de la première période intermédiaire au Nouvel Empire qui prouvent qu'un certain enseignement sportif était assuré en Égypte, pour la natation et le tir à l'arc en tout cas. Nous ne sommes toutefois pas informés sur la personne des instructeurs.   *Ph. Derchain*

DELLA VALLE, E., see our number 72110.

72174 DEMORIANE, Hélène, Champollion, *Connaissance des Arts*, Paris No 246 (août 1972), 30-39, with 12 ill. (11 in colour) and a colour ill. on cover.

Article on the life, travels and discoveries of Champollion on the occasion of the Champollion memorial year 1972.
On p. 71-73 there is also an introduction to the reading of hieroglyphs for the general public.   *L. M. J. Zonhoven*

72175 DEMORIANE, H., L'Égypte 150 ans après Champollion, *Connaissance des Arts*, Paris No 243 (mai 1972), 9-11.

Short note on the activities in the Champollion memorial year 1972, in France and Egypt.

72176 DERCHAIN, Philippe, Hathor Quadrifrons. Recherches sur la syntaxe d'un mythe égyptien, Istanbul, Nederlandsch Historisch-Archaeologisch Instituut in het Nabije Oosten, 1972 (19.5 × 26.7 cm; [X +]55 pp., 8 pl.) = Uitgaven van het Nederlandsch Historisch Archaeologisch Instituut te Istanbul, 28.; rev. *BiOr* 30 (1973), 209-211 (Erich Winter); *CdE* XLVIII, No 96 (1973), 292-294 (J. Cl. Goyon); *JEA* 60 (1974), 282-284 (J. Gwyn Griffiths).   Pr. fl. 48.50

Comme le sous-titre l'indique, l'auteur se préoccupe des structures selon lesquelles les Egyptiens ont associé les éléments de leur mythologie et de définir ainsi les significations qu'ils ont cherché à exprimer. Il examine ainsi un groupe d'une vingtaine de passages d'inscriptions des temples ptolémaïques où Hathor est décrite comme une déesse à quatre visages, pour indiquer sa qualité de souveraine de l'univers. Il montre que ce type iconographique remonte certainement au Moyen Empire car on y trouve une allusion dans les *Textes des Sarcophages*. Toutefois, les variations les plus subtiles sur ce thème n'apparaîtront qu'à Dendara où l'aspect quadruple est spécialement présent dans la partie axiale de la paroi du fond du temple et de la crypte centrale du mur sud.

L'équivalence exprimée dans certains textes de Hathor à quatre visages et de Temet, forme féminine d'Atoum, justifie la brève enquête à laquelle cette dernière est soumise, comme d'autres allusions ont nécessité le chapitre suivant "Hathor dans la barque solaire". On s'aperçoit que la déesse joue souvent auprès de Râ le rôle de pilote en même temps qu'elle est chargée d'une fonction érotique et que de double rôle permet aux décorateurs égyptiens de la faire alterner soit avec Maât soit avec Iousäas et Nebet Hetepet, qu'elle exprime l'idée d'un éros universel et primordial issu du Démiurge et qui indique le moteur qui l'incite à la création.

Dans un chapitre final intitulé "Du mythe à la philosophie", l'auteur montre que le système héliopolitain duquel dépend la construction qu'il vient d'étudier ne diffère que par les mythes de référence choisis d'une façon cohérente du système memphite, mais que l'un comme l'autre ont cherché à rendre compte de l'élan créateur, éros pour l'un, imagination pour l'autre.

Un index des textes étudiés et traduits termine l'ouvrage.

Ph. Derchain

72177 DERCHAIN, Philippe, Intelligenz als Karriere (*Neferti*, 10-11), *GM* Heft 3 (1972), 9-14.

The expression *qn.n gb3.f* (*Neferty* 10-14 and *Urk. IV*, 414,17) must be distinguished from the more frequently attested *qn gb3wy* or *qn 'wy* of the Ramesside Period. It signifies a person "whose arm has been industrious", i.e. a self-made man. The emergence of this concept is closely connected with the political and social situation at the beginning of the XIIth Dynasty.   *Dieter Mueller*

72178 DESANGES, Jehan, L'amphore de Tubusuctu (Mauretanie) et la datation de Teqêrideamani, *MNL* No 11 (Décembre 1972), 17-21.

Die Pyramide Beg. N. 28 gehört einem meroitischen Herrscher Teqêrideamani; Grabbeigaben weisen eine zeitliche Nähe zu den Pyramiden Beg. N. 15, 17, 18, 19 auf. Beg. N. 15 wurde bisher in die Epoche des Tiberius datiert, während Beg. N. 28 wegen eines demotischen Graffito von Philae, das einen König *Tqrrmn* nennt, um 266 n.Chr. angesetzt wurde. St. Wenig (vgl. Nr. 67600) nimmt jedoch einen König Teqêrideamani I. mit der Pyramide Beg. N. 28 in der Zeit des Trajan und einen König Teqêrideamani II. als Zeitgenossen des Trebonius Gallus an. Eine Amphore aus Beg. N. 28 erweist sich durch eine lateinische Inschrift als Importstück aus Tubusuctu (Tiklat) in Mauretanien. Amphoren der gleichen Provenienz fanden sich im Rom und Ostia; dort lassen sie sich in das zweite Viertel des 3. Jahr-

hunderts n.Chr. datieren. Beg. N. 28 gehört daher dem Herrscher
Teqêrideamani, der durch das Graffito in die Mitte des
3. vorchristlichen Jahrhunderts datiert wird, und man braucht
keinen zweiten König desselben Namens anzunehmen.

Inge Hofmann

72179 DESANGES, Jehan, Les raids des Blemmyes sous le règne de
Valens, en 373-374, *MNL* No 10 (Juillet 1972), 32-34.

In einer demotischen Inschrift des Isistempels von Philae vom
November 373 n.Chr. wird die Auseinandersetzung von *Ble.w*,
in denen die Blemmyer zu sehen sind, mit den Einwohnern
von '*Hbe.w* erwähnt. Damit ist wahrscheinlich Hibis gemeint.
Zur gleichen Zeit sind die Blemmyer aber auch am Roten Meer
nachzuweisen, wo sie die Halbinsel Sinai überfielen. In
Verbindung mit den Sarazenen zerstörten sie christliche Nieder-
lassungen und waren, da sie zweifellos von persischer Seite
unterstützt wurden, um 373-374 n.Chr. eine Quelle der Gefahr
für Valens.   *Inge Hofmann*

72180 DESROCHES-NOBLECOURT, Ch., Un buste monumental
d'Aménophis IV. Don prestigieux de l'Égypte à la France,
La Revue du Louvre et des Musées de France, Paris 22 (1972),
239-250, with 8 ill. and 1 colour pl.

Study of the monumental bust of Amenophis IV which has been
granted by Egypt as proof of its gratitude for the activities of
France in the Nubian campaign.
The royal statue comes from East Karnak and represents the
king naked and wearing a *pshent*, which for religious reasons
has been damaged afterwards. In the abnormal physical features
of the statue the author does not recognize the signs of a
disease; they were the result of a desire to translate the religious
ideas in the features of the royal body.

72181 DESROCHES-NOBLECOURT, Christiane, Pour remercier la
France de son œuvre de sauvegarde en Nubie, l'Égypte lui offre
un pharaon, *Connaissance des Arts*, Paris No 249 (novembre
1972), 96-97, with 1 colour ill.

The author discusses the colossal head of Akhnaton, presented
to the Louvre Museum by the Egyptian government. See our
preceding number.   *L. M. J. Zonhoven*

DESROCHES-NOBLECOURT, Christiane, see also our number 72525.

72182 DEVER, William G., Gezer, *Revue Biblique*, Paris 79 (1972),
413-418.

A short communication on the excavations at Tell Gezer, where especially stratum 7 yielded evidence of the relations with Egypt.
As to stratum 6, a destruction, possibly by Merenptah, is suggested. Stratum 7 belongs to the Amarna Period, in which the kings of Gezer may have occupied an important position, since ten letters from them were found in the Amarna correspondence. A destruction in stratum 8 may have been caused by Tuthmosis III in his first Asiatic campaign.

L. M. J. Zonhoven

72183 DEVER, William G., The 1971 Season of Excavations at Gezer (Israel), *AJA* 76 (1972), 208-209.

Summary of a paper.

72184 DEVER, W. G., Tel Gezer, *Israel Exploration Journal*, Jerusalem 22 (1972), 158-160, with 1 pl.

Field VI, stratum 7, belonging to the Amarna Age, yielded considerable quantities of Egyptian material. The destruction in stratum 8 may be due to Tuthmosis III.   *L. M. J. Zonhoven*

DEVER, William G., see also our number 72580.

72185 DEVRIES, Carl E., An Enigmatic Stone Object from A-Group Nubia, *Newsletter ARCE* No. 83 (October 1972), 25-26.

Abstract of a paper.
Mention is made of the occurrence of a number of palettes or grinding stones made of light-weighted stone among A-Group cemeteries at Qustul. On one specimen occurs incised carving or relief, which might be the earliest known example of incised relief.   *L. M. J. Zonhoven*

72186 DEVRIES, Carl E., To the Retiring Director of Chicago House at Luxor, *Newsletter ARCE* No. 81 (April 1972), 25-27.

A survey of Nims' activities in Egypt, on the occasion of his retirement as Director of Chicago House at Luxor.

L. M. J. Zonhoven

72187 DEWACHTER, Michel, La base d'une nouvelle statue de Senenmout, *BIFAO* 71 (1972), 87-96, with 3 pl. and 3 fig.

Publication of a statue base of black granite discovered by the author in 1971 near the entrance to the Valley of the Queens. It cannot be assigned to any of the many known statues of Senmut, but may have belonged to a copy of Cairo 42116 representing the famous dignitary with Hatshepsut's daughter Neferure.   *Dieter Mueller*

72188 DEWACIITER, Michel, Les cynocéphales ornant la base des deux obélisques de Louxor, *CdE* XLVII, Nos 93-94 (1972), 68-75.

Rappelant que les cynocéphales en adoration conservés au Louvre sous le No D.31 proviennent de la base de l'obélisque oriental de Louxor et non de celle de celui qui fut transporté à Paris, l'auteur réunit tous les exemples qu'il connaît de monuments analogues. Il distingue deux groupes, cynocéphales adossés et cynocéphales libres. On les trouve soit à la base des obélisques, soit au-dessus de la corniche d'une porte monumentale, soit avec certains autels. Le type en ronde bosse peut avoir été crée par Aménophis IV, mais a surtout été développé par Ramsès II.   *Ph. Derchain*

72189 DEWACHTER, Michel, Thèbes. Monuments en péril de la Vallée des Reines. La tombe de la reine Nebet-Taouy, *Archeologia*, Paris No 53 (décembre 1972), 18-24, with 7 ill. and 1 plan.

The author draws attention to the deplorable state of the tombs in the Valley of the Queens and studies one of them, no 60, belonging to Nebettaui, a daughter of Ramses II. The tomb has recently been partly cleared out and studied by the author as part of the C.E.D.A.E. program.
Comparing no 60 with nos 40 and 73 and other tombs Dewachter attempts to indicate its place within the evolution of the tomb in the period. He further discusses the remaining decorations as well as the role of princess Nebettaui, suggesting that she was a daughter of Queen Esenofre and later on queen-consort.

DEWEY, John R., see our number 72032.

72190 DIETRICH, M. und O. LORETZ, Die Schardena in den Texten von Ugarit, *in* : *Antike und Universalgeschichte*. Festschrift Hans Erich Stier zum 70. Geburtstag am 25. Mai 1972, Münster, Verlag Aschendorff, [1972] (= Fontes et Commentationes. Schriftenreihe des Institutes für Epigraphik an der Universität Münster. Supplementband 1), 39-42.

The authors first discuss the question whether the Šerdana occurring in the Amarna Letters are to be identified with the *Šrdn* from the time of Ramses II and III. Accepting the identity they suggest that the same people is meant with the word *ṯrtn* in the Ugaritic texts where they are mentioned together with other kinds of soldiers.

72191 DIXON, D. M., The Disposal of Certain Personal, Household and Town Waste in Ancient Egypt, *Man, Settlement and Urbanism* 647-650.

The author discusses the lavatories found in tombs and houses of the upper classes from the Archaic Period onwards, and the rubbish-heaps and abandoned buildings where a large proportion of the town and domestic refuse was dumped. He particularly mentions in this context the towns of Kahun, el-Amarna and Deir el-Medîna.

72192 DIXON, D. M., Masticatories in Ancient Egypt, *Journal of Human Evolution*, London and New York 1 (1972), 433-449, with 2 fig. (1 folding).

After a survey of the use of masticatories (quids) — substances chewed, for whatever purpose, without the intention of ingesting — in various parts of the world the author studies the evidence for ancient Egypt. The word for it may be *ḥpꜥw* (Pap. Ebers), though the verb *ḥpꜥ* has other meanings as well. Examples of quids in modern Egypt are mentioned, their use in pharaonic times being uncertain. The role of sugar cane was filled by papyrus. There is no evidence for the use of laudanum as masticatory, but that of natron is certain. The author points out that excavators have failed to recognize possible remains of masticatories.

Reprinted in : Population Biology of the Ancient Egyptians. Edited by D. R. Brothwell [and] B. A. Chiarelli, London and New York, Academic Press, 1973.

72193 DOBROVITS †, Aladár, Le chacal dans la barque, *Bulletin du Musée Hongrois des Beaux-Arts*, Budapest No 38 (1972), 3-12, with 1 ill.

Publication of a Ptolemaic stela in the Museum of Arts in Budapest. The upper register represents beneath the winged sun-disk a jackal standing in a papyrus-boat ; the second register contains an adoration scene of Osiris, Isis and Nephthys by the owner ; in the third a funerary text. This text contains ideas and phrases occurring in the *Book of the Dead*, ch. 102, as well as in some spells of the *Pyr. Texts*. The author also discusses the role of the jackal gods.

In a *Note additionelle* (p. 13) G[uillaume] W[essetzky] presents information about the posthumous article of Aladár Dobrovits. For an Hungarian version, compare p. 91-98.

72194 DONADONI, Sergio, Università degli Studi di Roma, *News-letter ARCE* No. 80 (January 1972), 22-25.

The excavation of Tomb No. 27 (Sheshonq) at Assasif was continued. The principal discoveries are in the field of epigraphy (biographical inscriptions).   *L. M. J. Zonhoven*

72195 DOTHAN, Trude, Anthropoid Clay Coffins from a Late Bronze Age Cemetery near Deir el-Balaḥ (Preliminary Report), *Israel Exploration Journal*, Jersusalem 22 (1972), 65-72, with 1 map, 1 plan and 5 pl.

At Deir el-Balaḥ, SW of Gaza, where previously a large number of anthropoid coffins, scarabs, shawabtis, and even Egyptian stelae have been found, excavations in 1972 brought to light three tombs with such coffins. They are of good quality, date from the Late Bronze Period, and may have belonged to members of the Egyptian army and Egyptianized local rulers and dignitaries.

72196 DOTHAN, Trude, בית־הקברות שליד דיר אל־בלח והקבורה בארונות־מתים דמויי־אדם בארץ־ישראל, *Qadmoniot*, Jerusalem 5 (1972), 21-25, with 1 map and 5 ill; rev. *ZAW* 85 (1973), 109 (J. Maier).

"The Cemetery near Deir el-Balaḥ and Burial in Anthropoid Sarcophagi in Eretz-Israel".

72197 DRENKHAHN, Rosemarie, Zur Anwendung der "Tagewähl-kalender", *MDAIK* 28 (1972), 85-94.

A comparison of historical dates from the New Kingdom with the calendars of lucky and unlucky days confirms that the Egyptians paid little attention to this distinction; the calendars are, in this respect, comparable to the horoscopes in modern newspapers.   *Dieter Mueller*

72198 DUNHAM, Dows, Ancient Egyptian and Near Eastern Acquisitions and Loans from the Horace L. Mayer Collection, *Boston Museum Bulletin*, Boston 70, No. 359 (1972), 14-21, with 1 pl. and 16 ill.

The article describes some objects from the collection of Horace L. Mayer placed on loan in the Boston Museum. Its major part has been acquired from the collection of Vassalli, an assistant of Mariette. Among the objects described are: two fragments of linen bearing inscriptions, which came from the Deir el-Bahari cache; a gold pendant representing a youthful king on a lotus, suggested to be Ramses II; and two kneeling statuettes, one of Necho II and one of Amenophis III.

Most of the museum numbers mentioned with the illustrations are now to be changed since the objects have been given to the Museum.

72199 DUNHAM, Dows, Recollections of an Egyptologist, Boston, Museum of Fine Arts, [1972] (21.8 × 28 cm; 55 p., 1 map, 37 ill. on cover).

Autobiographical sketch of the author as an excavator and Egyptologist, from his first job with Reisner at Gîza in 1914, through all his excavations in Gemmai, Gebel Barkal, Meroe, Naga ed-Dêr and Saqqâra, back to Gîza where he took part in the clearing of the burial chamber of queen Hetepheres, until his return to Boston in 1927. From that year onwards he worked in the Boston Museum. In 1946 he again visited Egypt and the Sudan.
The recollections contain many anecdotes related in a vivid style, from his excavating years as well as from his museum period. There are mentions of some colleagues such as Reisner and William Stevenson Smith, Miss Moss and Mrs Burney, etc. Several snapshots illustrate the scientific life of the author.

72200 DUPONT-SOMMER, André, Champollion et l'Académie des Inscriptions et Belles-Lettres. Discours pour la cérémonie du 20 octobre 1972 en l'honneur de Champollion, *Comptes rendus de l'Académie des Inscriptions et Belles-Lettres*, Paris, 1972, 544-556.

In his opening address of the session dedicated by the Académie to the memory of Champollion the author offers a survey of the life of Dacier as well as of Champollion. He particularly describes the relations between the Académie and the decipherer of the hieroglyphic writing.

72201 DUPONT-SOMMER, André, Champollion et ses amis, *Comptes rendus de l'Académie des Inscriptions et Belles-Lettres*, Paris, 1972, 677-690.

The author sketches Champollion's relations with several persons : his brother Champollion-Figeac; Joseph-Bon Dacier, the permanent secretary of the Académie des Inscriptions et Belles-Lettres; Jomard, member of the Commission d'Égypte; Young; various theologians, Champollion's opponents; the Pope Leo XII; and his admirer Signora Angelica Palli. Quoting from several letters, written mostly during his travels through Italy and Egypt, he shows Champollion in various moods, enthousiastic, indignant, etc.

72202 DZIERŻYKRAY-ROGALSKI, Tadeusz, Kadero — Recent Polish Research Post in the Sudan, *Africana-Bulletin*, Warszawa 17 (1972), 202-204, with 3 fig.

Kadero, 26 km von Khartum entfernt, wurde bereits 1955 entdeckt und beschrieben (vgl. unsere Nummer 3771). 1972 wurden zwei Gräber entdeckt; die Skelette lassen den Schluß zu, daß die Leichen auf der Seite liegend und mit angezogenen Beinen beigesetzt worden waren. Eines der Skelette aus Grab 2 gehörte einer Frau von ungefähr 50 Jahren. Perlenketten aus Karneol waren beigegeben.
Eine vorläufige Analyse datiert Kadero in die neolithische Kultur, und zwar später als Esh Shaheinab. *Inge Hofmann*

72203 DZIERŻYKRAY-ROGALSKI, Tadeusz, Remains of a Mummy of the Late Period Found in a Rock Tomb Discovered above the Temple of Queen Hatshepsut at Deir el-Bahari (Egypt) in 1970, *Études et Travaux*, Warszawa 6 (1972), 93-100, with 2 plans, 1 fig. and 2 ill.

Publication of the find of a mummy from the Late Period in a rock tomb above the temple of Hatshepsut. The modest remains of mummy and funerary equipment are described.

DZIEWANOWSKI, Andzrej, see our numbers 72489, 72490 and 72491.

72204 EDEL, Elmar, ✝ ☐ 𓀀𓀁 *nj-rmṯw-nswt* "ein Besitzer von Menschen ist der König", *GM* Heft 2 (1972), 15-17.

The name Ranke, *Personennamen I*, 225,23 should be read *ny-rmṯw-nswt*, following the pattern of several other names such as *ny-ibw-nswt* and *ny-ḫꜣswt-nswt*. This supports the reading *ny-mꜣʿt-rʿ* ("Lamares") for the name of Amenemhet III, which was rejected several years ago by W. Westendorf (see our No. 60750). *Dieter Mueller*

72205 EDWARDS, I.E.S., Jaroslav Černý. 1898-1970, *Proceedings of the British Academy*, London 58 (1972), 367-377, with portrait.

Obituary notice. Compare our number 70615.

72206 EDWARDS, I. E. S., Some reflections on the Tutankhamun Exhibition, *The Burlington Magazine*, London 114 (1972), 202-206, with 13 ill.

Some remarks on the Tutankhamun exhibition in the British Museum for the general reader.

72207 EDWARDS, I. E. S., The Tutankhamun Exhibition, *The British Museum Society Bulletin*, London 9 (February 1972), 7-11, with 4 ill. (one on cover).

The author gives some background information on the London exhibition, its preparations and the way the objects are displayed, as well as on the king himself and his tomb.

72208 EDWARDS, I. E. S., Tutankhamun's debt to the Rosetta Stone, *The Times*, London, October 20, 1972.

A short history of the decipherment of the Egyptian hieroglyphs.

EDWARDS, I. E. S., see also our number 72716.

EDZARD, D. O., see our number 72521.

EGGEBRECHT, Arne, see our number 72687.

EGLOFF, M., see our number 72369.

72209 ELANSKAYA, A. I., La loi de proportion en copte et la catégorie du temps en égyptien, *RdE* 24 (1972), 55-59.

Sous les termes français "loi de proportion", l'auteur entend "das Gesetz der Polarität" de Brunner (*ZÄS* 72 [1936], 139-141) et se réfère à l'inversion des emplois de *sdm.f* et de *sdm.n.f* dans les phrases affirmatives et négatives. Cette opposition et son dérivé en copte montrent selon l'auteur que le système verbal égyptien aurait été fondé essentiellement sur des notions de temps et non d'aspects.   *Ph. Derchain*

72210 ELANSKAYA, A. I., Коптология, *in* : *Азиатский музей* — Ленинградское отделение Института востоковедения АН СССР, Москва, Издательство "Наука",1972, 516-526.

"Coptic Studies".
A short history of Coptic studies at the Leningrad department of the Institute, whose egyptological activities are recounted in our number 72069. The present section deals with O. E. Lemm, P. V. Jernstedt and A. I. Jelanskaya.   *J. F. Borghouts*

72211 ERTMAN, Earl L., The Earliest Known Three-Dimensional Representation of the God Ptah, *JNES* 31 (1972), 83-86, with 2 ill.

The Norbert Schimmel Collection in New York has recently acquired a limestone head of a bearded man wearing a tight-fitting skull cap. It represents in all likelihood the god Ptah and is, if it indeed dates from the XIIth Dynasty, the oldest extant example of a Ptah statue known so far.

Dieter Mueller

72212 ERTMAN, Earl L., The "Gold of Honor" in Royal Representation, *Newsletter ARCE* No. 83 (October 1972), 26-27.

Abstract of a paper.
The form of a New Kingdom necklace of gold disk-shaped *shebyu* beads is traced, and its connection with the cult of Amon is speculated upon.   *L. M. J. Zonhoven*

72213 EVRARD-DERRIKS, Claire, A propos des miroirs égyptiens à manche en forme de statuette féminine, *Revue des Archéologues et Historiens d'Art de Louvain*, Leuven 5 (1972), 6-16, with 2 ill.

The nude feminine figures serving as mirror handles do not represent Hathor, Isis, or Astarte, but are those of young servants. The hair styles of these figures, and their postures are discussed in some detail.   *Dieter Mueller*

72214 The Facsimile Edition of the Nag Hammadi Codices. Codex VI + Introduction. Published under the Auspices of the Department of Antiquities of the Arab Republic of Egypt in Conjunction with the United Nations Educational, Scientific and Cultural Organization, Leiden, E. J. Brill, 1972 ([Codex VI]: 24 × 33 cm; XII p., 84 pl.; [Introduction]: 23 × 31 cm; II + 19 p., loose); rev. *BiOr* 30 (1973), 428-430 (R. Haardt); *OLZ* 69 (1974), 229-243 (Hans-Martin Schenke); *Rivista* 47 (1972), 47-48 (Tito Orlandi).   Pr. cloth fl. 160

Introduction. The brochure by the hand of James M. Robichon, meant for the entire series, discusses the discovery of the library, the history of its publication, and the contents of the facsimile edition. Added are inventories of the library.
Codex VI begins with a preface by the same author, both in Arabic and English.
The contents of the text have been studied by Martin Krause and Pahor Labib (our number 71335).
The plates present pictures of the outside of the cover (p. 1-2), of the codex as it was, opened at the centre, before the cutting of the sheets (pl. 3), and of all 78 pages in the original size as well as of some small fragments.

72215 The Facsimile Edition of the Nag Hammadi Codices. Codex VII. Published under the Auspices of the Department of Antiquities of the Arab Republic of Egypt in Conjunction with the United Nations Educational, Scientific and Cultural Organization, Leiden, E. J. Brill, 1972 (24 × 33 cm; XIV p., 136 pl.); rev. *WZKM* 65/66 (1973/74), 237-241 (R. Haardt).
     Pr. cloth fl. 195

Sequel to our preceding number.
The introduction by James M. Robichon, in Arabic and English,

presents general information concerning the codex and mentions earlier studies.

The plates reproduce the outside and inside of the cover and all 127 p., in the original size.

72216 FAIRMAN, H.W., Tutankhamun and the end of the 18th Dynasty, *Antiquity* 46 (1972), 15-18.

If Tutankhamun and Smenkhkare were indeed brothers, as a recent examination of their mummies suggests (see our No. 72301), one must conclude that their parents were Amenophis III and Sitamun. The article examines the chronological feasibility of this theory.   *Dieter Mueller*

72217 FAIRSERVIS, Jr., Walter A., Excavations at Hierakonpolis — A review, *Newsletter ARCE* No. 80 (January 1972), 33.

Abstract of a paper.
An evaluation of two seasons of field work at Hierakonpolis in 1967 and 1969.   *L. M. J. Zonhoven*

72218 FAIRSERVIS, Jr., W.A., Preliminary Report on the First Two Seasons at Hierakonpolis. Part I, *JARCE* 9 (1971-1972), 7-27, with 33 pl. (2 folding) containing 2 maps, 5 plans, 32 fig. and 11 ill.

An archaeological, geomorphological and ecological survey was started in 1967 and continued in 1968. Excavation of the Kôm el-Ahmar proceeded from the Town Wall to the "New Kingdom" wall of the Temple Area. Horemkhaʿufʾs tomb (Dyn. XVII) was recorded with the exception of the burial chamber. Compare our numbers 139 and 1598.
See also our numbers 72317, 72318 and 72761.
          M. Heerma van Voss

72219 FAIRSERVIS, Jr., Walter A., Preliminary Report on the First Two Seasons at Hierakonpolis. Part V. Summation and Conclusions, *JARCE* 9 (1971-1972), 67-68.

Compare our preceding number.
Phase C is to be placed after 3600 B.C. (radio-carbon years); it is found in three different areas. The palace facade is stratigraphically younger. There was a continuous occupation from the lowest level through the main occupation (Buildings I-IV). This is the conclusion from a seriation of ceramics and from the stratigraphy of the occupations.
Quibell was right in identifying a New Kingdom temple complex. This period means a revival for Nekhen.
          M. Heerma van Voss

72220 FANFONI-BONGRANI, L., La collezione egizia del Museo di Modena, *Oriens Antiquus* 11 (1972), 39-48, with 11 ill. on 6 pl. and 1 fig.

Le Museo Civico de Modène est né à la fin du siècle passé, de la fusion de plusieurs collections particulières. L'auteur décrit d'abord une dizaine de pièces importantes, notamment le sarcophage d'albâtre et un oushebti en faïence du Père divin Psamétik (voir notre no 71607). Elle signale quelques autres objets et finit par ceux faisant partie de la Galleria Estense, surtout un naos de basalte au nom de *Mwt-nbt.f* et un morceau de papyrus funéraire de Basse Epoque, dont une autre partie est conservée au Louvre.   *J. Custers*

72221 FAULKNER, R. O., Boat-Building in the Coffin Texts, *RdE* 24 (1972), 60-63.

L'auteur livre une traduction et un commentaire philologique des formules 189, 194 et 195 des *CT*, dans lesquelles le défunt, pour échapper au risque d'être contraint de se nourrir d'excréments dans l'au-delà se construit un canoé de papyrus avec lequel il gagnera le ciel (formules 189 et 195), ou hèle un bac pour le transporter (formule 194). Dans la formule 195, l'objectif du voyage semble être l'assimilation du défunt à la lune.   *Ph. Derchain*

72222 FAULKNER, Raymond O., The Book of the Dead. A Collection of Spells. Edited and Translated. From Papyri in the British Museum, New York, Printed for Members of the Limited Editions Club, 1972 (20.5 × 31 cm; Vol. I : The Texts : XXV + 157 p.; Vol. II : The Plates : continuous colour photographic facsimile).

With the exception of Spell 78, for which a translation published by the late Professor A. de Buck in the *JEA* 35 has been reproduced, the author has made his own translations. The only Spells not translated are those which virtually duplicate others, of which he gives translations, a small number which are too corrupt to yield intelligible renderings, Spells 162-165 which are later in the date of their composition than the Theban Recension of the *Book of the Dead*, and a further four Spells which the translator judged to be of no interest except to the professional scholar. A few Spells which had been numbered twice by nineteenth century Egyptologists have been allotted the numbers by which they are now usually designated. A five-page Glossary provides explanations and geographical details of technical words and place names.

The volume of plates is arranged as a continuous, folded sheet sixteen feet five inches in length. It consists of colour photographs of vignettes and the accompanying texts from the papyrus of Ani in the British Museum and brief descriptions of the scenes.

The book has been produced in a limited edition of 1,500 copies for the members of the Limited Editions Club.

I. E. S. Edwards

72223   FAULKNER, R. O., Coffin Texts Spell 313, *JEA* 58 (1972), 91-94.

This Spell similarly entitled but differing from nos. 148 and 312, appears to be a ritual relating to the demise of a king represented as Osiris, and the accession of his son in the form of Horus. Atum calls upon Thoth to visit Osiris in the Island of Fire (*iw nsrsr*) in the next world, then Horus asks Thoth to help establish him in his father's kingship. The tone of this suggests a text used at an actual royal demise as well as mythology. Translation presents difficulties as commented on by the late Prof. de Buck; there is confusion of suffix-pronouns, and there are no variant texts extant to help. Consequently a full translation with frequent footnotes is given.   *E. Uphill*

72224   FAULKNER, Raymond O., A Concise Dictionary of Middle Egyptian. Addenda and Corrigenda, Oxford, [Griffith Institute], 1972 (16.5 × 24.8 cm; 7 p.).

A list of additions and corrections to our number 62176.

72225   FAULKNER, R. O., *Ḥmt* "woman" as a feminine suffix, *JEA* 58 (1972), 300.

Examples are quoted to show that this word can be used as a suffix as early as the *Pyramid Texts*, and more rarely as the compound *st-ḥmt*.   *E. Uphill*

FAULKNER, Raymond O., see also our numbers 72257 and 72668.

FAVRE, Sébastien, see our number 72369.

FAVRO, F., see our number 72406.

72226   FAZZINI, Richard A., Some Egyptian Reliefs in Brooklyn, *Miscellanea Wilbouriana 1*, 33-70, with 39 ill (1 in colour).

The article discusses a large number of reliefs in the Brooklyn Museum, several of which not published previously. We mention : a stela in the form of a false door (no. L 69.19), probably from Abydos and from the VIth Dynasty; a stela from Nag' ed-Deir and one of Naqâda (nos 39.1 and 69.74.1), both from the First Intermediate Period; a relief from an early VIth Dynasty tomb representing the preparation of a bed, from Saqqâra (no. 71.10.1a-d); another part of a tomb-wall representing a nobleman spearing fish, with some deviations from the usual type (no. 69.115.2); a fragment from the upper terrace of the Hatshepsut temple, showing sailors rowing a boat (no. L 58.1.3); a sunk relief representing queen Nefertiti and bearing the name of Meritaten, from Karnak (no. L 69.38.1); a sunk relief representing a mourning scene from the Post-Amarna Period, from Saqqâra (no. 69.114); a Ramesside relief representing Amon, Ahmose-Nefertiry and Amenophis I, and with the name of Sethi II (no. L 68.10.2); several stelae from Sumenu, one of which with a curious scene representing three gods and an enigmatic text (no. 69.116.2); a late relief representing a woman with her child, copied from an XVIIIth Dynasty tomb (no. 48.74); some more reliefs from the Late Period by which the imitation of earlier periods is demonstrated; a glazed faience relief representing king Iuput (no. 59.17); and a chalice from Tûna el-Gebel with figures of men, plants and animals, of the Third Intermediate Period (no. 49.133; cfr our number 63493).

72227   FECHT, Gerhard, Der Vorwurf an Gott in den »Mahnworten des Ipu-wer« (Pap. Leiden I 344 recto, 11,11-13,8; 15,13-17,3). Zur geistigen Krise der ersten Zwischenzeit und ihrer Bewältigung, Heidelberg, Carl Winter. Universitätsverlag, 1972 (17.1 × 24.5 cm; 240 p.) = Abhandlungen der Heidelberger Akademie der Wissenschaften. Philosophisch-historische Klasse. Jahrgang 1972. 1. Abteilung; rev. *CdE* XLVIII, No 96 (1973), 283-284 (Dieter Mueller); *Mundus* 9 (1973), 119-120 (Waltraud Guglielmi); *Oriens Antiquus* 13 (1974), 248 (S[ergio] D[onadoni]); *Die Welt des Orients* 7 (1973-1974), 267-273 (F. Junge).

Pr. DM 68

The study is an extension of the ideas discussed by Otto in his lecture with the same title (our number 1972). The text of it had been completed in 1966, but publication being delayed the author has added a large number of "Nachträge" (p. 152-224) and even "Letzte Nachträge" (225-236), reference to which is to be found *in margine* in the original text.

Chapter I of Part A discusses the date of the *Admonitions*. Its metrical scheme is that applied since the XIth Dynasty, and from the contents of various passages it may be suggested that the version found in Pap. Leiden I 344 dates from the late XIIth Dynasty. This is stressed by the fact that several expressions and passages appear to be derived from other literary works of the Middle Kingdom. The original version, however, containing the theme of the work, certainly dates from the First Intermediate Period.

Chapter II deals with the composition of the *Admonitions* and the position of the "Reproach to God". The main conclusions are : 1. in this section, as well as in those preceding and following the author addresses the gods; 2. of a series of 5 sections, together constituting the speech of Ipuwer (?), of which Fecht demonstrates the inner construction, the "Reproach to God" is the centre; 3. the first half of the text consists of a litany without much of a composition and contains a complaint addressed to men.

Part B contains a copiously annotated translation of *Admon.* 11,11-13,8. Fecht i.a. attempts to demonstrate that the Reproach is addressed to the god(s) and thought to be pronounced in the hereafter. A summary of the composition is given on p. 108-119.

Part C deals with the "answer" (*Admon.* 15,13-17,3) and connected problems, such as the equal position of "the silent one" and "the violent one"; the negative predestination as responsibility of god; arbitrariness of men and the judgment of the dead.

Throughout the book, also where other texts are quoted, Fecht's method of translating is based on the metrical scheme which he finds reflected in the contents of the verses.

An index to the texts quoted on p. 237-240.

Cfr also the author's article : Ägyptische Zweifel am Sinn des Opfers. Admonitions 5, 7-9, *ZÄS* 100 (1973), 6-16.

72228 FENSHAM, F. C., W. F. Albright (24/5/1891-19/9/71), *Journal of Northwest Semitic Languages*, Leiden 2 (1972). 1-4.

Obituary article. See our number 71650.

FERNBERGER, Georg Christoph, see our number 72433.

72229 FEUCHT, Hans-Jürgen, Bemerkungen zum Artikel von Jürgen Horn, "Ägyptologie als Wissenschaft in der Gesellschaft" (Göttinger Miszellen, H.1, S.42-48), *GM* Heft 3 (1972), 49-56.

A reply to Horn's criticism of modern Egyptology and its methods (see our No. 72323). *Dieter Mueller*

72230 FIER, Richard, A Note on a New Concept Concerning Amarna Art, *Newsletter ARCE* No. 83 (October 1972), 27.

Abstract of a paper.

A theory that a light technique, called "casting of shadows" and in keeping with Akhnaton's new religion was employed during the Amarna Period. Also the reasons why are discussed. *L. M. J. Zonhoven*

72231 FISCHER, Henry G., Offerings for an Old Kingdom Granary Official, *Bulletin of the Detroit Institute of Arts*, Detroit, Michigan 51 (1972), 69-80, with 3 fig. and 5 ill.

The author studies the texts of the tomb chapel of Mery-nesut (compare our number 72547), containing offering formulae, a statement regarding payment for the tomb, and lists of offerings, as well as titles and names of the owner, his family, and the funerary priests designated to maintain the offerings.
Mery-nesut's most important title was "inspector of the archivists of royal documents", of the granary, as i.a. proves the title "strong-of-voice belonging to the granary", i.e., supervisor of the measurements of grain. His wife was "overseer of the dancers", which is nowhere else mentioned as a female title.
The author also publishes a limestone statue of Mery-nesut (Cairo J. E. 37713) and a limestone slab perforated with 21 round holes to serve as window (Cairo J.E. 37728), both found in the tomb.

72232 FISCHER, Henry G., *šḥ3.śn* (Florence 1774), *RdE* 24 (1972), 64-71, with 1 pl.

L'auteur propose de corriger la lecture du début de la stèle de Florence 1774 (Voir Varille, *Mél. Maspero* I, 553-566 et Bosticco, *Stele* I, 18, p. 25 = notre No 59078), et de reconnaître dans les premiers mots *šḥ3.sn* le nom du père du dédicant, qui s'appellerait alors lui-même *Mnṯw wsr* et non plus *S3 Mnṯw wsr*. A l'appui de sa thèse, il groupe une série de noms propres de l'Ancien et du Moyen Empire ayant la forme d'une proposition verbale à la 3e personne du pluriel. Le pronom dans ces formes renvoie implicitement aux dieux sous le M.E., à l'entourage du porteur du nom sous l'A.E.
Il propose en outre de faire de *Mnṯw wsr* fils de *Šḥ3.sn*, chef des cuisines du temple de Montou, l'intendant de la maison d'un dignitaire qui aurait pu être *Ny sw Mnṯw* connu par un monument daté de l'an 14 d'Amenemhet II (Louvre E. 3462). La stèle de Florence serait ainsi à dater de la fin du règne de Sésostris Ier et non plus de la XIe dynastie. Les deux monuments mentionnés sont reproduits photographiquement.

Ph. Derchain

72233 FORBES, R. J., Studies in Ancient Technology. Volume IX. Second, revised Edition, Leiden, E. J. Brill, 1972 (16 × 24.5 cm; X + 311 p., 8 tables, 48 ill. and fig. [including 6 maps, 3 folding]).

Second, revised edition of our number 64157. Sequel to our number 71193.

72234 FOSTER, John L., Impressions of a Fellow Traveller, *Newsletter ARCE* No. 81 (April 1972), 27-28.

A continuation of *Newsletter ARCE* July 1971.
The author produces a poetic translation of an inscription of Queen Nefertari in the Luxor temple. *L. M. J. Zonhoven*

72235 FOSTER, John L., Literary Translation of Ancient Egyptian Verse Texts, *Newsletter ARCE* No. 80 (January 1972), 34-35.

Abstract of a paper.
The three aspects of a poem (musical, pictorial and semantic) are only partly recoverable in Egyptian poetry, the characteristics of which are described. The problems of translating poetry are discussed. *L. M. J. Zonhoven*

72236 FOSTER, John L., Thought Couplets in the Hymn to the Nile, *Newsletter ARCE* No. 83 (October 1972), 27-28.

Abstract of a paper.
The verse lines of the Hymn to the Nile are composed in pairs, called "thought couplets" by the author, which term implies a stricter and more regular organization of the poetic structure than the older term "parallelism of members". *L. M. J. Zonhoven*

72237 FÓTI, László, Probleme des ägyptischen Schicksalbegriffes, *Annales Universitatis Scientiarum Budapestiensis de Rolando Eötvös Nominatae*. Sectio Classica, Budapest 1 (1972), 13-20.

Verfasser untersucht den zweisichtigen Schicksalbegriff in Parallele des *š3j ḥḏt* und *š3j km* als Mutterschwein, bzw. als sethianisches Tier. *V. Wessetzky*

72238 FRASER, P. M., Ptolemaic Alexandria. I. Text. II. Notes. III. Indexes, Oxford, At the Clarendon Press, 1972 (15.5 × 23.5 cm; [vol. I :] XVI + 812 p., 1 folding map; [vol. II :] XIV + 1116 p.; [vol. III :] VI + 157 p.); rev. *JEA* 60 (1974), 290-294 (J.R. Rea).

This thorough study of the city of Alexandria and its culture during the first three centuries of its existence is outside the scope of the *AEB*. By its very nature, however, it contains numerous references to Pharaonic Egypt, e.g. obelisks (p. 24-25), divinities such as Osiris and Isis, Harpocrates, Anubis, and their cults (246-276), the influence of ancient Egyptian medicine on Greek medical science (373-375), etc.

72239 FREEDMAN, David Noel, William Foxwell Albright In Memoriam, *BASOR* No. 205 (February, 1972), 3-13, with portrait (on cover).

Obituary article. Compare our number 71650.
For a biographical article cfr our number 70135.

72240 FREL, Jiři, A Ptolemaic Queen in New York, *Archäologischer Anzeiger*, Berlin (1971), 1971/72, 211-214, with 3 ill.

Publication of a almost life-sized head of a statue, at present preserved in the City Museum of New York and property of Joseph V. Noble. It is said to come from Samos and shows in workmanship and style the characteristics of the Egyptian tradition, although the general scheme and the proportions correspond to the pattern of classical Greek sculpture.
The author suggests it to represent Queen Arsinoe II.

FRY, E. I., see our number 72578.

72241 FULCO, William J., The God Rešep, *Dissertation Abstracts International. A. The Humanities and Social Sciences*, Ann Arbor, Michigan Vol. 32, No. 3 (September 1971), 1470 A.

Abstract of a doctor's thesis Yale University, 1971 (167 p.).
All iconographic material relating to Rešep is of Egyptian provenance, ranging from the mid-Eighteenth Dynasty through the Ramesside era to the Ptolemaic Period. Several suggestions on the role of Rešep are rejected or questioned, and some new interpretations of epitheta are given.   *L. M. J. Zonhoven*

72242 FUSCALDO, P., Las divinidades asiáticas en Egipto. Reshep y Qadesh en Deir el-Medina, *Revista del Instituto de Historia Antiqua Oriental*, Buenos Aires 1 (1972), 115-136, with 2 fig.

Nach dem Zeugnis von Stelen, Amuletten, Skarabäen und Ostraca genossen unter den zahlreichen asiatischen Gottheiten, die insbesondere während des Neuen Reiches in Ägypten Fuß gefaßt hatten, in Dêr el-Medine Reschep und Qadesch, gern in Verbindung mit Min, besondere Beliebtheit, Reschep als Heilsgottheit, Qadesch als Göttin der Liebe. Diese Beliebtheit schreibt Verf. einen syrischen Kolonie zu, die sich in Dêr el-Medine angesiedelt hatte. Auf sie gehe auch eine neue Haltung des Menschen zur Gottheit zurück, die sich in größerer "responsabilidad individual" und "justificación por la fe" äußere und in den ex-votos von Dêr el-Medine ihren Niederschlag finde.
          I. Gamer-Wallert

FUSCALDO, Perla, see also our number 72607.

72243 GABALLA, G. A., New Light on the Cult of Sokar, *Orientalia* 41 (1972), 178-179, with 2 pl.

In addition to our number 69191 the author publishes a scene from the Memphite tomb chapel of Mose containing the earliest known example of the sacrifice of an oryx and the offering of its head to Sokar. The author gives the text with translation and a short commentary.

72244 GABALLA, G. A., Some Nineteenth Dynasty Monuments in Cairo Museum, *BIFAO* 71 (1972), 129-137, with 5 fig. and 5 pl.

The author publishes three monuments of the Cairo Museum: 1. A stela of the overseer of the works May (Nr 14.10.69.1; for May, cfr our numbers 3345 and 3518); the inscription mentions buildings erected under the supervision of May. 2. A block from Mitrahîna with the name of queen Twosre (JdE Nr 45568). 3. The lower part of a stela of two stone masons (*sȝktyw*) of Ramses II, from Abydos (JdE Nr 21801).

72245 GAGNERIN, Bernard, Une source capitale pour la recherche à Genève : la Fondation Martin Bodmer, *Genava*, Genève 20 (1972), 5-54, with 59 ill.

The author describes pieces from the enormous collection of documents belonging to the "Fondation Martin Bodmer", recently connected with the University of Geneva.
On p. 8-10 are depicted the photographies of a squatting statue of the general Sebekhotep (dated to 1250 B.C.) and an ostracon with some lines from the instructions of Khety (ll. 7,9-8,2).

72246 GALAND, Lionel, A propos d'une comparaison entre les écritures libyco-berbère et méroitique, *MNL* No 9 (June 1972), 6-8.

Bezugnehmend auf einen Artikel von Zawadowski (vgl. unsere Nr. 71649), der eine Ähnlichkeit zwischen der Form und dem phonetischen Wert von 9 Zeichen des Libyco-Berberischen und des Meroitischen festgestellt hatte, gelangt Verfasser zu dem Ergebnis, daß besonders die libyschen Zeichen für *f*, *t* und *n*^{y} sehr strittig sind, zumal sie horizontal geschrieben werden und somit jünger sind als die libysche vertikale Schrift.
Vgl. auch unsere Nr. 72805. *Inge Hofmann*

72247 GAMER-WALLERT, Ingrid, El vaso canopo de la coleccion Ramon Fernandez Canivell (Malaga), *Trabajos de Prehistoria*, Madrid 29 (1972), 267-271, with 1 ill.

Publication of a small canopic vase with a lid shaped as the head of a baboon, though the inscription mentions Duamutef. It has originally belonged to a priest of Wadjyt, Mistress of 'Imt, called Wahibre-khu, and dates from the XXVIth Dynasty. It may have been found in a tomb from the 7th-6th century B.C. in the neighbourhood of Malaga.

72248 GEORGE, Beate, Versuche zur Gewinnung eines ägyptischen Menschenbildes aus dem Weltbild des Amduat im Rahmen der vergleichenden Religionswissenschaft, *GM* Heft 3 (1972), 15-20.

The *Amduat*, which deals with the journey of the sun through the netherworld, asserts that its knowledge is useful for life in this world as well. This claim might be based on the belief in the identity of macrocosm and microcosm. In order to substantiate this hypothesis, the author draws a comparison between the *Amduat* and certain religious concepts from China, Tibet, and Europe.   *Dieter Mueller*

van GERVEN, Dennis P., see our number 72032.

GIANGERI, P., see our number 72110.

GIANNESSI, G., see our number 72110.

72249 GILLINGS, Richard J., Mathematics in the Time of the Pharaohs, Cambridge, Massachusetts and London, the MIT Press, [1972] (18×25.5 cm; XII + 286 p., 1 map, numerous tables and fig., frontispiece); rev. *Janus* 59 (1972), 239-248 (E.M. Bruins).

In this edition the author has furnished an almost complete survey of our present knowledge on ancient Egyptian mathematics. The latest suchlike work up to now, though less extensive, was that of K. Vogel (our number 58605). Older again are parts in the works of B. L. van der Waerden (the original Dutch edition of "Science awakening", our number 1593, is from 1950) and O. Neugebauer (1934 and 1951). Separate editions appeared, devoted to the famous Rhind Papyrus (A. Eisenlohr, 1877; T. E. Peet, 1923; A. B. Chase, 1927-1929) and the Moscow Papyrus (W. W. Struve, 1930). For the rest one is dependent on studies of special problems, to be found in journals on either Egyptology or Mathematics. In his Bibliography (p. 267-275) Gillings mentions all those works, several of which deal with various possible interpretations of unclear texts. It is to be understood, though regrettable, that the Bibliography is not complete with regard to non-English literature : for instance, K. Vogel's dissertation "Die Grundlagen der ägyptischen Arithmetik in ihrem Zusammenhang mit der 2:n Tabelle des Papyrus Rhind", München, 1929, has been omitted.

In 22 chapters the author discusses the more common subjects of ancient Egyptian mathematics, as also various special problems. He always very accurately mentions the disputable points and their interpretations, giving all references. We mention, for instance, chapters 6 and 7 (45-89) on the well known 2:n table which is on the recto of the Rhind Papyrus, and an elaborate discussion of the problem why, from so many possibilities, it was this table that has been chosen by the Egyptians. Then the famous problems 10 and 14 of the Moscow Papyrus on the (supposed) area of a hemisphere and on the volume of a truncated pyramid (chapters 17 and 18, p. 185-201). Other chapters still are on the writing of numbers, the two-thirds table, the red auxiliary numbers, various distribution problems, more simple problems of areas and volumes, equations of the first and the second degree, progressions, Egyptian weights and measures, squares and square roots.

There follow 14 appendices (232-266), concerning, among other things, the Egyptian calendar, and the contents of the Rhind and Moscow papyri.

To the Egyptologist who is interested in ancient Egyptain mathematics the book is recommended since it is very well readable and the author is very clear in his explanation of the disputable questions. Because of the latter and the good documentation it is also important for the mathematic-historian.

A. Smeur

72250 GILULA, Mordechai, Enclitic Particles in Middle Egyptian, *GM* Heft 2 (1972), 53-59.

A summary of the doctoral dissertation submitted to the Senate of the Hebrew University in Jerusalem in 1968.

Dieter Mueller

72251 GILULA, Mordechai, The Negation of the Adverb in Demotic, *JAOS* 92 (1972), 460-465.

The author studies the sentence of Pap. Insinger 13/23 the structure of which with twice the occurrence of *in* appears to be unique; the first *in* belongs to the sentence being partner to *bn-iw n*, the second is the negation of *r-db3 swg*. Hence the sentence contains the negation of an adverbial phrase as well as coupling this phrase with the negation of the predicative nexus of what might be a cleft sentence. The correct translation is: "It is not he who consorts with a fool who perishes (but) not because of stupidity".

Gilula points out the similarity between the negation of an adverb and that of the emphatic sentence throughout the Egyptian language. The sentence here discussed contains the earliest known example of *in* outside the combination *bn.... in*, constituting an indication for the development towards the independent status of Coptic ⲁ̅ⲛ.

At the end the *n* after *bn-iw*, which occurs almost exclusively in the Pap. Insinger, is briefly discussed.

72252 GINOUVÈS, R., Informatique et archéologie, *BSFE* No 63 (Mars 1972), 9-18.

The author discusses the function of the computer in the archaeology, stressing the necessity to create an exact terminology. Compare our number 71621.

72253 GIVEON, R., An Egyptian Official in Gezer?, *The Israel Exploration Journal*, Jerusalem 22 (1972), 143-144.

Note to the position of a certain *Har-u-a-si* (= *Hr-wd3*) mentioned on a clay tablet of the 7th century B.C. found at Gezer. He may have been a descendant of an Egyptian taken captive by an Assyrian ruler, who acted in Gezer as an Assyrian major (*ha-za-nu*).

72254 GIVEON, R., Egyptian Temples in Canaan, *Bulletin Haaretz Museum*, Tel-Aviv 14 (1972), 57-62, with 2 plans.

The author discusses literary and archaeological evidence for the possible occurrence of Egyptian temples in Palestine. He concludes that these are not (yet) known, the Timna temple (and that of Serabît el-Khâdim) being unique.

72255 GIVEON, Raphael, Le temple d'Hathor à Serabit-el-Khadem, *Archeologia*, Paris No 44 (janvier-février 1972), 64-69, with 7 ill.

The author gives a description of the history of the temple of Hathor at Serabît el-Khâdim and of the cult of the goddess. Although expeditions to the mines seem not to have taken place in the time of Akhnaton, there was found a relief fragment in the Amarna style. *L. M. J. Zonhoven*

72256 GIVEON, R., תצליל, חתחור כאלת הגיונה בסיני, Haifa Vol. 6 (1972), 5-10, with 4 ill. and 3 fig.

"Hathor as Goddess of Music in Sinai". (not seen).

72257 GLANVILLE, S. R. K., Wooden Model Boats. Revised and completed by R. O. Faulkner. Drawings by Grace Huxtable, [London], The Trustees of the British Museum, 1972 (28.5 × 36.4 cm; [VI+] 77 p., 66 fig., 12 pl., frontispiece in colour) = Catalogue of Egyptian Antiquities in the British Museum, 2; rev. *JEA* 60 (1974), 266-267 (E.P. Uphill).

The volume has been prepared by the late Professor Glanville and completed by Dr. Faulkner, with contributions of Mrs. Huxtable and Mr. Shore.

31 model boats or parts of them are carefully described, all

technical details such as date, provenance, measures, preservation, etc. being added. For the complete boats there is indicated to which type they belong, according to the classification of Reisner. All objects are depicted on the plates, while most of them and some of their important details are illustrated by line drawings.

A glossary on p. 68; a concordance between collection numbers and catalogue numbers on p. 77.

72258 GLODLEWSKI, Włodzimierz, Faras à l'époque méroïtique, *Études et Travaux*, Warszawa 6 (1972), 185-193, with 1 map and 2 plans.

Noch im 12. Jahrhundert v.Chr. war Faras eine Insel, bis der westliche Nebenarm des Nil austrocknete. Die Entvölkerung Unternubiens aufgrund geo-politischen Ursachen dauerte bis 300 v.Chr. an, zu welchem Zeitpunkt eine Erhöhung des Nil-Wasserstandes und die Einführung der Sakieh wieder verbesserte Lebensbedingungen boten. In meroitischer Zeit war Faras eines der bedeutendsten Zentren Unternubiens. Zu Beginn der Wiederbesiedlung Faras' im 3. vorchristlichen Jahrhundert wurden die Tempel des Neuen Reiches niedergerissen. Die Blütezeit der Siedlung lag im 1. und 2. Jahrhundert n.Chr. Einen weiten Raum in der Beschreibung nimmt der "Westpalast" ein, der als Regierungssitz des *pesate* (mer. *pešto*) angesehen wird. Dieser soll später nach Karanog verlegt worden sein. Verschiedene Grabtypen des meroitischen Friedhofs von Faras werden besprochen, besonders diejenigen, die den *peštoleb* als letzte Ruhestätte dienten.   *Inge Hofmann*

72259 GODRON, Gérard, Revision de quelques textes hagiographiques coptes de Vienne, *Muséon* 85 (1972), 91-95.

Some corrections to Till's publication of the *Koptische Heiligen- und Märtyrerlegenden* I (1935) and II (1936), and to Lefort's article *Un martyr inconnu* (our number 1424).

72260 GOEDICKE, Hans, "The Book of Memphis", *JARCE* 9 (1971-1972), 69-72.

Compare our abstract 69385,1.

The author proposes a different translation: "Indeed, an honor (*tsw*) is it to be in the gazette of the Court (*inb*)... the saying of the Lord, the grace of the vizier or the announcement (*dm*) of an administrative document (*srw*)".

                                    M. Heerma van Voss

72261 GOEDICKE, Hans, The Letter to the Dead, Nag' ed-Deir N 3500, *JEA* 58 (1972), 95-98.

The writer stresses the ambiguity of form and use of "implicit insinuations" which constitute major difficulties in the understanding of such texts, and quoting Simpson's remark that his study (our no. 70505) was tentative in many respects offers some suggestions as a commentary and also a translation. He sees the letter as representing the sick child (or descendant) of Pepi-seneb turning to his father (or ancestor) to alleviate his misery which he ascribes to the influence of demons.

E. Uphill

72262 GOEDICKE, Hans, Tax Deduction for Religious Donations, *JARCE* 9 (1971-1972), 73-75.

Djefa-Hapi permitted holders of leases ('*ḥtyw*) to donate part of their tax-dues to the local funerary cult. This innovation is stipulated in his second and in his eighth contract.

M. Heerma van Voss

72263 GOEDICKE, Hans, Zu zwei Stellen im Papyrus Westcar, *WZKM* 63/64 (1972), 1-5.

The first note is to Pap. Westcar 7, 20 : *nḏ-ḥrt im3ḥw pw* (cfr 8,1). This cannot be a non-verbal sentence with nominal predicate and *pw* as the logical subject, since then *pw* would follow immediately after the predicate *nḏ-ḥrt*. The author suggests to read *nḏ[.i] ḥrt*, "[I] asked after the condition".
In Pap. Westcar 10, 10-11 (and 17-19 and 24-26), in the descriptions of the birth of the children, there occurs the word *nḥbt*, which is hard to explain. Goedicke suggests to read ⸺ *ḥbt*, "without exception", and to connect it with the preceding *rwḏ ḳsw.f*.

72264 GOLDWATER, Leonard J., Mercury. A History of Quicksilver, Baltimore, York Press, 1972 (16 × 23.5 cm; XI + 318 p., fig.).

The book is a comprehensive and richly diverse account of mercury in its every aspect — its occurrence and exploitation, its physical properties, the history of its varied use, especially in medicine, and its peculiar lore, both ancient and modern. Of particular interest to Egyptologists are the sections on mercury in the occult arts (pp. 21-31), ancient commerce in mercury (58-60), the early knowledge and uses of it (72-85 — especially 74-76 re Egypt), and its early medical applications (199-214 — especially 199-201), as well as the notes on terminology (292-302 — especially 292). More specifically, there are important addenda to Lucas in the discussion (75-76) of an early analysis (1826) of a red pigment, revealing the presence of cinnabar mixed with iron oxide, and the reference (76) to two more recent analyses made by the author, one of red pigment on a sherd from el-Amarna, the other of the red colour on a fragment of Ptolemaic cartonnage, both of which indicated the presence of a mercuric pigment, which must have been either cinnabar or mercuric oxide — assuming no accidental contamination.

J. R. Harris

72265 GOLTZ, Dietlinde, Studien zur Geschichte der Mineralnamen in Pharmazie, Chemie und Medizin von den Anfängen bis Paracelsus, Wiesbaden, Franz Steiner Verlag, 1972 (16.7 × 24 cm; X + 455 p.) = Sudhoffs Archiv Beiheft 14.

In this book on names of minerals, in a few instances Egyptian words are mentioned. Akkadian *nitiru*, "Sodium, Potassium" and Greek νίτρον derive from Egyptian *ntrj* (p. 73 and 165). In her discussion of the word ἄσημος the author wonders whether this word is perhaps to be derived from the Egyptian loan-word *ḥsmn* (related to Akkadian *ešmaru* and Hebrew *ḥašmal*, "Elektron"), which first meant "alloy" and later on "bronze" (p. 188). The Arabic word for "Antimontrisulfid", *iṯmid* might have developed from Egyptian *msṯm*, from which Greek στίμμι (στίβι) was derived (p. 238).
For a more extensive discussion of the word ἄσημος compare Robert Halleux, *CdE* XLVIII, No. 96 (1973), 370-380.

L. M. J. Zonhoven

72266 GOPHNA, Ram, Egyptian First Dynasty Pottery from Tel Halif Terrace, *Museum Haaretz Bulletin*, Tel-Aviv 14 (December 1972), 47-56, with a map, 2 fig. and 1 ill.

The author, discussing the problem whether the impressive quantity of Egyptian pottery found at various places in south Palestine points to Egyptian domination during the Ist Dynasty, studies the sherds found near Tel Halif in this region. In view of the abundance and ordinary quality of the Egyptian material settlement seems to be the obvious explanation. There are still a number of questions to be solved.

72267 GOPHNA, Ram, ‏אחר מצרי מימי השושלת הראשונה ליד עין־הבשור‎ *Qadmoniot*, Jerusalem 5 (1972), 14-15, with 2 maps and 2 ill.; rev. *ZAW* 85 (1973), 108 (J. Maier).

"A First Dynasty Egyptian Site near 'En-haBesor".
For a summary by Yochanan Agam, see *GM* 8 (1973), 58.

72268 GOUDSMIT, S. A., Not for the Art Trade, *Expedition*, Philadelphia, Penn. 14, Number 4 (Summer 1972), 13-16, with 1 fig. and 8 ill.

Article for the general reader discussing forgeries and means to establish authenticity. The illustrations are partly depicting objects from the author's own collection. Of one of them he argues from some abnormal details that it is genuine.

72269 GOYON, Jean-Claude, Confirmation du pouvoir royal au nouvel an [Brooklyn Museum Papyrus 47.218.50], [Le Caire], Institut français d'Archéologie orientale et Brooklyn Museum, [1972] (20.1 × 27.3 cm; [VI+]142 p., 1 plan, 4 fig, 3 tables and 9 pl. including 7 with hieroglyphic texts) = Bibliothèque d'Étude 52.

Pap. Brooklyn 47.218.50 can be dated to the Fourth Century B.C. and probably represents the copy of a document from the New Kingdom. It consists of twenty columns of text and was apparently designed as a liturgical guide or program for the ceremonies in commemoration of the royal accession, performed during the epagomenal days and the first nine days of the new year. The predominant role of Re, and the references to the layout of the temple in which the rites were performed, suggest that it may have come from Heliopolis.

After a detailed description of the papyrus and a thorough analysis of the ritual, its localities, and the time and purpose of its celebration, the author turns to the translation of the text, followed by a commentary with copious notes and several indexes.

The Plate Volume (Wilbour Monographs 7) has appeared in 1974.   *Dieter Mueller*

72270 GOYON, Jean-Claude, Rituels funéraires de l'ancienne Égypte. Introduction, traduction et commentaire, Paris, Les Éditions du Cerf, 1972 (12.5 × 19.5 cm; 357 p., 4 fig. [one folded]); series: Littératures anciennes du Proche Orient, 4; rev. *BiOr* 30 (1973), 219-221 (Erhart Graefe); *CdE* XLVIII, No 95 (1973), 66-67 (J. López); *JEA* 59 (1973), 259 (J. Gwyn Griffiths). Pr. NF 75

Apart from a preface the volume consists of three parts, respectively dealing with the *Embalmment Ritual*, the *Ritual of the Opening of the Mouth* and the *Books of Respirations*. Each part contains a bibliography, an introduction and the translations with notes.

The text of the *Embalmment Ritual* is known from Pap. Bulaq III and Pap. Louvre 5158 (compare our number 2554). In the introduction Goyon describes the course of the mummification process (p. 24-41).

The introduction to Part II deals with the origin of the *Ritual of the Opening of the Mouth*, the ancient text, and the ritual itself. The translation divides the Ritual into several parts: Preliminaries, the Play of the Animation of the Statue, the Rites of Upper Egypt, the Rites of Lower Egypt, the Ceremony of Dressing, the Funerary Repast, and the Final Rites.

Characteristic for the *Books of Respirations* are the great variations in formulas and their organization. They are divided by the Egyptians themselves into two Books, the first one being the oldest. Goyon discusses origin and date of the manuscripts and title and formation of the composition. He first translates Book I (Isis), followed by a list of sources; than Book II (Thoth), consisting of six texts; and at the end a number of extracts from texts IIA and IV, of which several different traditions are known.

Indexes on p. 319-348; a list of papyri used for Part III on p. 349-350.

72271 GRABAR, André, Deux images tirées de la vie de saint Pachôme, *RdE* 24 (1972), 72-79, with 1 pl. and 1 fig.

Deux peintures de l'église moldave de Sucevitsa (vers 1600) ont illustré deux épisodes de la vie de Saint Pachôme. La première relate l'hostilité du saint à la perfection de l'œuvre matérielle, cause d'orgueil en montrant comment il fit endommager par ses moines l'église trop belle à ses yeux qu'il venait de faire construire, l'autre l'effort des démons pour le faire rire et ainsi le désarmer, en transportant à grand renfort de cables, une simple feuille d'arbre. *Ph. Derchain*

72272 GRAEFE, Erhart, Beethoven und die ägyptische Weishcit, *GM* Heft 2 (1972), 19-21.

Ludwig van Beethoven, who died in 1827, cannot have copied the famous inscription in the temple of Neith at Sais from Champollion-Figeac's book *Egypte Ancienne*, which was only published in 1835, but may have found it in Plutarch's *De Iside et Osiride*, 9, 14. *Dieter Mueller*

72273 GRAY, P. H. K., Egyptische mummies doorgelicht, *Spiegel Historiael* 489-492, with 5 ill.

"Egyptian mummies X-rayed".
Radiological investigation, while leaving mummies intact, offers results important for both Egyptology (presence of human bones in the wrappings, determination of age and sex, information on embalming techniques, discovery of amulets or other objects) and Palaeo-pathology (average age of males and females, diseases and injuries). *L. M. J. Zonhoven*

72274 GRAY, P. H. K., Notes Concerning the Position of Arms and Hands of Mummies with a View to Possible Dating of the Specimen, *JEA* 58 (1972), 200-204, with 5 tables.

A table of figures derived from 111 mummies X-rayed since 1963, giving details of date (by Dynasty) of the mummy, position of arms and hands, and the sex. Conclusions reached show that all dynastic mummies have the arms extended, Ptolemaic prefer them crossed on the breast, and Roman revert to the extended position.   *E. Uphill*

72275 GREENE, D. L., Dental Anthropology of Early Egypt and Nubia, *Journal of Human Evolution*, London and New York 1 (1972), 315-324, with 3 tables.

Durch die Ausgrabungen während der letzten Jahre kam genügend Material für eine dental-anthropologische Untersuchung Ägyptens und Nubiens zusammen. Die Analyse der Zahnmorphologie von Angehörigen der Badari-Kultur, des meroitischen Reiches, der X-Gruppe und der christlichen Kultur zeigte eine erstaunliche biologische Kontinuität, so daß Massenbewegungen einwandernder Völker in Frage gestellt werden müssen. Die Ursachen für die Veränderung der Zähne seit dem Pleistozän werden diskutiert.
Wieder abgedruckt in : Population Biology of the Ancient Egyptians. Edited by D. R. Brothwell [and] B. A. Chiarelli, London and New York, Academic Press, 1973.   *Inge Hofmann*

72276 GRELOT, Pierre, Documents araméens d'Égypte. Introduction, traduction, présentation, Paris, Les Éditions du Cerf, 1972 (12.5 × 19.5 cm; 533 p., 2 maps, 4 plans); series : Littératures anciennes du Proche-Orient. Collection publiée sous la patronage de l'école biblique et archéologique francaise de Jérusalem; rev. *BiOr* 31 (1974), 119-124 (E. Lipiński); *Phoenix* 19 (1973), 303-304 (K. R. Veenhof); *Revue Biblique* 80 (1973), 466-469 (B. C[ouroyer]); *ZAW* 84 (1972), 385 ([G. Fohrer]).

After an introduction dealing with the life of mercenaries, both Arameans and Jews, the Aramaic language as used by the scribes and the various categories of documents the book discusses the sources, presenting for each of them a translation with textual notes and extensive comments. All together 108 documents are discussed, divided into four parts. Part I contains sources from daily life, contracts, accounts, letters, etc., while in two separate chapters documents from two families are dealt with. Part II is devoted to administrative texts, part III to religious life, Jewish as well as non-Jewish, and part IV to literary texts, particularly the novel of 'Aḥîqar.
In part V the onomastic material is discussed, with a list of all names in the sources. The appendices contain a list of month names, a table of various types of money, and two of measures of capacity.
Indexes on p. 515-525.

72277 GRIESHAMMER, Reinhard, O. D. Berlev, Trudovoe naselenie Egipta v epochu srednego carstva, Akademija Nauk SSSR - Institut vostokovedcnija, Isdatel'stvo "Nauka", Moskva 1972, *GM* Heft 2 (1972), 61-62.

A summary of our number 72070.

GRIESHAMMER, Reinhard, see also our numbers 72088 and 72537.

72278 GRIFFITHS, J. G., Antécédents de la Triade divine dans l'Égypte préhistorique, *Bollettino del Centro Camuno di Studi Preistorici*, Campo di Ponte, Brescia 9 (1972), 104-105.

Report of a lecture.

72279 [GRIFFITHS, J. Gwyn], Editorial Foreword, *JEA* 58 (1972), 1-4.

72280 GRIFFITHS, J. Gwyn, The Symbolism of Red in Egyptian Religion, *Ex Orbe Religionum* 81-90.

Although frequently associated with Seth, the color red is not exclusively considered to be malevolent. The author lists numerous examples where it has a positive connotation as the color of amulets, of sacred animals, of mummies, etc.

Dieter Mueller

72281 GRIFFITHS, K. Bosse, Une idole en pierre de l'Égypte préhistorique, *Bollettino del Centro Camuno di Studi Preistorici*, Capo di Ponte, Brescia 9 (1972), 104.

Report of a lecture.

72282 GRIMM, Günter, Thebanische Mumienporträts?, *Archäologischer Anzeiger*, Berlin (1971), 1971/72, 246-252, with 5 ill.

Discussion of the problem whether there are mummy portraits painted on wood which came from Thebes. The author deals with various mentions about such objects by early Egyptologists such as Champollion and Salt, but has to conclude that there is at present no definite proof.

72283 GRIMM, Günter, Two Early Imperial Faience Vessels from Egypt, *Miscellanea Wilbouriana 1*, 71-100, with 16 ill. (2 in colour).

Study of two Egyptian faience vases from the 1st century A.D. (nos 70.93.1 and 70.89.3), the motifs of their decoration being compared with those of a large number of similar pieces in other collections, many of which represented by photographs.

72284 GRINSELL, Leslie V., Guide Catalogue to the Collections
from Ancient Egypt, Bristol, City Museum, 1972 (14.6 × 21 cm;
[I+]84 p., frontispiece, map, 40 ill., colour ill. on cover).

The catalogue of the Egyptian objects in the Bristol City
Museum, mainly originating from excavations by Petrie and
Emery, begins with a general introduction to Egyptology in
South-West Britain and a history of the collections. After short
notes on the country and the chronology of Egypt, a synopsis
of each period (from Prehistoric up to Greek, Roman and
early Christian times) is given, together with a description of
the objects.
Of the objects we mention : from the Old Kingdom a relief from
the tomb of Nefermaat (inv. No. H 3571), from the Middle
Kingdom a quartzite head of Nebhepetre Mentuhotep (inv.
No. H 5038), and from the New Kingdom a black granite
head of Tuthmosis IV (inv. No. H 5037).
The book ends with a short lexicon of deities, a chapter on
funerary customs, a glossary, an enumeration of the principal
sites from which the objects originate, and a catalogue of the
objects described.   *L. M. J. Zonhoven*

72285 GROENEWEGEN-FRANKFORT, H. A., Arrest and Move-
ment. An Essay on Space and Time in the representational
Art of the ancient Near East, New York, Hacker Art Books,
Inc., 1972 (16.5 × 24.3 cm; XXVI + 222 p., 47 fig., 94 pl.); rev.
BiOr 30 (1973), 18-19 (Ingrid Gamer Wallert); *CdE* XLIX,
No. 97 (1974), 90-92 (Claude Vandersleyen); *JARCE* 10 (1973),
117 (Earl L. Ertman); *JEA* 60 (1974), 272-276 (John Baines);
JNES 34 (1975), 145 (David P. Silverman).

American edition of our number 1816.

GROSSMANN, Peter, see our number 72357.

72286 Groupe d'Études Méroitiques (Paris), REM = Répertoire
d'Épigraphie Méroitique REM 1001-1110. Enregistrement des
Textes. Données simplifiées. Données Septembre 1971, diffusion
Mars 1972 (70 p.).

Register von 110 meroitischen Texten (REM 1001-REM 1110),
zu deren Beschreibung und Bibliographie unsere Nummern
68373, 69381, 69382, 70347 zu vergleichen sind. Der Schlüssel
zur Textanalyse ist in 70261 gegeben.   *Inge Hofmann*

72287 Groupe d'Études Méroitique (Paris), REM = Répertoire
d'Épigraphie Méroitique REM 1001-1110. Index simplifié.
Données Septembre 1971, diffusion Mars 1972 (50 p.).

Index zu den 110 meroitischen Texten (REM 1001-REM 1110), die im Register (unsere Vorgehende Nr.) analysiert und transliteriert wurden.   *Inge Hofmann*

72288 GRUEN, Stephan W., The meaning of ☰𐄷 in Papyrus Harris 500, verso (= Joppa 1, 5), *JEA* 58 (1972), 307.

The writer suggests *snny* is in fact not a reduplicated verb (3ae inf.) but a substantive meaning 'charioteer'.   *E. Uphill*

72289 GRUMACH, Irene, Untersuchungen zur Lebenslehre des Amenope, München-Berlin, Deutscher Kunstverlag, 1972 (21 × 29.6 cm; [VIII+] 198+41 [unnumbered] p.) = Münchner Ägyptologische Studien. Herausgegeben von Hans Wolfgang Müller, Heft 23; rev. *JARCE* 10 (1973), 105 (Hans Goedicke); *JEA* 59 (1973), 266-268 (P. V. Johnson); *Journal of Biblical Literature* 92 (1973), 598-600 (Ronald J. Williams); *Orientalia* 43 (1974), 125-128 (K. A. Kitchen); *ZAW* 85 (1973), 125-126 ([G. Fohrer]).   Pr. DM 55

In the introduction to her literary analysis the author discusses prosody and composition of the Instruction which appears to follow a definite scheme, proving that we here possess an original work, although the copies preserved date from the XXVIth and XXVIIth Dynasty.
Comparison with *Prov.* 22,17-23,11 and isolation of the units there finding a parallel proves that there has existed an earlier composition on which also the author of *Prov.* was dependent (compare our number 3649). This "Old Instruction", dated by Miss Grumach to the time of Horemheb, is reconstructed in transcription on the three first (unnumbered) pages of the appendix.
The main part of the book consists of a translation of the three titles and the thirty chapters, each followed by comments on the translations, the prosody, the sources and the contents. In a concluding section (p. 182-185) the author indicates the way in which Amen(em)ope used the "Old Instruction" and other sources in order to develop his own point of view in accordance with the religious thoughts of his time.
A bibliography on p. 186-189; indexes on p. 193-198. In the Appendix apart from the "Old Instruction" the entire text of Amenope in transliteration with indications as to its metric scheme.

72290 GUILLAUMONT, Antoine, Copte ⲘⲈϨⲘⲞⲞⲨ = "puiser de l'eau", *RdE* 24 (1972), 80-83.

L'expression copte reprise dans le titre de l'article, composée du verbe ⲘⲞⲨϨ qui signifie littéralement remplir, constitue un

décalque de l'araméen מִלָּא מִיָא, litt. "remplir l'eau", qui a le
même sens. On en tire un indice sur l'origine du texte utilisé
pour établir la traduction copte de l'Ancien Testament, qui ne
saurait être dans ce cas l'original hébreux, mais un targum.

Ph. Derchain

72294 HAIKAL, Fayza Mohammed Hussein, Two Hieratic Funerary
Papyri of Nesmin. Part Two. Translation and Commentary,
Bruxelles, Fondation Égyptologique Reine Élisabeth, 1972
(22.1 × 28 cm; 76 p.) = Bibliotheca Aegyptiaca 15; rev. *BiOr* 30
(1973), 398-399 (L. Kákosy); *JARCE* 10 (1973), 106-107
(Hans Goedicke); *JEA* 59 (1973), 268 (R. O. Faulkner); *JNES* 33
(1974), 265 (Mordechai Gilula).

Sequel to our number 70242.
The present volume consists of two chapters, each containing
translation with comments of one of the texts originally belonging
to Nesmin.
Pap. BM 10209 consists of a manual for the glorifications to
the dead at the Festival of the Valley. The series of spells is a
compilation from earlier religious texts composed for the benefit
of the king, consisting of three parts: part 1 and 3 are said to
be recited by a lector priest, part 2 by Isis (represented by a
priestess). The papyrus is a palimpsest, traces of the original
demotic legal document still being visible. On top of sheet
1 indications by Nesmin concerning placing the papyrus with
his mummy.
In a special chapter Miss Haikal discusses the Festival of the
Valley and its history from the Middle Kingdom to the
Graeco-Roman Period. In the present text virtually no mention
of Amon occurs; possibly it was meant to be recited during
the sacred meal which private.tomb owners still celebrated in
the Late Period.
The second chapter deals with Pap. B.M. 10208, containing the
text of a ritual to be performed during the funerary celebration
for Osiris in the month Khoiak. It may be compared with
Pap. B.M. 10188 (Pap. Bremner-Rhind) and Pap. Berlin 3008,
the "Songs" and the "Lamentations" of Isis and Nephthys
respectively, though the three differ considerably. Like the
"Lamentations" the present text may have been appended to
a *Book of the Dead*, it being stated that the ritual was
performed for the benefit of the original owner.
Bibliography (p. 67-73) and indexes to Egyptian words (74-76)
at the end.

HALAND, Randi, see our number 72528.

72291 HABACHI, Labib, The Destruction of Temples in Egypt, *in :*
Medieval and Middle Eastern Studies in Honour of Aziz Suryal
Atiya. Edited by Sami A. Hanna, Leiden, E. J. Brill, 1972,
192-198, with a map.

The author rejects the view of O'Leary (*Bulletin de la Société
d'Archéologie Copte* 4, 1938, 51-57) that the destruction of
Egyptian temples in the Delta was largely due to the Christians.
Many other factors contributed to the destruction, such as
neglect, and their use as a quarry to provide stones for other
buildings, which happened in all ages. Many temples were
even used as Christian churches.

72292 HABACHI, Labib, Nia, the $w^c b$-Priest and Doorkeeper of
Amun-of-the-Hearing-Ear, *BIFAO* 71 (1972), 67-85, with 7 fig.
and 6 pl.

Of the priest and doorkeeper Nia there are known the following
objects, all to be dated to the XIXth Dynasty : 1. a limestone
dyad in Munich (Aeg. Staatssammlung Nr 28 = GL. W.A.F. 25,
according to our number 72687, p. 78); Nia is here called Entia;
2. stela Turin Nr 1585, with in the middle register a rare scene
of Nia's wife sitting on a chair and four of her children wailing
and gesturing in mourning in front of her; in the lower register
prayers on behalf of Nia; 3. offering table Turin Nr 1753;
4. shawabti Turin Nr 2556; 5. a box for canopic jars, Turin
Nr 2444; 6. a wooden pectoral, Turin Nr 6831, with a
scarab bearing the text of *BD* chapter 30 and Nia's name
inserted in it. After describing these objects the author discusses
Amon-of-the-Hearing-Ear, who was probably identical with
Amon-Who-Hears-the-Prayers, and Nia himself and his family.

72293 HABACHI, Labib, The Second Stela of Kamose and his
Struggle against the Hyksos Ruler and his Capital, Glückstadt,
Verlag J. J. Augustin, 1972 (21 × 29.7 cm; 67 p., 32 fig., 8 pl.)
= Abhandlungen des Deutschen Archäologischen Instituts
Kairo. Ägyptologische Reihe. Band 8; rev. *Aegyptus* 52 (1972),
210-211 (E. Bresciani); *Anthropos* 68 (1973), 972-973 (Inge
Hofmann); *BiOr* 31 (1974), 249-251 (M. Gitton); *CdE* XLIX,
No. 97 (1974), 98-102 (Robert Hari); *Mundus* 10 (1974), 23-24
(Waltraud Guglielmi); *ZDMG* 125 (1975), 149-151 (Winfried
Barta).   Pr. DM 72

After an Introduction in which previous studies on the stela
are mentioned chapter I deals with its discovery in the foundation
of a fragmentary statue of Ramses II besides the colossus of
Pinodjem in the forecourt of the Karnak temple. All seven
other blocks with texts and reliefs found in the foundations
of these two statues are published, among which scenes of the

heb-sed festival of Amenophis III and the representation of a temporary palace. The author also publishes the texts and scenes on the sides of the stela, which has been made out of a pillar from a chapel of Sesostris I.

Chapters II and III contain a description of the stela and a translation, accompanied by notes. The text is divided into ten sections, each part being headed by a copy of the relevant lines, in which Habachi's restorations are noted.

Chapter IV discusses the two Kamose stelae. They cannot have been twins, their dimensions being different, and they may not have been standing next to each other since they were reused in different places. However, using the same style and phraseology, they belong certainly together. The author gives a translation of the Carnarvon Tablet (after Gunn and Gardiner, *JEA* 5 [1918], 45-46), underlining those passages which have survived on the fragments of the first stela, followed by the continuous translation of the second stela. There follows a discussion of some important points, such as : a possible Nubian campaign of Kamose; the question where the stela refers to actual events and where it merely states boasts and threats; the role of Pi-Hathor (Gebelein) in the period.

The last chapter is devoted to various historical problems. The "chief of the treasurers" Neshi, who is stated to have been charged with the carving of the text, may be identical with the person of that name in the inscription of Mes. Other texts from the XVIIth Dynasty such as that of Emḥab (cfr our number 69114) may contain allusions to Kamose's campaign. At the end the author discusses the position of Avaris, once more arguing, partly on account of fresh material, that it has to be sought in the Khata'na-Qantîr area.

Among the plates there are two presenting a very clear photograph of the stela.

HAENY, Gerhard, see our number 72357.

HAGMANN, Diego, see our number 72360.

72295 HAMMOND, Mason, assisted by Lester J. BARTSON, The City in the Ancient World, Cambridge, Massachusetts, Harvard University Press, 1972 (16.5 × 24 cm; XVI + 617 p., 13 maps); series : Harvard Studies in Urban History; rev. *Aegyptus* 53 (1973), 191-194 (Nicola Criniti); *BiOr* 31 (1974), 56-58 (H. W. Pleket).   Pr. bound $ 20

After quoting Wilson for a characterization of the Egyptian civilization (compare our number 61746) there follows a description of the country, the population and the prehistoric cultures. The second section is devoted to a brief survey of the

Egyptian history. In his conclusion the author stresses the conservatism and centralization of the government in the hands of the pharaoh. Hence the citics had no independent existence and played no major role in the history or economy.
An annotated bibliography to this chapter on p. 428-433.

HANNA, Sami A., see our number 72291.

72296 HARANT de Polžic et Bezdružic, Christophe, Voyage en Égypte. Introduction, traduction et notes de Claire et Antoine Brejnik, [Le Caire], Institut français d'Archéologie orientale du Caire, 1972 (16.5 × 19.5 cm; 311 p., 1 pl., 13 fig.) = Collection des voyageurs occidentaux en Égypte, 5.

The author, a well known soldier and statesman, was one of the protagonists of protestant Bohemia before the Thirty Years War, and has been beheaded by order of the Emperor Ferdinand II in 1620.
In 1598 he visited Palestine and Egypt. In his diary he pays much attention to the population and its customs, but his description of the antiquities is rather short (cfr p. 184-195). An astonishing representation of the pyramids is reproduced on p. 187.

72297 HARI, Robert, Un cône funéraire inédit, *CdE* XLVII, Nos 93-94 (1972), 76-81, with 1 ill. and 1 fig.

L'auteur publie un cône funéraire d'un type inconnu au Corpus de Davies-Macadam (notre No 57131), dédié par un certain *Nb 'nn sw* à ses parents X et *Mry.t*, par ailleurs non identifiés. La formule se présente sous une forme originale.

Ph. Derchain

72298 HARI, Robert, Deux scarabées royaux inédits, *Aegyptus* 52 (1972), 3-7, with 3 ill., and 6 fig. on 2 pl.

Ces deux scarabées en stéatite blanche, acquis à Louqsor, datent des règnes d'Amenemhat III et de Mineptah. L'inscription du premier présente des difficultés d'interpretation; quatre pièces contemporaines portent une légende analogue. Les signes rappelleraient autant de qualités du roi, avec plusieurs thèmes se rapportant à la Basse Égypte. Le second scarabée a en place de la tête un visage négroïde. Un croisillage "en hérisson" tient lieu d'élytres et constitue une sorte de coiffure exotique. Le texte commémore une campagne militaire indéterminée, mais que le type même de l'objet inciterait à situer en Nubie ou au-delà.

J. Custers

HARPER, James E., see our number 72171.

72299 HARRIS, James E., Another Look at the Chronology of the New Kingdom Pharaohs, *Newsletter ARCE* No. 83 (October 1972), 28.

Abstract of a paper.
The x-ray examination of the mummies of the New Kingdom Pharaohs provided a "biological time-clock" helpful for reconsideration of the chronology of the New Kingdom.

L. M. J. Zonhoven

72300 HARRIS, James E., A Radiographic Survey of the New Kingdom Pharaohs, *Newsletter ARCE* No. 80 (January 1972), 35.

Abstract of a paper.
The royal mummies in the Cairo Museum were radiographically examined from top to toe, the evidence from which can be combined and compared with the historical documentation.

L. M. J. Zonhoven

72301 HARRISON, R. G. and ABDALLAH, A. B., The Remains of Tutankhamun, *Antiquity* 46 (1972), 8-14, with 1 pl.

An X-ray examination of the mummy of Tutankhamun in the Valley of the Kings revealed a striking resemblance to the mummy from Tomb 55, now believed to be that of Smenkhkare. Both have the same blood group, and may very well have been brothers.
See also our number 72216.

Dieter Mueller

72302 HASSAN, Ali, Waren die Außenseiten der Pyramiden in Giza farbig?, *MDAIK* 28 (1972), 153-155.

The recovery of several painted blocks from the casings of the pyramids of Kheops, Khefren, and Mycerinos, suggests that their upper layers were painted red, probably in imitation of the red granite used at the base.

Dieter Mueller

72303 HASSAN, Fekri A., Note on Sebilian Sites from Dishna Plain, *CdE* XLVII, Nos 93-94 (1972), 11-16, with 1 map and 1 fig.

Dans la plaine de Dishna, à mi-chemin de Qena et de Nag Hammadi, sur la rive droite du Nil, l'Expédition de la Southern Methodist University (Dallas, Texas) dirigée par F. Wendorf a découvert deux sites caractérisés par une industrie sébilienne que l'auteur rapproche de celle qui fut identifiée au Soudan et à Ballana, plus ancienne que celle de Kom Ombo. Elle appartient à l'échelon Sébilien I, et est datable de 10.550 a.C. (± 230).

Ph. Derchain

72304 HAYCOCK, B. G., Landmarks in Cushite History, *JEA* 58 (1972), 225-244, with 1 map.

The importance of local Sudanese cultures in antiquity is stressed, and the point made that however important Egyptian influence might have been, the dynamism of these indigenous peoples often reached an apex when the Pharaohs were too feeble to intervene in the south. Also noted is the growing readiness of scholars to accept Cushite artistic achievements as distinctive, and recognize this civilization as 'African'. This is manifested by such things as the apparent growth of writing and literacy even in minor villages of Nubia in late Meroitic times, while the inscriptions found by Garstang at Meroe and by Hintze at Musawwarât suggest literacy was quite widespread near the capital much earlier, and the author agrees with Millet in seeing this as evidence that the replacement of Egyptian hieroglyphic or demotic by simple alphabetic Meroïtic scripts increased the ability to write. He therefore rejects Adams' view of a 'static culture or cyclical development'. Late Meroïtic development of N. Nubia was made possible by the introduction of the *saqiya* or animal-driven waterwheel. Continuity from Napatan to Meroïtic times has now been stratigraphically shown by the excavations at Meroe, even perhaps lasting until the local X-Group period. Philae texts published by Junker tend to show that the new towns of Ptolemy VI were mainly on sites of the disused New Kingdom settlements. It is possible that as the Roman market for the products of S. Cush fell off with supplies from India and elsewhere, the decline of Meroe set in.   *E. Uphill*

72305 HAYES, William C., A Papyrus of The Late Middle Kingdom in the Brooklyn Museum [Papyrus Brooklyn 35.1446]. Edited with Translation and Commentary, [New York], The Brooklyn Museum, [1972] (21.5 × 28 cm; [IV+] 185 p., 14 pl. with opposite transcription in hieroglyphs) = Wilbour Monographs 5; rev. *BiOr* 30 (1973), 207-209 (O. D. Berlev); *CdE* XLVIII, No. 95 (1973), 84-87 (Bernadette Menu).   Pr. bound $ 8

Reprint of our number 3943.
On the unnumbered p. 3 a few errata are mentioned, and a list of articles and books dealing with the present papyrus.

72306 HEERMA VAN VOSS, M., Over het oudegyptische Dodenboek, *De Ibis*, Amsterdam 3 (1972), 51-54, with a fig.

Our number 67252 in an abridged form.

72307 HELCK, Wolfgang, Das Datum der Schlacht von Megiddo, *MDAIK* 28 (1972), 101-102.

R. O. Faulkner's emendation "year 23, 1. *šmw*, day 20" (instead of "21") in *Urk. IV*, 657, 1 is probably unjustified. The entry *Urk. IV*, 652, 13-14 is to be read "Day 19 : One awakens in the royal tent; (departure) for the town of 'Aruna". If the army arrived there on the twentieth, the battle at Megiddo can very well have taken place on the twenty-first.

Dieter Mueller

72308 HELCK, Wolfgang, Die Ritualdarstellungen des Ramesseums. I, Wiesbaden, Otto Harrassowitz, 1972 (18.1 × 25 cm; [V+] 182 p.) = Ägyptologische Abhandlungen. Herausgegeben von Wolfgang Helck und Eberhard Otto, 25; rev. *BiOr* 31 (1974), 253-255 (Michel Gitton); *Mundus* 9 (1973), 124-125 (Hellmut Brunner).   Pr. DM 48

Publication of the texts to the ritual scenes on the walls of the Ramesseum. Each text is given in written hieroglyphs, accompanied by a translation. There are no notes or comments.
The texts are published in the following order : both sides of the first pylon (p. 1-20); the Osiride pillars and 3 columns at the eastern side of the second court (21-53); the architraves and capitals of this court (54-57); the pillars and columns at its western side (58-90); both sides of the wall in front of the hypostyle hall (90-105); the columns of this hall and their architraves (105-137); the western wall of the hypostyle hall (137-146), the astronomical room (146-170) and the inner room behind it (171-182). The volume contains no table of contents, while the author uses numbers differing from those of *PM* II, 2nd edition. There are small plans at the beginning of each section.
A second volume with the plates will follow.

72309 HELCK, Wolfgang, Der Text des Nilhymnus, Wiesbaden, Otto Harrassowitz, 1972 (17.7 × 25 cm; [IV+] 87 p.); series : Kleine ägyptische Texte; rev. *CdE* XLVIII, No. 95 (1973), 80-82 (B. van de Walle); *JNES* 34 (1975), 150 (Dieter Mueller).

Pr. DM 14.80

On p. 1-2 a list of the manuscripts containing the *Hymn to the Nile*. The text itself, in written hieroglyphs, all known variants of each line under each other, is given on p. 3-85. The author has added some notes and a translation to each of the 14 sections into which the hymn is divided. He also gives what to his opinion may have been the original text of each section. At the end a short note (p. 86-87) on the text history, in which the relationship between the various manuscripts, all from the Ramesside Period, is discussed.

72310 HELCK, Wolfgang, Zu den "Talbezirken" in Abydos, *MDAIK* 28 (1972), 95-99.

The author defends his thesis that the so-called "funerary palaces" at Abydos housed the royal statue. In the corresponding section of Djoser's complex, fragments of a royal statue have been found. They bear the name of the king, followed by that of Imhotep — presumably because the latter acted as "crown-prince" during the dedication ceremonies. *Dieter Mueller*

72311 HELCK, W., Zur Frage der Entstehung der ägyptischen Literatur, *WZKM* 63/64 (1972), 6-26.

Literature in Egypt has never been merely a story or a spontaneous expression of feeling; in accordance with the character of the civilization it always has an aim, it has to be effective, to create Maat.

From this principle Helck explains the development from the mention of regnal years and royal acts to literary royal inscriptions; from the mention of the name of a tomb owner and legal documents concerning his funerary cult to auto-biography; from proverbs to the instructions. In his opinion the *Instruction of* Hordedef dates from the First Intermediate Period, shortly earlier than Merikare; that of Ptahhotep is somewhat older, Kagemni again older, but still later than the VIth Dynasty. They were ascribed to persons already famous and venerated. In the XIIth Dynasty originated the political literature, to which Helck also reckons the *Admonitions of Ipuwer*.

Other genres are those originating from the initiation talk which transferred the knowledge of the community to the younger generation and developed i.a. to the *Dispute of the Man and his Ba*; and the stories placed in a historical context and intending to stimulate Maat, though growing from popular stories, beginning in the XIIth Dynasty with that of the general Sisenet, down to the Setne-novels.

At the end the author points out the parallel development in religious literature, from ritual texts to theological texts and hymns.

72312 HELCK, Wolfgang, Zur Herkunft der sogenannten 'Phö-nizischen' Schrift, *Ugarit-Forschungen*, Kevelaer/Neukirchen-Vluyn 4 (1972), 41-45; rev. *Phoenix* 19 (1973), 284-287 (K. R. Veenhof).

The author rejects the theory that the "Phoenician" writing has been a conscious invention. He argues that from the time before 1000 B.C. so few texts remain because they have been written on papyrus, hence in Egyptian hieratic script. For Phoenician texts in this script the so-called syllabic orthography will have been used, from which the "Phoenician" signs were thus derived. He draws up a table from which this is apparent for 16 out of 22 signs, choosing his examples from various Egyptian papyri from the early XIIIth Dynasty.

Helck also stresses the gradual development of "Phoenician" writing, during which some signs, still present in the South Arabian script, got lost. For these too he proposes hesitantly Egyptian prototypes.

HELCK, Wolfgang, see also our number 72432.

72313 HELLER, Angela, Siegfried Morenz. Verzeichnis seiner Schriften, *ZÄS* 99,1 (1972), IV-X.

Bibliography. Compare our number 72086 and *ZÄS* 100, 1 (1973), 76 (Ergänzung).
The same bibliography has also been published in *Jahrbuch. Sächsische Akademie der Wissenschaften zu Leipzig*. 1969-1970, 1972, 238-247.

72314 HERBERT, Kevin, Greek and Latin Inscriptions in the Brooklyn Museum, Brooklyn N.Y., The Brooklyn Museum, 1972 (22.6 × 28.5 cm; XVIII + 95 p., 28 pl., 2 coloured ill. on frontispiece) = Wilbour Monographs 4; rev. *Erasmus* 24 (1972), 750-751 (Jean Leclant).   Pr. bound $ 8

The author has published a number of various objects in the Brooklyn Museum all provided with a description, translation and commentary.
From the rich contents we mention the numbers 13-20 (p. 34-42) comprising mummy labels of which some are written both in Greek and Demotic. Interesting is a completely preserved mummy with its wrapping (no. 12, p. 32-39). Finally we may point to several magical amulets of various gods. We mention in particular a rare amulet of the goddess Maat (no. 27, p. 54-55) and a superb amulet of the lion-headed god (no. 24, p. 49-51).
The book is concluded with indices, concordances and plates.
R. L. Vos

72315 HEYLER, André et Jean LECLANT, Préliminaires à un répertoire d'épigraphie méroïtique (REM) (suite), *MNL* No 10 (Juillet 1972), 1-9.

REM 1111 - REM 1137 umfaßt die meroitischen Texte, die zwischen 1968 und 1970 publiziert wurden und gibt das Inventar mit Bibliographie wieder. *Inge Hofmann*

HINTZE, Fritz, see our number 72086.

72316 HINTZE, Ursula, Siebente Grabungskampagne in Musawwarat es Sufra 1968 und der Wiederaufbau des Löwentempels 1969/70, *Ethnographisch-Archäologische Zeitschrift*, Berlin 13 (1972), 259-271, with 1 plan, 9 ill. (one on cover).

Die Kampagne 1968 beschäftigte sich hauptsächlich mit der "Großen Anlage"; die bisher aufgestellten 8 Bauperioden konnten bestätigt werden. Die ältesten aus Steinquadern erbauten Anlagen scheinen in die Zeit des Königs Aspelta zurückzugehen, die jüngsten, die in einer "Plattenbauweise" errichtet wurden, dürften in die spätmeroitische Phase (1.-3. Jahrhundert n.Chr.) zu datieren sein. In der sogenannten "Westkapelle" (Raum 516) standen zwei Säulen mit Kartuschen, die mit großer Wahrscheinlichkeit den Namen des Königs Arnekhamani enthalten. Im Zentraltempel lagen u.a. eine Bronzemünze Ptolemaios' III. und ein Elefantenzahn. Insgesamt 140 Inschriften konnten aufgenommen werden, davon 1 demotisch, 18 altnubisch, 1 griechisch, 1 lateinisch und die übrigen meroitisch.
Es kann als gesichert angenommen werden, daß Musawwarat es Sufra ein Wallfahrtsort war, dessen Haupttheiligtum, die "Große Anlage", wahrscheinlich Amun geweiht war. Tempel 300 scheint Kultstätte des Götterpaares Arensnuphis und Sebiumeker gewesen zu sein. Das Gebäude III A war wohl eine christliche Kirche, zu der ein kleiner Friedhof gehörte. Im Nordfriedhof liegen Gräber der nachmeroitischen Zeit.
Abschließend folgt ein Bericht über den Wiederaufbau des Löwentempels, der am 14. Januar 1970 unter starker Beteiligung der sudanesischen Öffentlichkeit feierlich eingeweiht wurde. *Inge Hofmann*

72317 HOFFMAN, Michael, Preliminary Report on the First Two Seasons at Hierakonpolis. Part III. Occupational Features at the Kom el Aḥmar, *JARCE* 9 (1971-1972), 35-47, with 7 tables and 14 fig. on 2 pl.

Compare our number 72218.
From the archaeological remains much variety is apparent. That the area surrounded by the walls was not occupied completely at once is likely; shifts are probable. *M. Heerma van Voss*

72318 HOFFMAN, Michael, Preliminary Report on the First Two Seasons at Hierakonpolis. Part IV. Test Excavations at Locality 14, *JARCE* 9 (1971-1972), 49-66, with 12 tables and 13 fig. on 4 pl.

Compare our number 72218.
The author deals with stratigraphy, chronology, artifacts, lithic, wooden and ceramic material. His pottery classification distinguishes straw tempered, grit tempered and untempered (plum-red) wares.   *M. Heerma van Voss*

72319 HOFMANN, Inge, Eine meroitische Stadt in Wadai?, *MNL* No. 9 (June 1972), 14-18.

The author mentions a report of a journey by the Tunesian Sheikh Zain el Âbidîn, published in 1847, during which he found in Wadai — between Darfur and Chad — in the neighbourhood of Wara the remains of a town and some stone coffins, in which i.a. inscribed copper plates, gold coins and stone statues. Excavating the ruins he found columns and portals with a representation of the sun.
The mysteries of this town cannot yet be unravelled.

72320 HOFMANN, Inge, Eine neue Elefantengott-Darstellung aus dem Sudan, *JEA* 58 (1972), 245-246, with 1 pl.

In 1970 the German expedition of Musawwarat es Sufra discovered a graffito on the eastern outside wall of Temple 300, which appears to be an elephant-headed figure wearing a sun disk. The elephant god was worshipped in Meroïtic religion and this representation may be compared with the elephant statue at Wad Ban Naga and paralleled with the Indian god Gaṇeśa.   *E. Uphill*

72321 HOFMANN, Inge, De ontcijfering van het Meroïtisch, *Spiegel Historiael* 472-478, with 9 ill., 1 map and 3 fig.

"The decipherment of Meroitic".
After an introduction on the history and the culture of the Meroitic Kingdom, in which Egyptian influence as well as important independent traits are distinguished, the author discusses the Meroitic alphabet, the hieroglyphic and cursive writing and the importance of Griffith and Lepsius for the decipherment. She stresses the grammatical and lexicographical problems for translation of the texts, which some day may be solved with the help of computer analysis.   *L. M. J. Zonhoven*

72322 HOLTHOER, Rostislav, Two Inscribed Akhenaten Blocks from el-Ashmunein, *Studia Orientalia*, Helsinki 43, 5 (1972), 1-8, with 2 ill. and 3 fig.

Publication of two inscribed blocks from the Akhnaton temple seen by the author in Hermopolis. The first one, similar to that published by Roeder (our number 69520, pl. 201) under no. PC 190, i.a. mentions the name of Akhnaton's granddaughter . . . . . . tasheri; the other contains a name of the king himself.

72323 HORN, Jürgen, Ägyptologie als Wissenschaft in der Gesellschaft, *GM* Heft 1 (1972), 42-48.

Critical analysis of the history and aims of German egyptology and its future.
For a reply, see our numbers 72229 and 72536.

72324 HORN, Jürgen, Bohairisch ṀⲠⲀⲚⲦⲉ- statt ṀⲠⲀⲦⲉ- (S ṀⲠⲀⲦⲉ-), *GM* Heft 1 (1972), 8-10.

The form ṀⲠⲀⲚⲦⲉ- with ⲛ occurs almost exclusively in one text, the Encomium on Makarios of Tkow. The author presents suggestions for its explanation.

72325 HORN, Jürgen, Methodologische Überlegungen zur Interpretationskategorie "Religion" in der ägyptologischen Forschung, *GM* Heft 3 (1972), 43-48.

A summary of H. G. Klippenberg, Der religiöse Mensch als soziales Wesen (*in : Evangelische Kommentare* 5, 1972, 423-426). The author describes Klippenberg's theory of the unity of religion and society in the ancient world, and insists on its applicability to Egyptological research.   *Dieter Mueller*

72326 HORN, Jürgen, Ⲥ ⲭ̄ⲛ̄ ⲙ̄ⲙⲟⲛ /Ⲃ ⳉⲁⲛ ⲙ̄ⲙⲟⲛ in der Doppelfrage. Eine lexicographische Bemerkung, *GM* Heft 1 (1972), 28-29.

The expression, usually rendered as "or not", in fact indicates the alternative to the first part of the question. Hence in some instances it has to be translated in an other way.

72327 HORN, Siegfried H., Palestinian Scarabs at Andrews University, *Andrews University Seminary Studies*, Berrien Springs, Michigan 10 (1972), 142-146, with 1 pl.

Publication of 8 scarabs, 5 of which (nos 2-5 and 8) belonging to a hoard allegedly found in the Samaria area. Four of them date from the First Intermediate or Hyksos Periods, two bear the prenomen of Tuthmosis III, and one, representing a king on a chariot, may date from Sethi II.

72328 HORNUNG, Erik, Ägyptische Unterweltsbücher. Eingeleitet, übersetzt und erläutert, Zürich und München, Artemis Verlag, [1972] (10.2 × 17 cm; 525 p., 114 fig.); series : Die Bibliothek der Alten Welt. Reihe der Alte Orient; rev. *Mundus* 9 (1973), 211-212 (Hellmut Brunner).   Pr. DM 58

The volume contains translations with some notes of four books on the netherworld, the *Amduat*, the *Book of Gates*, the *Book of Caverns* and the *Book of the Earth*, followed by short abstracts from related texts such as the *Litany of Re*, the *Books of Day* and *of Night*.

In his preceding introduction Hornung stresses that the Egyptians conceived death as the place of regenerating the existence, as the sun-god rejuvenated himself during the night. Hence these books are no means to conquer the death, but guides to banish the dangers during the journey through the netherworld by knowledge. The author briefly describes the belief in the netherworld from ancient times onwards, the various books on it and their occurrences in the tombs, as well as their principle motifs, e.g. the journey of the sun, body and soul of the dead, the care for the blessed and the punishment of the damned. In the last section he explains the problems of translating these texts and mentions their main editions. Notes, bibliography and a vocabulary at the end.

72329 HORNUNG, Erik, Probleme der Erfassung und Darstellung ägyptischer Geschichte, *in*: *Antike und Universalgeschichte*. Festschrift Hans Erich Stier zum 70. Geburtstag am 25. Mai 1972, Münster, Verlag Aschendorff, [1972] (= Fontes et Commentationes. Schriftenreihe des Instituts für Epigraphik an der Universität Münster. Supplementband 1), 17-25.

A brief description of the Basel project to document all aspects of Egyptian history; the two samples at the end illustrate the sections on Neb-ka and Amenophis I.

Dieter Mueller

72330 HUARD, Paul et Jean LECLANT, Problèmes archéologiques entre le Nil et le Sahara, *Études Scientifiques*, Le Caire, Sept.-Dec. 1972, 5-93, with 2 maps, 10 fig. and 13 ill.; rev. *BiOr* 30 (1973), 405-407, with 4 ill. on 2 pl. (Inge Hofmann).

Die Studie ist im wesentlichen ein Vergleich zwischen Felsbildern der Sahara und dem Niltal während der Perioden vom frühen Neolithikum bis in rezente Zeit. Für die Stufe der Jäger, gekennzeichnet durch mehr oder weniger naturalistische Wild-tierdarstellungen, werden mehr als 20 Kulturzüge heraus-gearbeitet, die sich auf Felsbildern beider Kulturräume fest-stellen lassen. Die Hirtenperiode ist charakterisiert durch die Darstellung domestizierter Tiere, insbesondere von Rindern; in Bezug auf Viehzucht und Ackerbau wird das Problem der jeweiligen Entstehung und Diffusion diskutiert. Streitwagen und Pferde halten die Autoren in Ägypten von den Hyksos übernommen und von dort nach Westen und Süden verbreitet. Das Eisen im Sudan und seine Verbreitung wird besprochen, abschließend das Problem des Kamels im Niltal und der Sahara.   *Inge Hofmann*

72331   HUBERT, Emmanuelle, Les "mystères" de l'Égypte avant Champollion, *Archeologia*, Paris No 52 (novembre 1972), 46-53, with a map and 7 ill. (1 in colour).

Survey of the knowledge about ancient Egypt previous to Champollion.

HUMPHREYS, S. B., see our number 72578.

HUXTABLE, Grace, see our number 72257.

72332   Искусство Древнего Египта. Живопись. Скульптура. Архитектура. Прикладное искусство, Москва, Издательство Изобразительное Искусство, 1972 (22.2 × 28.2 cm; 28 p., 24 ill., 158 pl. [63 in colour], ill. on endpapers); rev. *Asien. Afrika. Lateinamerika* 2 (1974), 1023 (Steffen Wenig).   Pr. руб. 6 коп. 97

"The Art of Ancient Egypt. Painting, Sculpture, Architecture, Applied Art".
The short text by R. Shurinova contains a survey of Egyptian art history. The illustrations and plates, of good quality, mostly represent well known objects, from the Ist Dynasty until the end of the New Kingdom. For scholars the book may be of importance because of the objects from the Pushkin Museum, Moscow, and the Ermitage, Leningrad.

72333   IVERSEN, Erik, Obelisks in Exile. Volume Two. The Obelisks of Istanbul and England, Copenhagen, G.E.C. Gad Publishers, 1972 (21.7 × 35.2 cm; 169 p., 1 fig. and 40 pl. containing 3 plans, 1 map and numerous ill. and fig., 2 ill. on cover); rev. *Rivista* 47 (1972), 121-125 (Sergio Donadoni).

Fortsetzung unserer Nummer 68296.
Von den einst mindestens fünf Obelisken in Konstantinopel sind heute noch zwei erhalten. Alle Nachrichten von Reisenden, alle bildlichen Wiedergaben sind sorgfältig zusammengestellt. Den 390 n.Chr. von Theodosius auf dem Hippodrom wiedererrichteten Obelisk hatte Thutmosis III. 1454 v.Chr. südlich des 7. Pylons von Karnak aufstellen lassen. Der im vorigen Jahrhundert im Serailbezirk gefundene Porphyr-Obelisk stand möglicherweise einmal in der Nähe der Apostelkirche. Der von der Noticia dignitatum Constantinopolitanae erwähnte Obelisk im Gebiet des Strategiums könnte mit dem Obelisk Priuli

identisch sein, der nach Pierre Gilles um 1550 aus dem
Topkapi-Serail entfernt wurde; dieser kann deshalb nicht
identisch sein mit dem Obelisken, den Graves 1792 während
seines Istanbuler Aufenthalts im Palastbezirk sah.
Unter den Obelisken Englands werden ausführlich behandelt
die beiden Obelisken Nektanebos' (BM 523-524), ehemals
wahrscheinlich für eines der hermopolitanischen Thotheiligtümer
bestimmt, der von Ptolemäus VII. und Cleopatra III. vor dem
1. Pylon des Isistempels auf Philae errichtete "Bankes-Obelisk"
und der von Amenophis II. auf Elephantine aufgestellte
"Alnwick-Obelisk". Am berühmtesten wohl ist die sog. "Nadel
der Cleopatra", von Thutmosis III. einst für den Tempel in
Heliopolis in Auftrag gegeben, von Oktavian nach Alexandria
gebracht und dort aufgestellt, 1877 schließlich nach London
überführt, wobei sie um ein Haar in der Biskaya versunken wäre.
Noch kein Jahrzehnt lang in England ist schließlich der 1964
in Qasr Ibrim gefundene Obelisk der Hatschepsut. Eine Liste
kleinerer Obelisken und Fragmente von solchen in britischen
Sammlungen und ein ausführlicher Index beschließen das Werk.

I. Gamer-Wallert

72334 JACOBSOHN, Helmuth, Gestaltwandel der Götter und des
Menschen im alten Ägypten, *Eranos-Jahrbuch*, Zürich 38 (1969),
1972, 9-43.

In two sections the author follows the awakening of self-
consciousness in ancient Egypt.
Section 1 deals with the Old Kingdom. The author first discusses
the *Monument of Memphite Theology*, describing how Atum,
the primordial god and creator, is explained to be an emanation
of Ptah. Although the two are identified, the creation came
into being through heart and tongue of the latter, that is : man
realized that he himself was involved in the realization of the
gods and projected this in the god Ptah. Referring to an
earlier lecture (our number 70277) the author sketches the
mystery of Ka-mutef in connection with the aristocratic self-
understanding of man in the Old Kingdom. He illustrates the
optimistic naivety of the officials by quoting from the
Instruction of Ptahhotep.
The second section is devoted to the crisis of the First
Intermediate Period and its consequences for the development
of self-consciousness. The author quotes largely from the
Admonitions and the *Dispute of a Man with his Ba*. The latter
demonstrates that also non-royal persons could attain a unity
with their ba, which is relatively independent from the gods.
In some stelae from Deir el-Medina a later stage of this process
of individualization finds its expression.

72335 JACQUET, Jean, Fouilles de Karnak Nord. Quatrième campagne 1971, *BIFAO* 71 (1972), 151-160, with 2 folding plans and 8 pl.

Sequel to our number 71296.
The article deals with the excavations on two sites, one (fouille A) East of the enclosure of Montu and North of the enclosure of Amon, and the other (fouille H) within the enclosure of Montu to the East of the temples of Montu, Harpreʿ and Maʿat. The former is intended to uncover the plan of a monument of Tuthmosis I, which appears to be of an unusual form. Several baker's ovens and a number of objects, among which re-employed blocks, have been discovered. The study of the pottery will prove to be of value for future excavations in Upper Egypt.

72336 JACQUET-GORDON, Helen, Concerning a Statue of Senenmut, *BIFAO* 71 (1972), 139-150, with 5 fig. and 5 pl.

During the 1970-1971 season of excavations at Karnak North fragments of a block statue have been found which appear to belong to a statue of Senenmut holding princess Nefrure on his lap, found near the IXth pylon and published by Daressy, *ASAE* 22 (1922), 248-252.
Nowhere apparently the names of Amun or of Senenmut have been intentionally damaged, though the author is inclined to suggest to a very careful recutting of them; moreover, there are traces that the name of Hatshepsut has been altered in that of Tuthmosis III.
Probably the statue was originally placed in the newly discovered temple of Tuthmosis I (cfr our preceding number).

72337 JACQUET-GORDON, Helen, A Donation Stela of Apries, *RdE* 24 (1972), 84-90, with 1 pl.

Cette stèle, vue dans le commerce au Caire, fait mention d'une donation faite en l'an 1 (?) par Apriès à Min d'Imet (Nebecheh), dont elle porte la plus ancienne mention actuellement connue. L'auteur réunit à cette occasion, dans une note de son commentaire de la stèle, la documentation relative à ce culte peu connu. Une photographie et un facsimile au trait de la stèle illustrent l'article.   *Ph. Derchain*

72338 JACQUET-GORDON, Helen and Charles BONNET, Tombs of the Tanqasi Culture at Tabo, *JARCE* 9 (1971-1972), 77-83, with 1 table, 2 fig., and 9 ill. on 3 pl.

There was no X-Group occupation at Tabo. Apparently, the Third Cataract was the frontier between this and the Ushara-Tanqasi-Tabo-Group. The two cultures had many traits in

common. The authors divide these into three groups : I. those
common to Meroitic civilization and to both underlying
cultures; II. those due to close contact with the Romano-
Egyptian civilization; III. those apparently indigenous to the
two cultures.
Probably, both were originally closely related, and are to be
associated with the Noba or Nubian peoples.

M. Heerma van Voss

72339   JAIRAZBHOY, R. A., Did the Ancient Egyptians Reach
America?, *The Illustrated London News*, London 260/6889
(August 1972), 40-41, with 3 ill.

The author argues that there is evidence for Egyptian influence
upon the Olmec civilisation in Mexico.

72340   JAMES, T. G. H., The Archaeology of Ancient Egypt, London-
Sydney-Toronto, The Bodley Head, [1972] (19.4×25.3 cm;
143 p., 2 maps, 5 plans, 1 section, 20 fig., 47 ill., 8 colour pl.,
frontispiece, colour ill. on wrapper); rev. *Palestine Exploration
Quarterly* 105 (1973), 116-117 (E. P. Uphill).   Pr. bound £1.95

Although intended for the general public this book will be
consulted with profit by Egyptologists since the author, apart
from the "obligatory" subjects such as the tomb of Tutankhamon, deals with some less known excavations.
After a preface and an introduction to Egyptian history there
follow eleven chapters mainly devoted each to a particular site
and a particular scholar. They follow the Egyptian chronology,
from Petrie's excavations at Nagâda (chapter 2) to those of
Emery at Ballâna and Qustul. Chapter 6, however, deals with
a historical event, the expulsion of the Hyksos, discussing i.a.
the Carnarvon tablet and the stelae of Kamose, while chapter
11 is devoted to Champollion and the decipherment of
hieroglyphs. We mention here particularly chapter 8, about
Bruyère's work at Deir el Medîneh and the study of the
ostraca by Černý, and chapter 9, about Montet's excavation
of the royal tombs at Tanis.
At the end of the book a postscript, a bibliography and an index.
There has also appeared an American edition, New York,
Henry Z. Walck, 1972 (Pr. $8.95).

72341   JAMES, T. G. H., Gold Technology in Ancient Egypt. Mastery
of Metal Working Methods, *Gold Bulletin*. A quarterly review
of research on gold and its applications in industry, Johannesburg 5, Number 2 (April 1972), 38-42, with 7 ill. (6 in colour).

Description of the gold mining in ancient Egypt so far as
known to us, and of several techniques of the gold workers.

The author points to some problems still unsolved, e.g. where the gold has been washed. There is no evidence of any technique of refining. The gold workers employed the same techniques as modern craftsmen, such as hammering the metal into a heavy sheeting; use of thin foil and gold leaf; cloisonné work; casting and the use of moulds by the help of which gold foil was beaten into the required shape

The *Gold Bulletin* is obtainable from the Research Organization, Chamber of Mines of South Africa, 5 Holland Street, Johannesburg, South Africa.

72342 JAMES, Harry [T.G.H.], An Open Letter to Dr. Rosalind Moss, *JEA* 58 (1972), 5-6, with frontispiece.

A tribute to Dr. Rosalind Moss.

72343 JANKUHN, Dieter, Das Buch "Schutz des Hauses" (*s3-pr*). Dissertation zur Erlangung der Doktorwürde der philosophischen Fakultät der Georg-August-Universität zu Göttingen, Bonn, Rudolf Habelt Verlag GmbH, 1972 (14.6 × 20.8 cm; [VIII +] 180 + 1 p., 3 pl. [2 folded]); rev. *CdE* XLVIII, No. 95 (1973), 99-102 (Jean-Claude Goyon).

The inventory of the temple library in Edfou lists, among other magical books, a work entitled "Protection of the House", whose text is preserved on the north side of the enclosure wall; fragments of it have also been found on the architraves of the mammisi of Edfou, and in the crypts of the Hathor temple at Dendara.

This doctoral thesis is primarily devoted to the study of the Ptolemaic ritual. After a brief survey of earlier references to the practice of protecting buildings by magical means, the three extant versions are reproduced section by section, then translated and annotated. The commentary is brief and concentrates on the mythological allusions that make up the bulk of the text; however, special attention is paid to its connection with the New Year. A brief comparison with related books, and several indexes conclude this thesis.

Dieter Mueller

72344 JANKUHN, Dieter, Steckt hinter dem Gott "Rwtj" eine Erinnerung an den rituellen Königsmord?, *GM* Heft 1 (1972), 11-16.

Discussion of the god *Rwty* and the *pr-Rwty*. The god is connected with death and resurrection; he performs the ritual coronation of the dead in the *pr-nms* (*CT* IV, 77b-80d). On account of African parallels the author suggests that *pr-Rwty* is the building in which in prehistoric times the king was ritually killed by being buried alive. The corpse was laid in a hide of a bull and pressed until dry; the author connects this with the *'Imy-wt*.

72345 JANSSEN, Jac. J., Jean François Champollion, de grondlegger van de Egyptologie, *Spiegel Historiael* 452-461, with 7 ill. and 2 fig.

"Jean François Champollion, the founder of Egyptology".
An article on the occasion of the 150th anniversary of the publication of the "Lettre à M. Dacier".
The author deals with the life of Champollion, the history of the decipherment of the hieroglyphs, the writing system, and the developments in language and writing.

L. M. J. Zonhoven

72346 JANSSENS, Gerard, Contribution to the Verbal System in Old Egyptian. A New Approach to the Reconstruction of the Hamito-Semitic Verbal System. Uitgegeven door de Sektie niet-Westerse filologie bij de fakulteit Letteren en Wijsbegeerte, Leuven, Uitgeverij Peeters, [1972] (16.6 × 25.3 cm; 56 p.) = Orientalia Gandensia VI; at head of title : Rijksuniversiteit Gent; rev. *BiOr* 30 (1973), 211-212 (Alessandro Roccati); *JARCE* 10 (1973), 112-114 (David Lorton); *Orientalia Suëcana* 21 (1972), 142-144 (Frithiof Rundgren).

The author basing his argument on the material collected in Edel's *Altägyptische Grammatik* — he nowhere refers to actual texts — discusses various forms of the Old Egyptian verbal system, establishing strong parallels with the Semitic system. He also pays attention to vocalisation problems.
In section I Janssens distinguishes between three *sdm.f*-forms, corresponding with Sem. preterite, jussive and imperfect. In section II he attempts to prove that the active *sdmw.f* is a variant of the imperfective *sdm.f*. In section III he argues that the suffix of the *sdm.f*-form was originally an object pronoun converted into the subject. For this object/subject conversion, fundamental for some following sections, see also section XIII. Section IV explains that the *t* in *ywt* and *ynt* is an old accusative mark indicating direction, while section V compares *n.f* in the *sdm.n.f*-form with Sem. *lahū*, "to him", also used to express the object of the action, in Eg. converted into the subject. Section VI argues that the imperfective form *mrr.f* in fact contains an active infinitive, the Old Egyptian possessing two infinitives, *mrr* and *mrt*.
The following sections deal with the verbal noun, the participles and the relative forms, the verbal adjective (*.tyfy*), the passive forms *sdmw.f* and *sdmm.f*, and the Old Egyptian passive voice

formed by the affix *.ty* (= Edel's passive *sḏmt.f*-formation). The last sections are devoted to the use of the infinitive instead of the verb, continuing a finite verb or a participle (XIV), the pseudo-participle (XV), the imperative (XVI) and the augment *ya.* and its preservation or elision.

72347 JANTZEN, Ulf, Ägyptische und orientalische Bronzen aus dem Heraion von Samos, Bonn, Rudolf Habelt Verlag GmbH, 1972 (22 × 30 cm; VIII + 108 p., 85 pl.) = Samos Band 8; at head of title: Deutsches Archäologisches Institut; rev. *Acta Archaeologica Academiae Scientiarum Hungaricae* 25 (1973), 420-421 (L. Castiglione); *AJA* 77 (1973), 236-237 (Oscar White Muscarella); *BiOr* 30 (1973), 198-200 (George A. Hanfmann).
Pr. DM 120

In this catalogue of the bronzes found during the excavations of the Heraion on Samos until 1965 (later discoveries are not included) the first chapter (p. 5-37) is devoted to the 132 Egyptian objects. Only three of them have been published previously.

In the preliminary remarks to the chapter the author states that only very few bronze objects found in Greece are known, though some more may today be preserved in small museums and excavator's storerooms.

The objects are arranged according to technique, size and type. The following groups are distinguished: large hollow cast human and apis figures (29 instances); small hollow cast figures and fragments (23); animal figures (21), being falcons, apis-bulls and cats; solid cast figures (21); ibis figures of various materials, of which only the bronze parts are preserved (7); and various kinds of objects, among which a mirror, a sistrum, parts of furniture, etc. Each object is separately described, while each category is followed by a technical discussion. The author, not being an Egyptologist, has refrained from dating the bronzes, nor did he study them in the context of Egyptian art.

We mention here particularly: the mirror, discussed by Peter Munro (p. 33-34) and dated by him to the early Saite Period; an aegis and a Bes figure, previously studied by Parlasca (cfr our number 4790); the torso and head of a male figure, a priest clad in a panther skin (original height 66 to 68 cm), with traces of gilding. The last group of objects provisionally called fans (p. 37; cfr pl. 35) is only with hesitance arranged among the Egyptian objects, as well as the so-called leaf-stands, very curious objects which may perhaps belong to them.

JARITZ, Horst, see our number 72357.

72348 JEFFREYS, M. D. W., A Triad of Gods in Africa, *Anthropos*, Freiburg/Schweiz 67 (1972), 723-735.

Die Göttertriaden innerhalb der Igbo-Religion — die allerdings auch in anderen religiösen Systemen Afrikas vorkommen — lassen Verf. an eine Beziehung zwischen den Kulturen des Nigerbeckens und des Niltales denken. Hinsichtlich der meroitischen Religion wird Budge (1928) zitiert, der Osiris mit Apedemak gleichsetzt.   *Inge Hofmann*

72349 JOHNSON, Janet H., The XXXth Dynasty As Seen in a Demotic Source, *Newsletter ARCE* No. 83 (October 1973), 28-29.

Abstract of a paper.
On basis of new readings in the Demotic Chronicle the author draws new historical conclusions, i.a. on the relationship of Nectanebo I and Tachos, his son and successor.
L. M. J. Zonhoven

72350 JUNGE, Friedrich, Ägyptologie und modernes Ägypten, *GM* Heft 1 (1972), 49-51.

An appeal to connect specialized egyptological knowledge with modern Egypt.

72351 JUNGE, Friedrich, Einige Probleme der *sḏm.f*-Theorie im Licht der vergleichenden Syntax, *Orientalia* 41 (1972), 325-338.

L'auteur admet les bases suivantes : a) l'égyptien a possédé à l'origine une conjugaison à préfixes, pareille à celle des langues sémitiques; b) dans l'histoire d'un idiome, les fonctions survivent aux formes, et plusieurs formes peuvent se succéder pour une même fonction. L'article vérifie les conséquences logiques à tirer de ces principes quant à la genèse du présent *sḏm.f.* Il envisage sous cet angle le pseudoparticipe, puis le participe passif, l'infinitif, et enfin développe les idées typologiques de Satzinger (notre N° 68519). Aucune théorie, conclut-il, n'arrache la conviction. Il estime en revanche avoir rémontré logique l'inconciliabilité de deux thèses : d'un côté l'origine préfixale, de l'autre la dérivation de participe ou d'infinitif. Les tenants des avis traditionnels doivent selon lui se prononcer contre une stricte parenté entre égyptien et langues sémitiques, et s'abstenir d'établir des comparaisons entre ces langues.
J. Custers

72352 JUNGE, Friedrich, Funktionsverschiebung bei Hieroglyphenzeichen, *GM* Heft 2 (1972), 47-48.

The author examines the interchangeable use of ⸚, ⸚, 𓊮, ⸚ and 𓏛 in the *Coffin Texts*.   *Dieter Mueller*

72353 JUNGE, Friedrich, Über die Wünschbarkeit theoretischer Diskussion in der Ägyptologie, *GM* Heft 2 (1972), 63-65.

Theory and practice of Egyptology in a rapidly changing social and scientific environment warrant a critical discussion.

Dieter Mueller

72354 JUNGE, Friedrich, Zur Funktion des *sḏm.ḥr.f*, *JEA* 58 (1972), 133-139.

A discussion of the specialized uses of this construction as found in the studies of Westendorf and Reineke on Egyptian medical texts and mathematical papyri, outside what was dealt with by Gardiner and Erman in their Egyptian Grammars. Examples are quoted from P. Rhind (63, 50 etc.) and P. Kahun (18,40), for calculating, from scientific observations (P. Eb. 788 etc.), in the diagnosis formula in medicine, in drug preparation (P. Hearst 25 etc.), and also from Coptic Texts. *E. Uphill*

72355 JUNGE, Friedrich and Wolfgang SCHENKEL, Göttinger Konkordanz zu den altägyptischen Sargtexten, *GM* Heft 3 (1972), 37-38.

The authors intend to produce a concordance of all seven volumes of the Coffin Texts with the help of a computer.

Dieter Mueller

72356 KADISH, Gerald E., A Report on the Epigraphic and Archaeological Work at the Temple of Osiris *ḥkȝ ḏt* During May-July, 1971, *Newsletter ARCE* No. 80 (January 1972), 36.

Abstract of a paper.

72357 KAISER, Werner, Dino BIDOLI†, Peter GROSSMANN, Gerhard HAENY, Horst JARITZ und Rainer STADELMANN, Stadt und Tempel von Elephantine. Dritter Grabungsbericht, *MDAIK* 28 (1972), 157-200, with 10 pl. and 9 fig. including 4 plans.

Continuation of our Nos 70291 and 71303. The German Archaeological Institute has continued its work on the temples of Satis and Khnum, and the centers of habitation at Elephantine. The finds made during this season include a wooden cylinder seal of the Old Kingdom, several statues of the Middle Kingdom, and a stela of King Sethnakhte (20th Dyn.). *Dieter Mueller*

72358 KÁKOSY, László, Az egyiptomi öröklét fogalom, *Antik Tanulmányok*, Budapest 19 (1972), 165-174, with 2 ill.

"Der ägyptische Begriff der Ewigkeit".
Der Ewigkeitsbegriff verfügt über verschiedene religionsmytho-

logische Inhalte. Neben der Würdigung der bisherigen Theorien über *nḥḥ* and *ḏt* befasst sich der Verfasser mit anderen Ewigkeitssymbolen und Begriffe.   *Vilmos Wessetzky*

72359   KÁKOSY, László, Ptah als Orakelgott, *Annales Universitatis Scientiarum Budapestiensis de Rolando Eötvös Nominatae.* Sectio Classica, Budapest 1 (1972), 9-12.

Ptah besass mindestens seit dem Neuen Reich die Rolle eines Orakelgottes. Dazu dürften die mythologischen Verbindungen mit den Widdergötter beigetragen haben und als Schöpfergott konnte er ebenfalls in die Zukunft sehen. Die in der griechischen Paroimia-Literatur auftauchende Meinung über Ptah als Orakelgott war also in der Ideenwelt der ägyptischen Religion verwurzelt.   *V. Wessetzky*

72360   KAPLONY, Peter, Altägyptischer Totenglaube, *in* : Diego Hagmann, *Das dritte Leben.* Entwicklungsmöglichkeiten im Ruhestand, Basel, Verlag Die Pforte, [1972], 59-63.

Survey for the general reader about the belief concerning death in Egypt.

72361   KAPLONY, Peter, Der Papyrusarchiv von Abusir, *Orientalia* 41 (1972), 11-79 and 180-244, with 1 table.

This is the first extensive study of the corpus of Abûsîr papyri (for the publication see our number 68486), divided into six parts.
Part I is devoted to form and contents of the various categories of documents : labour lists (either tabulated monthly or simple lists), lists of deliveries (also either tabulated or not), of persons, inventories and inspection notices, and letters. In several instances the categories appear to overlap. A mass of details are discussed, e.g. the corrections in the text (p. 30) and private names composed with royal names (32). At the end a section with general remarks, e.g. about the economic dependence of the pyramid from the Sun-Temple of Neferirkare. Deliveries to the pyramid, insofar not used by its priests and workmen, may have gone to its clients, who also in other instances sent deliveries to the pyramid.
In part II the author discusses the technical administrative terms, elucidating many details of the organisation. Part III deals with the prosopography, presenting a list of all names occurring in the documents, followed by conclusions, e.g. that the persons belong to one or two generations and are to be dated to the reigns of Djedkare, Unas and Teti. Part IV contains lists of words for objects such as parts of buildings,

furniture, vessels, wood, stone and metals, food and beverages, etc. Part V is devoted to the inspection marks; part VI to expressions of accountancy. Together parts II, IV, V and VI contain a fairly complete glossary to the corpus.

72362 KAPLONY-HECKEL, Ursula, Neue demotische Orakelfragen, *Forschungen und Berichte* 14 (1972), 79-90, with 1 pl.

The article, the author's Habilitationsvortrag, begins with a general survey of the function of oracles in ancient Egypt, after which six texts are published : Pap. Berlin P 13.584, Pap. Heidelb. dem. 23, and four from the collection Michaelides. The latter constitute a closed group, together with a fifth one which is very obscure; they have been written by the same hand and on the same day (year 3, I *prt* 12).
The texts are published in photograph and facsimile, with transliteration, translation and comments. At the end a discussion of the situation in which they were written.

72363 KARIG, Joachim Selim, Vorschläge zur graphischen Kennzeichnung von Materialien, *GM* Heft 3 (1972), 39-41, with 2 fig.

The author recommends various forms of hatching to indicate geological formations and building materials.

Dieter Mueller

72364 KARKOWSKI, Janusz, The Problem of the Origin of the Thutmoside Blocks Found in Faras, *Études et Travaux*, Warszawa 6 (1972), 83-92, with 1 table and 2 fig.

In Faras the Polish excavators have found 417 fragments of decorated blocks originating from New Kingdom temples, bringing the total of blocks there discovered up to 565, of which 365 belong to the Tuthmosid Period. They belonged to the higher parts of a temple built by Hatshepsut and adopted by Tuthmosis III; neither the lower part, possibly still *in situ*, nor the foundations have been discovered. According to the texts the temple was dedicated to Horus of Buhen, Satis and Anukis. The author suggests as one possible explanation that the blocks belonged to the temple at Buhen now removed to the Khartoum Museum.

72365 KASSER, Rodolphe, Bibliothèque gnostique X. L'Hypostase des Archontes, *Revue de théologie et de philosophie*, Lausanne 105 (1972), 168-202.

Continuation de notre No 70303.
Introduction et translation avec des notes de l'Hypostase des Archontes, le quatrième écrit du codex II de Nag' Hammadi.

72366 KASSER, R., Fragments du livre biblique de la Genèse cachés dans la reliure d'un codex gnostique, *Muséon* 85 (1972), 65-89, with 1 fig.

Publication of three Coptic fragments recovered from the cartonnage of Nag Hammadi Codex VII. They contain *Gen.* 32:5-21 and 42:27-38, and apparently belong to a codex of unusual age. It seems to have comprised the second half of the *Book of Genesis*, and predates the year AD 345 perhaps by as much as half a century.   *Dieter Mueller*

72367 KASSER, Rodolphe, L'hypostase des archontes. Propositions pour quelques lectures et reconstitutions nouvelles, *in*: *Essays on the Nag Hammadi Texts* in Honour of Alexander Böhlig. Edited by Martin Krause, Leiden, E. J. Brill, 1972 (= Nag Hammadi Studies, 3), 22-35.

After comparing the two editions of the *Hypostasis of the Archons* by Bullard (our number 70101) and Nagel (our number 70404) the author proposes a number of emendations and restorations.

72368 KASSER, R., La surligne a-t-elle précédé le "djinkim" dans les textes bohaïriques anciens?, *RdE* 24 (1972), 91-95.

L'auteur tente de fixer l'âge d'apparition des deux systèmes d'accents servant à marquer les limites des syllabes en copte, utilisés respectivement dans le saïdique et les dialectes apparentés et le bohaïrique. Malgré l'enrichissement considérable de la documentation apporté par les découvertes des Kellia, fournissant des textes bohaïriques antérieurs à ceux que l'on connaissait jusqu'ici, il n'est pas prouvé que la surligne soit un système plus ancien que le "djinkim", mais il reste vraisemblable qu'ils aient été inventés parallèlement dans deux écoles de scribes indépendantes.   *Ph. Derchain*

72369 KASSER, Rodolphe, avec la collaboration de Sébastien FAVRE et Denis WEIDMANN, Kellia. Topographie, Genève, Georg. Librairie de l'Université, [1972] (26.8 × 36.4 cm; 232 p., 163 plans, fig. and ill. [5 in colour], 49 maps [1 unnumbered], 5 loose folding maps [1 in colour]) = Recherches suisses d'archéologie copte dirigées par Rodolphe Kasser, Volume II; rev. *Orientalia* 43 (1973), 141-143 (H. Quecke).

Sequel to our number 67319. Compare our number 69322. The present volume on the Franco-Swiss campaigns contains the results of the topographical researches from 1966 to 1968.
Chapter I describes the topographical methods followed and the plans resulting from them. Chapter II contains remarks on

the Coptic habitation, chapter III a general inventory of the 1555 Coptic buildings of which at least traces had been found at the end of October 1968.

Chapter IV, by S. Favre, deals with a monastery at Quṣûr 'Îsâ (buildings 57, 72/18, 74), with its mural paintings and inscriptions (studied by Kasser), and a note on the pottery by M. Egloff.

Chapter V consists of four tables of concordances; chapter VI of an index to the vocabulary of the inscriptions (words, personal names, etc.). Chapter VII contains a brief note on Zone A, by J.-C. Pasquiér and R. Pesenti.

72370   KEEL, Othmar, Die Welt der altorientalischen Bildsymbolik und das Alte Testament. Am Beispiel der Psalmen, [Zürich, Einsiedeln, Köln], Benziger Verlag / [Neukirchen], Neukirchener Verlag, [1972] (20.5 × 29.5 cm; 366 p., 480 fig., 24 pl.); rev. *Biblische Zeitschrift* 18 (1974), 152-153 (Vinzenz Hamp); *Revue Biblique* 80 (1973), 603 (R. Tournay); *ZAW* 85 (1973), 267 ([G. Fohrer]).   Pr. bound DM 90

General commentary on the Book of Psalms, lavishly illustrated by pictures from the entire Ancient Near East including ancient Egypt. Accordingly a large proportion of the drawings and some of the photographs picture Egyptian representations from stelae, wall reliefs, papyri, etc.

After an introduction in which i.a. the iconography is discussed there follow chapters on representations of the world, the powers of destruction, the temple, representations of gods, the king, and man before god. The text contains numerous references to Egypt, the captions to the pictures however are mostly verses of the Psalms.

72371   KEMP, Barry J., Fortified Towns in Nubia, *Man, Settlement and Urbanism* 651-656, with 2 plans and 1 pl.

Discussion of the question to what extent Egyptian town design and fortification is reflected in the colonial settlements in Nubia.

During the New Kingdom fortifications around Nubian towns were largely symbolic, being unmodified copies of the Egyptian temple enclosure wall, although in contrast to the custom in Egypt residential buildings were included in the enclosures.

During the Middle Kingdom two types of fortification existed, one for the flattish grounds North of the Second Cataract and one for the hilly grounds of this region. Both may have been genuine defenses, the former being possibly of Egyptian type, the latter adapted to the geographical environment.

72372 KEMP, Barry J., Temple and Town in Ancient Egypt, *Man, Settlement and Urbanism* 657-680, with 1 diagram and 4 plans.

The author begins with an outline reconstruction of a temple economy during the New Kingdom, discussing its landed property, the "offerings" (a term for all kinds of goods presented to the god), the taxes (a difficult problem because of the absence of demarcation between the spheres of state and temple), the costs of running the temple establishment, the temple trade, etc.
As regards the temple's influence on settlement the author distinguishes two types : a) the new foundations on non-urban sites, e.g. mortuary temples. He describes the town of Kahun, the settlement behind the temple of Amenhotep III and that in Medinet Habu. To this category also belong many settlements in Nubia where the economy may have been dominated by the temples. b) temples within existing communities which had other bases for their economic life. The only archaeological material for this type comes from el-Amarna. Although at first sight almost all inhabitants seem to have been connected with the temple the occurrence of large numbers of silos and storehouses proves them to be first and foremost landholders, though craftsmen appear to be living among them in the North and South suburbs. In fact, el-Amarna will have had the appearance of a series of villages, and so may have been the appearance of all Egyptian towns. Their economic structure was based on farm centres, the temple only being a major one.

72373 K[ENYON], K[athleen] M., Father Roland de Vaux, O.P., *Levant*, London 4 (1972), V-X.

Obituary article. See our number 71654.

KERVAN, Monique, see our number 72794.

KIECHEL, Samuel, see our number 72433.

72374 KIRWAN, L.P., An Ethiopian-Sudanese Frontier Zone in Ancient History, *The Geographical Journal*, London 138 (1972), 457-465, with 1 map.

Die günstigen geographischen Bedingungen vor allem während der Trockenzeit führten nicht zu friedlichem Austausch zwischen den Nachbarvölkern im aksumitischen und meroitischen Reich, die, umweltsmäßig verschieden, auch kulturell und politisch andersartig orientiert waren. Dabei wird Meroe nach der Invasion von 24/22 v.Chr. als römischer Satellit bezeichnet. Kriegerische Auseinandersetzungen sind durch aksumitische Inschriften aus der 1. Hälfte des 4. Jahrhunderts n.Chr. belegt.

Die aksumitischen Invasionen mögen der Hauptfaktor des wirtschaftlichen Niederganges des meroitischen Reiches südlich des 3. Kataraktes gewesen sein und dazu geführt haben, daß sich ein neues Machtzentrum im Gebiet zwischen dem 1. und 2. Katarakt bildete. *Inge Hofmann*

72375 KISS, Zsolt, Les fouilles polonaises en Égypte et au Soudan en 1971, *Africana-Bulletin*, Warszawa 17 (1972), 198-202.

Beschrieben werden : 1. die Ausgrabungen im Gebiet südöstlich vom Kôm el-Dikka in Alexandria, wo in hellenistischer und römischer Zeit ein Wohnquartier lag; 2. die Arbeiten in Deir el-Bahari, wo die Dokumentation und Rekonstruktion der dritten Terrasse des Hatschepsut-Tempels fortgeführt wurden; 3. die Ausgrabungen in Dongola, vornehmlich im sogenannten "kreuzförmigen" Gebäude.
Es wird kurz hingewiesen auf weitere Forschungen in dem prähistorischen Gebiet in der Nähe von Kadakol. *Inge Hofmann*

72376 KITCHEN, K. A., Ramesses VII and the Twentieth Dynasty, *JEA* 58 (1972), 182-194, with 1 table.

A hitherto overlooked sandstone doorjamb found in Deir el-Medineh tombs has an inscription in which Ramesses VII refers to Ramesses VI as 'his father'. While such evidence is not entirely certain it is strongly indicative of their relationship. The Medinet Habu procession of princes shows Ramesses VI as a son of Ramesses III. A genealogical table lists up to six generations from Setnakht to Ramesses XI, showing a succession from Ramesses III by two queens of ten sons, three of whom became kings, and three grandsons as later kings with their descendants. *E. Uphill*

72377 KITCHEN, K. A., Ramesside Inscriptions. Historical and Biographical. V. Fascicle 2, Oxford, B. H. Blackwell Ltd, [1972] (20.4 × 29 cm; 64 p. [= p. V, 65-128]); rev. *BiOr* 30 (1973), 397-398 (W. Helck); *JARCE* 11 (1974), 108 (Hans Goedicke); *JEA* 60 (1974), 279-280 (C.H.S. Spaull). Pr. £ 1.50.

A continuation of our number 70314.
The inscriptions of the 2nd Libyan War at Medinet Habu are continued. Next follow several rhetorical stelae, Syrian War Scenes from Medinet Habu and Karnak, and some small inscriptions concerning wars and Royal Sports. Under the general heading "Works of Peace : Festivals of the Gods", the author gives the Theban Calendar of Feasts texts from Medinet Habu and the Ramesseum. *L. M. J. Zonhoven*

72378 KITCHEN, K. A., Ramesside Inscriptions. Historical and Biographical. V. Fascicle 3, Oxford, B.H. Blackwell Ltd, [1972] (20.3 × 28.8 cm; 64 p. [= p. V, 129-192]); rev. *BiOr* 30 (1973), 397-398 (W. Helck); *JARCE* 11 (1974), 108 (Hans Goedicke); *JEA* 60 (1974), 279-280 (C.H.S. Spaull). Pr. £ 1.50

A continuation of our preceding number.
The Works of Peace : Festivals of the Gods are continued with the texts of the Theban Calendar of Feasts at Medinet Habu and the Ramesseum.
Next follow the inscriptions of the Festival of Opet from the temple of Ramses III at Karnak and from Medinet Habu.

L. M. J. Zonhoven

72379 KITCHEN, K. A., The Third Intermediate Period in Egypt (1100-650 B.C.), London, Aris & Phillips Ltd, [1972; misprinted as 1973] (14.2 × 22.2 cm; XVIII + 525 p., 9 maps, 2 plans).

See our volume 1973 for the abstract.

72380 KLASENS, A., Cheops en zijn pyramide, *Natuur en Techniek*, Heerlen 40, No. 10 (Oktober 1972), 488-499, with 1 map, 1 fig. and 7 ill., colour ill. on cover.

After sketching the knowledge about Ancient Egypt in Antiquity and afterwards the author discusses some theories of the pyramidologists as well as some more serious explanations of the pyramids and their builders in former ages. He also gives a survey of the present knowledge concerning Cheops.

72381 KLASENS, Adolf, Walter Bryan Emery. 1903-1971, *Proceedings of the British Academy*, London 58 (1972), 379-392, with a portrait.

Obituary article. See our number 71651.

72382 KLASENS, A., Rijksmuseum van Oudheden [te Leiden], *Nederlandse Rijksmusea*, 's Gravenhage 92 (1970), 1972, 255-266.

On p. 258 the author describes the transfer of the temple of Tâfa, donated by the Egyptian government to the Netherlands, and on p. 262 the acquisitions of the year 1970, among which 6 paleolithic axes, Naqâda pottery, 2 stelae dated to the end of the Old Kingdom or to the First Intermediate Period, and a shawabti of Sethi I. *L. M. J. Zonhoven*

72383 KÖHLER, Ursula, Der Berliner Totenpapyrus (P 3127) und seine Parallelen. Die engen Beziehungen dieser Totenpapyrus-Gruppe zu den Vignetten des Totenbuches, *Forschungen und Berichte* 14 (1972), 45-58, with 2 pl.

Pap. Berlin P 3127 and its eight parallels constitute a special group of papyri from the XXIst Dynasty for which the vignettes of the *Book of the Dead* or parts of them are used as models.

The author distinguishes between three groups of themes: those connected with the judgment of the dead; those connected with the course through the pylons and rooms of the Netherworld; those connected with the triumph and rise of the sun. Each of them is extensively discussed, while the plates depict not only Pap. Berlin P 3127, but also the parallels Pap. Berlin P 3128 and *BD* of Isisemkhab and of Tentosorkon in Cairo.

72384 KÖHLER, Ursula, Einige Überlegungen zu den verwantschaftlichen Beziehungen zwischen Horus und Seth in Pap. Chester Beatty No. I, *GM* Heft 1 (1972), 17-20.

The author argues that in the *Contendings of Horus and Seth* the indication of the former as *śn śry* means "nephew" and of the latter as *śn ꜥꜣ* "uncle". Seth is merely called the brother of Isis, not of Osiris. We have here an example of the so-called avunculate, the predominant position of mother's brother, on account of which Seth was able to contest the inheritance of Horus.

72385 KOROSTOVTSEV, M., La classification des propositions (phrases) simples en néo-égyptien, *RdE* 24 (1972), 96-100.

Malgré l'apparente variété des types de propositions verbales et nominales en néo-égyptien, on peut admettre qu'elles expriment toutes une même structure linguistique, à l'exception de la proposition nominale d'identité (à prédicat nominal). Il ressort de cette analyse que le verbe égyptien est traité comme un substantif.   *Ph. Derchain*

72386 KOROSTOVTSEV, Michail A., Les verbes diffus, *ZÄS* 99,1 (1972), 17-20.

L'auteur retourne aux "verbes diffus", phénomène archaïque. A comparer notre No 68349.   *M. Heerma van Voss*

72387 KOROSTOVTSEV, M. A., Древний Египет и христианство, *Наука и религия* 3 (1972), 56-61.

"Das alte Ägypten und das Christentum". Populär-wissenschaftlicher Artikel (nicht gesehen).

72388 KOSACK, Wolfgang, Zwei koptische Texte aus der Bonner Universitätsbibliothek, *Muséon* 85 (1972), 419-424, with 4 pl.

Publication of a fragmentary Coptic papyrus with description of a scene from the mass, and an ostracon with a drawing and part of a predication by Apa Epiphanius used as writing exercise.

72389 KRAUSE, Martin, Ein Fall friedensrichterlicher Tätigkeit im ersten Jahrzehnt des 7. Jahrhunderts in Oberägypten, *RdE* 24 (1972), 101-107, with 1 pl.

Publication d'un ostracon copte appartenant à l'University College de Londres (sans numéro), relatif à une affaire indistincte, à propos de laquelle l'expéditeur de la lettre demande aux intéressés de s'entendre. Le commentaire s'efforce de clarifier les rôles et de préciser la signification historique du document, dont certains protagonistes sont connus par ailleurs.
Ph. Derchain

72390 KRAUSE, Martin, Grusswort an den Jubilar, *in* : *Essays on the Nag Hammadi Texts* in Honour of Alexander Böhlig. Edited by Martin Krause, Leiden, E. J. Brill, 1972 (= Nag Hammadi Studies, 3), 1-4.

Short biography of A. Böhlig.

72391 [KRAUSE, Martin], Verzeichnis der Veröffentlichungen von Alexander Böhlig, *in* : *Essays on the Nag Hammadi Texts* in Honour of Alexander Böhlig. Edited by Martin Krause, Leiden, E. J. Brill, 1972 (= Nag Hammadi Studies, 3), 5-15.

List of publications of A. Böhlig.

72392 KRAUSE, Martin, Zur "Hypostase der Archonten" in Codex II von Nag Hammadi, *Enchoria* 2 (1972), 1-20.

Verfasser behandelt die in Codex II von Nag Hammadi über-lieferte Schrift über "das Wesen der Archonten". Der Artikel enthält zwei Teile. Im ersten Teil werden die von einander abweichenden Textlesungen und -ergänzungen, denen man in früheren Ausgaben des Textes begegnet, besprochen. Im zweiten Teil wird kurz über die literarische Beschaffenheit des Textes gesprochen.
R. L. Vos

KRAUSE, Martin, see also our number 72367.

72393 KRAUSPE, Renate, "Zeugnisse altägyptischer Handwerks-kunst" — Sonderausstellung des Ägyptischen Museums des Karl-Marx-Universität, *Wissenschaftliche Zeitschrift der Karl-Marx-Universität*. Gesellschafts- und sprachwissenschaftliche Reihe, Leipzig 21 (1972), 363-365.

Short notice on an exhibition of the Ägyptisches Museum Leipzig, with special attention to the productive process anteriorating the finished products in the fields of sculpture, pottery, wood- and metal working.
L. M. J. Zonhoven

72394 KROMER, Karl, Österreichische Ausgrabungen in Gizeh (VAR). Vorbericht über die Frühjahrskampagne 1971, Wien-Köln-Graz, Hermann Böhlaus Nachf., 1972 (15.3 × 23.8 cm; 46 p., 1 map, 4 fig., 4 ill. on 2 unnumbered pl., 27 pl.) = Österreichische Akademie der Wissenschaften. Philosophisch-historische Klasse. Sitzungsberichte, 279. Band, 5. Abhandlung; rev. *BiOr* 31 (1974), 71-72 (Fekri A. Hassan).   Pr. ÖS 120

Preliminary report of the Austrian excavation at Gîza South of the causeway of Mycerinus in 1971, during which a fairly extensive area appeared to be covered by the debris of a living quarter which is to be dated on account of the finds (stone vessels, pottery, seals and impressions, architectural remains) to the Ist-IIIrd Dynasties. The author argues that the debris came from a settlement which had to be demolished in order to make room for the pyramids. It seems less probable that the material was first used for the building-slopes since then it would have been more mixed, whereas the excavators found it highly concentrated in the small area investigated during this campaign.

72395 KUENTZ, Ch., A propos du nom démotique, copte et nubien du henné, et de son emploi comme anthroponyme, *RdE* 24 (1972), 108-110.

L'article se compose de deux notes :
1) Le nom sémitique (hébr. *kôfer*) du henné est à l'origine de l'appellation de cette plante en démotique, copte, grec et nubien.
2) On connaît en Égypte quelques exemples de l'emploi de ce mot comme anthroponyme, aux époques hellénistique et copte. Le rapprochement avec des noms sémitiques homophones araméens ou sud-arabiques reste toutefois hasardeux.

Ph. Derchain

72396 KUHLMANN, Klaus-Peter und Wolfgang SCHENKEL, Vorbericht über die Aufnahmearbeiten im Grab des *Jbj* (Theben Nr. 36), *MDAIK* 28 (1972), 201-211, with 1 plan and 2 pl.

A preliminary report on the work in the Saite tomb of Iby (TT No. 36), followed by a concise description of its decoration and its architecture.   *Dieter Mueller*

72397 KUHN, K. H., A Coptic Limestone, *Muséon* 85 (1972), 415-417, with 1 pl.

Publication of an "ostracon", at present preserved in the Gulbenkian Museum at Durham. The Sahidic text, a bail bond by a third party not involded, is presented in photograph with transcription, translation and comments.

72398 LABAT, René, William F. Albright - Albrecht Goetze, *Journal Asiatique*, Paris 260 (1972), 213-214.

Obituary notice. See our number 71650.

72399 LACAU, Pierre, Études d'égyptologie. II. Morphologie, Le Caire, Publications de l'Institut français d'Archéologie orientale du Caire, 1972 (20 × 27.5 cm; VIII + 379 p.) = Bibliothèque d'étude, 60.

Sequel to our number 70331, also prepared for publication by Gérard Roquet, who added the indexes.
The book consists of 12 articles, three of which have appeared earlier, namely IV (= our number 2921), VII (= 2924) and XII (= 4055), the others being hitherto unpublished.
I (p. 1-15). The third weak radicals *w* and *i̯*, which were not written but the existence of which appears from some Coptic biliteral words with a long vowel (e.g. N H B).
II (17-41). The verbal prefix *w*. After arguing that several verbs known to us as biliteral have originally been triliterals, e.g. IIIae inf., Lacau studies verbs which may contain a prefix *w*., e.g. *wb3*, *wḫ3*, *wdi̯*, etc. Its meaning seems to be "to put into action" or "into a permanent state".
III (43-104). The nominal suffix *.w*, fem. *.wt*. Discussion of a number of categories of substantives on *.w* and feminines on *.wt* (in Middle Egyptian usually written *.yt*). The *.w* has consonantal value. Parallel formations in Semitic languages are mentioned. Conclusions on p. 103-104.
V (111-173). The plurals of the substantive. The development of the expression of plural is studied, from the suffix *.w* which caused a vowel modification, through its dropping, leaving merely the vowel modification as indication of the plural, to the last stage in Coptic in which only traces are left, the plural being mainly expressed by the article.
VI (175-218). The demonstrative. Proceeding from the writing *pi̯* for *pw* when used as copula (mainly in the *Pyr. Texts*) various demonstratives are studied. In the plurals with *i̯* this is argued to be an prothetic vowel; the older plural was *nw*.
VIII (265-278). Analogy in Egyptian. Lacau refers to examples among the pronouns, verbs, substantives and prepositions.
IX (279-284). The prothetic *i̯.* in substantives, used when the first two consonants follow each other immediately and made pronunciation difficult, e.g. in some plurals and pronominal forms of substantives.
X (285-291). The collectives on *.wt/.yt* and the sign ı ı ı, in which the determinative indicates either plural sense and a sound, or sense alone (the grammatical form being singular), or even the final *.w* indicating the abstract.

XI (293-294). The plurals of the type *.ww*, of which the first *.w* is either the third radical or the masc. suffix.
Extensive indexes on p. 319-373.

LAMBDIN, Thomas O., see our number 72408.

72400   LAMBERG-KARLOVSKY, C. C., Tepe Yaḥya 1971. Mesopotamia and the Indo-Iranian Borderlands, *Iran*, London 10 (1972), 89-100, with 4 fig. and 4 pl.

During the excavations at Tepe Yaḥya (S.E. Iran) there was found in level IA (c. 0-500 A.D.) a green glazed faience figure of a baboon, representing Thoth (h. 8.2 cm); see plate I.

72401   LASKER, G. W., The Potential Relevance of Studies of Ancient Egyptian Populations for the Microevolutionary Study of Modern Populations, *Journal of Human Evolution*, London and New York 1 (1972), 137-139.

General remarks about the value of the study of mummies and skeletons to the problems of human population biology.
Reprinted in : Population Biology of the Ancient Egyptians. Edited by D. R. Brothwell [and] B. A. Chiarelli, London and New York, Academic Press, 1973.

72402   LAUER, Jean-Philippe, Recherches et travaux à Saqqarah (campagnes 1970-1971 et 1971-1972), *Comptes rendus de l'Académie des Inscriptions et Belles-Lettres*, Paris, 1972, 577-600, with 1 plan, 6 ill. and 8 pl. (= p. 593-600).

Sequel to our number 70335.
The author first deals with the continuation of reconstruction works in the *heb-sed* court of the Djeser-complex. He then discusses his researches in the area of the Sekhemkhet pyramid, where the descent to the Southern tomb used by the tomb robbers has been found.
The third section is devoted to work in and around the pyramids of Teti I and Merenre. In the former more fragments with texts have been found, up to a total of 2400 pieces. There also came to light the contents of a canopic vessel and other fragments of the original funerary equipment. Reconstruction works in and outside the pyramid were continued.
Of the pyramid of Merenre the entrance, obstructed since Maspero, has been reopened, and three blocking slabs have been removed. The author presents a description of the present state of the pyramid chambers, where the well preserved basalt sarcophagus and the granite canopic box have been found. The style of the Pyramid texts here is described. In the sanctuary East of the pyramid an offering table and an

elliptical basin were discovered. The unfinished state of the relief fragments may indicate the premature death of the pharaoh.

72403 LAUER, J.-Ph. et J. LECLANT, Mission archéologique de Saqqarah. I. Le temple haut du complexe funéraire du roi Téti, Le Caire, Institut français d'Archéologie orientale du Caire, 1972 (20.3 × 27.3 cm; VIII + 114 p., 91 fig., 24 pl., 1 folded plan, 3 sections [2 folded]) = Bibliothèque d'étude 51.

The volume contains a complete description of the remains of the Upper Temple of Teti situated on the Eastern side of his pyramid.

In chapter I a survey is given of the results of earlier excavations, mainly those of Quibell, of Firth, and of Sainte Fare Garnot with the present authors in 1951-52 and 1956.

Chapter II describes the architecture of the temple and all its parts : the causeway ending at the SE corner of the temple complex, an oblong forecourt, the entrance hall, a court with a portico, and the temple proper with i.a. on the axis a room with five niches originally containing statues, and the sanctuary. The remains of storerooms on both sides are also discussed. There are further sections on the satellite pyramid discovered by Quibell, on a chapel on the N. face of the main pyramid, on the height and sections of the temple, and on its proportions. The authors i.a. demonstrate the application of the "sacred triangle" with sides proportional to the numbers 3, 4 and 5.

Chapter III is devoted to the decoration of the temple. It contains an inventory of all blocks with relief fragments found by the excavators, each of which is fully described, with line drawings of the more important pieces. A separate section mentions blocks which appear to come from other buildings, some objects found and three graffiti. There follows a list of relief blocks mentioned in a manuscript of Gunn and not re-discovered, and one of blocks and objects published by earlier excavators, mainly by Quibell.

Three more blocks, probably socles of statues, and two others are described in an addendum.

The plates bear photographs of the area of the excavations and various details as well as of the main relief fragments, including those found by Quibell.

72404 LAUFFRAY, Jean, Abords occidentaux du premier pylône de Karnak. Le Dromos, la tribune et les aménagements portuaires, Kêmi 21 (1971), 77-144, with 5 pl., 4 plans (2 folding), 15 fig. (5 folding) and 21 ill.

1. La Tribune dite "débarcadère" s'appuyait sur un mur où étaient inscrits des maxima de crue. Les datations possibles

vont du règne de Séti II à celui de Sheshonq Ier. Un kiosque de bois devait abriter un reposoir bien en vue. Des blocs remployés appartiendraient à une chapelle de Shapénoupet (II?). La tribune devait jouer un grand rôle comme lieu d'apparition divine lors des cérémonies, qui se déroulaient encore sous Ptolémée V. Les 45 inscriptions nilométriques confirment les relations d'Amon "l'Ancien" avec l'eau, principe de vie.

2. Les quais constituèrent une digue protectrice après les dégâts provoqués par une crue violente, sous Herihor ou Osorkon III. Au sud, un retour à angle droit surplombe les aménagements portuaires.

3. La rampe ancienne réutilise deux piédestaux de Pinedjem. Le clergé en procession devait y remplir d'eau les vases thériomorphes de la triade thébaine (voir notre No 72715). Psamétik II usurpa dans les inscriptions les cartouches de Taharqa. La rampe Nord plus fruste semble contemporaine des quais.

4. Les niveaux successifs du Dromos et le remploi d'un décret lagide imposent pratiquement pour le dernier aménagement une date romaine. Des canalisations et des plantations d'arbustes furent renouvelées, et devaient donc être importantes. Peut-être y eut-il un bassin ancien plus proche du Nil. Avant Pinedjem, l'avenue ramesside subsistait, apparemment infléchie vers une ancienne tribune.

5. Le petit temple romain paraît avoir été dédié au culte impérial.

6. Des constructions byzantines et gréco-romaines entouraient le dromos. Les restes d'édifices d'époque pharaonique y attesteraient l'existence d'une enceinte.

7. La trouvaille de monnaies grecques, d'amulettes et de céramiques signalerait des cultes populaires pratiqués ici.

J. Custers

72405 LAUFFRAY, Jean, Ramadan SA'AD, Serge SAUNERON [and Pierre ANUS], Rapport sur les travaux de Karnak. Activités du "Centre Franco-Égyptien des temples de Karnak" (Campagne de travaux 1969-70), *Kêmi* 21 (1971), 53-76, with 10 ill., 1 fig. and 2 plans.

La campagne a été assez bousculée cette année encore, mais a fourni d'importants résultats. Voir notre No précédent pour le Dromos et ses abords. Une tranchée dans la Grande Cour a révélé l'existence d'un étroit espace axial rempli de terre meuble. Le vestibule d'Aménophis IV s'appuyant au IIIe pylône a été démonté. A l'angle N-W du IVe pylône, l'édifice de Thoutmosis IV avait connu plusieurs remaniements (voir aussi notre No 72431). Une ancienne porte a été dégagée dans la Cour de la Cachette. Voir, pour les travaux du IXe pylône, notre No 72629. R. Sa'ad s'apprêtait à publier le socle du Colosse Sud et les "talatat" qu'il contenait. Les sondages au nord du Portique septentrional des Bubastites ont démontré une longue occupation et livré des objets disparates. A l'angle S-E du Lac sacré sont apparues six maisons, l'angle d'une enceinte et une porte d'Amasis. Tout le décor peint de la crypte Sud du Temple d'Opet a pu être reconstitué. La documentation sur les travaux de Karnak s'organise et comprend un classement mécanographique.   *J. Custers*

72406 LAUSAROT, P. Michelin, C. AMBROSINO, F. FAVRO, A. CONTI and E. RABINO MASSA, Preservation and Amino Acid Composition of Egyptian Mummy Structure Proteins, *Journal of Human Evolution*, London and New York 1 (1972), 489-499, with 2 schemes, 4 tables and 1 colour pl.

Report of an investigation into the chemical and physico-chemical state of preservation of structure proteins in the tissues of a XIIth Dynasty mummy.
Reprinted in : Population Biology of the Ancient Egyptians. Edited by D. R. Brothwell [and] B. A. Chiarelli, London and New York, Academic Press, 1973.

72407 LAVER, A. B., Precursors of Psychology in Ancient Egypt, *Journal of the History of the Behavioral Sciences*, Brandon, Vermont 8 (1972), 181-195.

The well documented article deals with various aspects of what is known about psychology from Egyptian texts.
The author i.a. discusses the words for heart, *ib* and *ḥȝty*, arguing that the heart was conceived to be the seat of life and the source of all psychological activities, whereas the function of the brain was not recognized. The texts about the dead show a confused and contradictory conception of their psychology. The concepts of name (*rn*), *bȝ*, *kȝ* and shadow (*šwt*) are discussed. The conclusion is that the evidence for Egyptian psychology constitutes an accidental and biassed sample and does not contain a conception relevant to ours.

72408 LAYTON, Bentley and Thomas O. LAMBDIN, A Dictionary of Coptic Gnostic Literature, *ZÄS* 98, 2 (1972), 156.

Announcement of a Harvard project to compile a comprehensive Coptic-English dictionary of all Coptic Gnostic texts.
                                                           Dieter Mueller

72409 [LECLANT, J.], [Bernard Bruyère], *BSFE* No 63 (Mars 1972), 5.
Obituary notice. Compare our number 72812.

72410 LECLANT, Jean, Champollion, la pierre de Rosette et le déchiffrement des hiéroglyphes, Paris, 1972 (22.2 × 27.7 cm; 11 p.) = Comptes rendus de l'Académie des Inscriptions et Belles-Lettres, Paris, 1972, 557-565.

In this lecture the author relates the history of the Rosetta stone and its study, and he describes Champollion's way to the decipherment of the hieroglyphs as well as the contents of the *Lettre à M. Dacier*.

72411 LECLANT, Jean, L'enregistrement par l'informatique du répertoire d'épigraphie méroitique, *BSFE* No 63 (Mars 1972), 45-50.

Die mehr als 800 meroitischen Texte wurden in dem Répertoire d'Épigraphie Méroitique (REM) zusammengestellt (vgl. unsere Nummern 68373, 69381, 69382, 70347). Jedes "Wort" eines "Satzes" soll in seinem Kontext registriert und seine grammatikalische Struktur analysiert werden. Die Registrierung erlaubt, die Texte sehr schnell auf alle sich bietenden Möglichkeiten durchzusehen. Bisher sind 110 Texte (REM 1001 bis REM 1110) registriert und mit einem korrespondierenden Index versehen worden.   *Inge Hofmann*

72412 LECLANT, Jean, L'enregistrement des textes méroïtiques selon les procédés de l'informatique, *MNL* No 11 (Décembre 1972), 34-35.

Es wird ein Überblick über die Entwicklung zur Erstellung des Répertoire d'Epigraphie Méroitique (REM) gegeben. Bisher liegen Index und Konkordanz der Texte REM 1001 - REM 1110 vor (vgl. unsere vorige Nummer). Jetzt werden die Texte von Faras REM 0501 ff. und von Kawa REM 0601 ff. in Angriff genommen.   *Inge Hofmann*

72413 LECLANT, Jean, Fouilles et travaux en Égypte et au Soudan, 1970-1971, *Orientalia* 41 (1972), 249-291, with 47 ill. on 32 pl.

Sequel to our number 71355.
The present report consists of 32 numbers for Egypt, 14 for the Sudan and 13 for other countries. We mention : the excavations at Gîza, at Saqqâra, at Karnak and on the left bank of Thebes (29 different activities), the surveys between Sonqi and Alasha and that South of the Dal Cataract, the excavations at Sedeinga and Tabo, and the discovery of rock-drawings at Gebel Gorod (9 ill.). From the other countries finds are mentioned, i.a. from Israel, Cyprus and Lebanon (Kamid el-Loz and Khalde).
Indexes on p. 289-291.

72414 LECLANT, Jean, Les fouilles méroitiques de Sedeinga (Nubie soudanaise), *Revue française d'Histoire d'Outre-Mer*, Paris 59, No 214 (1972), 505-506.

Es handelt sich um einen Vortrag über die Ausgrabungen von Sedeinga, durchgeführt von M. S. Giorgini seit Ende 1964. Die Nekropole der meroitischen Epoche enthielt mehrere Hundert Gräber, die z.T. in die Napata-Zeit zurückreichen. Unter den Funden verdienen besondere Beachtung die Glaswaren, vor allem die beiden Kelche mit ägyptisierenden Darstellungen und einer griechischen Inschrift.   *Inge Hofmann*

72415 [LECLANT, J.], [André Heyler], *BSFE* 63 No (Mars 1972), 6. Obituary notice. Compare our number 72813.

72416 LECLANT, Jean, Histoire de la diffusion des cultes égyptiens, *Annuaire. École Pratique des Hautes Études. Ve section - sciences religieuses*, Paris 79 (1971-1972), 197-201.

Fortsetzung unserer Nummer 71356.
Untersuchungen vor allem anhand von neuerer Literatur zum Thema der Verbreitung ägyptischer Kulte in Italien, Griechenland, Frankreich; die Zusammenstellung von Karten über das Vorkommen ägyptischer oder ägyptisierender Objekte in den Provinzen des römischen Reiches, besonders der Iberischen Halbinsel, Großbritannien und Ungarn wird weiter verfolgt. In Bezug auf die meroitistische Forschung war man mit Problemen der Textregistrierung befaßt, mit Untersuchungen über den meroitischen Gott Apedemak, einer Opfertafel aus den Ausgrabungen von Sedeinga und einem beschrifteten Ostrakon aus Saï.   *Inge Hofmann*

72417 LECLANT, J., Remarques préliminaires sur le matériel égyptien et égyptisant recueilli à Chypre, *in*: Πρακτικὰ τοῦ πρώτου διεθνοῦς κυπρολογικοῦ συνεδρίου. Λευκωσία, 14-19 απριλίου 1969. τόμος Α,1 — Αρχαῖου τμῆμα, Λευκωσία, ἑταιρεία κυπριακῶν Σπουδῶν, 1972, 81-84.

The author sketches the history of the Egyptian and Egyptianized material from Cyprus and the relations between both countries through the ages. Very few traces are known from the Old and Middle Kingdoms, and again from the Third Intermediate Period, whereas there is rich material from the New Kingdom. In the late 7th century B.C. some kind of *koinè* has developed throughout the Eastern Mediterranean, in which style the Egyptian component plays an important part, while in the 6th century the presence of Cypriots in Egypt has been attested. The main periods for the present subject, however, are those of the Ptolemies and the Romans.

72418 [LECLANT, J.], [Siegfried Schott], *BSFE* No 63 (Mars 1972), 5.

Obituary notice. See our number 71652.

72419 LECLANT, Jean, Sur quelques livres récents concernant l'Égypte ancienne, *Revue Historique*, Paris 96, CCXLVIII (1972), 117-130.

Review article of our following numbers : 65178 (English edition, London, Weidenfeld & Nicolson, 1967); 69345; 68045; 71560; 66526; 69445; 67505 and 66005.

72420 LECLANT, J., avec la collaboration de Gisèle CLERC, Inventaire bibliographique des Isiaca (IBIS). Répertoire analytique des travaux relatifs à la diffusion des cultus isiatiques. 1940-1969. A-D, Leiden, E.J. Brill, 1972 (15.7 × 23.8 cm; XVIII + 191 p., 21 pl., frontispiece) = Études préliminaires aux religions orientales dans l'empire romain publiées par M. J. Vermaseren, 18; rev. *Acta Archaeologica Academiae Scientiarum Hungaricae* 25 (1973), 422 (L. Castiglione); *BiOr* 29 (1972), 131 (anonymous); *CdE* XLVII, Nos 93-94 (1972), 170-172 (Michel Malaise); *Revue de l'Histoire des Religions* 185 (1974), 99-100 (P. Barguet); *WZKM* 65/66 (1973/74), 278-279 (Erich Winter). Pr. cloth fl. 80

In his preface the author explains aims and limits of this bibliography. Although dealing with Isiaca in the Graeco-Roman world the limits of the latter are rather vague, ancient Greece and in some instances Phoenicia being included. As regards the divinities, not only Isis herself with her group, including e.g. Serapis, Anubis, etc., but also Thoth and in some instances Ammon, that is, all Egyptian gods of which the cults diffused around the Mediterranean, are taken into account.

The present first volume contains 346 publications, alphabetically arranged according to the name of the author (here only those beginning with the letters A-D). Each number also contains a summary of the publication.

Very extensive indexes (p. 126-188) largely enhance the usefulness of the volume.

Volume II (E-K) has appeared in 1974.

LECLANT, Jean, see also our numbers 72142, 72315, 72330, 72403 and 72717.

72421 LEEK, F. Filce, Bite, Attrition and Associated Oral Conditions as Seen in Ancient Egyptian Skulls, *Journal of Human Evolution*, London and New York 1 (1972), 289-295, with 1 table.

Remarks to attrition of the dental cusps, caries, pathological

changes in the alveolar walls and abnormalities of the temporo-
mandibular joints in ancient Egyptian skulls.
Reprinted in : Population Biology of the Ancient Egyptians.
Edited by D. R. Brothwell [and] B. A. Chiarelli, London and
New York, Academic Press, 1973.

72422 LEEK, F. Filce, Did a Dental Profession Exist in Ancient
Egypt during the 3rd Millennium B.C.?, *Medical History*,
London 16 (1972), 404-406.

The author adduces arguments against the opinion of Gha-
lioungui (see our number 71199) that the existence of an
organized dental profession during the Old Kingdom has been
proved. He particularly studies the two teeth joined by gold
wire found by Junker at Gîza, at present in the Roemer-
Pelizaeus Museum, the evidence of which is far from conclusive.

72423 LEEK, F. Filce, The Human Remains from the Tomb of
Tut'ankhamūn, Oxford, Printed for the Griffith Institute at the
University Press by Vivian Ridler, 1972 (22.5 × 28.5 cm; [VIII+]
29 p., 2 fig., 24 pl.) = Tut'ankhamūn's Tomb Series 5; rev.
BiOr 30 (1973), 402-403 (Lennart Diener); *JEA* 60 (1974), 280
(David M. Dixon); *Man* 8 (1973), 482 (Don Brothwell).

The volume consists of three chapters. Chapter I contains
Extracts from Howard Carter's Diary bearing on the opening
of the coffins and the examination of the mummy by Dr. Derry
and Saleh Bey. Chapter II, *The Anatomical Report on the Royal
Mummy*, contains the report by Dr. Derry hitherto unpublished,
and the author's own remarks on account of the skeletal
investigation in 1968 and a few other notes of Derry. The
author stresses that the original investigation has been
exhaustive; the cause of the king's death cannot be established.
Chapter III deals with *The Other Human Remains* found in the
tomb, namely two mummified foetuses in miniature coffins.
There are two Appendixes, one on abdominal incisions and
one on the ages between which the epiphyseal ends become
fully calcified (an indication of the age of the deceased person).
The plates show photographs taken by Harry Burton, except
pls 21-22 which represent x-rays of the head and the trunk.
Notes to the plates on p. 27-29.

72424 LEEK, F. Filce, Teeth and Bread in Ancient Egypt, *JEA* 58
(1972), 126-132, with 5 pl. and 2 tables.

Sugar has been stated to be the cause of much dental disease
in modern man, but ancient man's sweetener — honey —
would not have had the same bad effect on his teeth. Yet
a wide survey of Egyptian skulls from the predynastic period

until Ptolemaic times shows extensive dental decay, here discussed, and the causes shown to be among other things grit contained in the bread. Illustrations are provided of children's and adult's teeth, the method of grinding flour, and X-ray photos of bread samples. Inorganic residue in samples proved to be quartz, feldspar, amphible, mica and greywacke.

E. Uphill

LEEK, F. Filce, see also our number 72136.

72425 von LEMM, Oscar, Kleine Koptische Studien. I-LVIII. Unveränderte, um ein Vorwort von Peter Nagel, Halle/Saale vermehrter Nachdruck der 1899-1910 in der Petersburger Akademie-Schriften erschienenen Stücke, Leipzig, Zentralantiquariat der Deutschen Demokratischen Republik, 1972 (18.8 × 27.1 cm; X+ 682 p., 3 pl.) = Subsidia Byzantina Volumen 10.

Pr. cloth M 125

Reprint of seven articles, together consisting of 58 separate studies, which originally have appeared in the Bulletins and Memoirs of the Imperial Academy of Sciences at Petersburg and have been reedited in 1907-1912.
The short preface by Peter Nagel sketches the history of Coptic studies and the importance of von Lemm's work.

72426 von LEMM, Oscar, Koptische Miscellen. I-CXLVIII. Unveränderter Nachdruck der 1907-1915 im "Bulletin de l'Académie Impériale des Sciences de St. Pétersbourg" erschienenen Stücke. Herausgegeben von Peter Nagel, Halle/Saale, unter Mitarbeit von Kurt Kümmel, Leipzig, Zentralantiquariat der Deutschen Demokratischen Republik, 1972 (18.1 × 27.1 cm; [X+] 542 p.) = Subsidia Byzantina Volumen 11.   Pr. cloth M 105

Reprint of 27 articles, together containing 148 miscellanies, originally published in the Bulletin of the Imperial Academy of Sciences at Petersburg. The first 100 numbers have been reedited in 1914, the second volume with numbers 101-148 has never appeared.

72427 LENGER, Marie-Thérèse, La XXVIe Session de la Société internationale Fernand de Visscher pour l'histoire des droits de l'antiquité. Bordeaux, 15-18 septembre 1971, *Revue internationale des droits de l'antiquité*, Bruxelles 19 (1972), 497-521.

Pour une paraphrase de la communication de A. Théodoridès, *L'influence du Droit sur la société et de la société sur le Droit dans l'Égypte pharaonique*, voir p. 502-505.

L. M. J. Zonhoven

72428 LESKO, Barbara S., Three Reliefs from the Tomb of Mentuemhat, *JARCE* 9 (1971-1972), 85-88, with 3 ill. on a pl.

Publication of three more relief fragments from Theban Tomb 34; compare p. 60 of our number 60572.
It concerns Nr. 51.4.2 in the M. H. de Young Memorial Museum of San Francisco, and Nrs. 53.Eg.II.39 and .40 in the Seattle Art Museum, Seattle. The author identifies a picture of Shepenmut, wife of the tomb-owner, and locates one or two of the fragments.   *M. Heerma von Voss*

72429 LESKO, Leonard H., The Ancient Egyptian Book of Two Ways, Berkeley-Los Angeles-London, University of California Press, 1972 (17.3 × 26 cm; XII + 148 p., 1 ill.) = University of California Publications. Near Eastern Studies 17; rev. *BiOr* 31 (1974), 247-249 (Ph. Derchain); *CdE* XLVIII, No. 96 (1973), 284-287 (P. Barguet); *JARCE* 11 (1974), 95 (Dieter Mueller).
                                                                    Pr. $ 5

In the introduction the author states that texts of the *Book, of Two Ways* occur on 14 published and 4 unpublished coffins, all of which come from el-Bersha. The present study is a pioneering attempt in translating them, based on what the author considers to be the best versions. Then the three main versions and their differences are discussed (compare our number 71363). The author also offers a survey of the religious traditions reflected in the text : the myths of Osiris, that of Re, as well as the roles of Thoth and Horus son of Re.
The main part of the volume consists of a translation with notes of the text, divided into IX sections (p. 11-133).
In the conclusion (134-138) the author states that the Egyptians considered the text to be a book, as may be seen from the colophons, and that various versions are sometimes found on one and the same coffin. Probably version C is the earliest one, its goal being to guide the deceased to a life besides Osiris, while that of the other versions is to join Re. Section VI, however, presents a tradition that makes Thoth's abode the goal of the deceased. Section IX ties together these traditions and relates them to one another. Probably the intention of the priest composing the definitive text was to show the religion of Re to be superior. There also may have been an intention to break down earlier class distinctions. At the end the author discusses relations between the *Book of Two Ways* and chapters of the *Book of the Dead*.
Indexes to *CT* spells, *Book of the Dead* parallels, and a vocabulary on p. 140-148.

72430 LESKO, Leonard H., The Field of Ḥetep in Egyptian Coffin Texts, *JARCE* 9 (1971-1972), 89-101.

A translation, accompanied by notes, of *Coffin Texts* 464-468. These spells constitute the earliest versions of *Book of the Dead* 110. The author discusses them, their interrelations and their arrangement on the coffins.   *M. Heerma van Voss*

72431 LETELLIER, Bernadette, Découverte d'une tête colossale de Sésostris III à Karnak, *Kêmi* 21 (1971), 165-176, with 2 pl., 4 ill. and 7 fig.

Cette tête, découverte en février 1970 au N-W du IVe pylône, montre une ressemblance frappante avec les colosses 42.011 et -012 du Caire. Seule la barbe tressée distingue ce visage carré, individuel et vivant, de celui du 42.011. Le pschent harmonieux subsiste en entier. Un enduit blanchâtre épais et un trou à la section du cou font songer à une restauration voire à un remploi. Le reste du corps n'avait pas été dissocié, comme l'indiquent des fragments de granit rose trouvés aux alentours. Les traits, se rapportant à un type d'âge moyen, n'ont de stylisé que les sourcils, où des chevrons gravés décrivent une arête de poisson. Cette technique, rare en Égypte, n'est attestée que dans la seconde moitié de la XIIe dynastie et à la IIe Période Intermédiaire.   *J. Custers*

72432 Lexikon der Ägyptologie. Herausgegeben von Wolfgang Helck und Eberhard Otto. Band I, Lieferung 1, Wiesbaden, Otto Harrassowitz, 1972 (20 × 28 cm; XXVIII p. + 160 col., 1 map, 2 ill.); rev. *JEA* 60 (1974), 264-265 (Kate Bosse-Griffiths); *Mundus* 9 (1973), 209-210 (Hellmut Brunner); *WZKM* 65/66 (1973/74), 270-275 (Erich Winter).   Pr. DM 38

The first fascicle of the *Lexikon* begins with a preface by the editors in which they explain method, scope and problems of the present work.
There follow a list of abbrevations and a provisional list of periodicals and serieses quoted in abbreviation.
The first fascicle deals with the lemmata from *A-Gruppe* to *Altes Testament*. Although the lemmata are in German, some articles are in French or English, each being signed by the initials of its author, the names of which are given on the endpaper. Each article is followed by bibliographical notes.
Some of the articles are fairly long, particularly those dealing with general subjects which have never before been discussed in this way, e.g. *Abgaben und Steuern* (col. 3-12), *Abstraktionsvermögen* (col. 18-23), *Ägypten im Selbstbewußtsein des Ägypters* (col. 76-78), *Akten* (col. 118-129).

Apart from Egyptian names and toponyms there are also articles about foreign names which are of importance to Egyptian history (e.g. *Addu-nirari, Aitakama*). Although Hellenistic and Christian Egypt in general are excluded, as well as "das Nachleben" (the legacy), some names and toponyms which are important for ancient Egyptian history and culture have shortly been mentioned, e.g. *Alexander "der Große"* and *Alexandria*.

72433 von LICHTENSTEIN, H.-L., S. KIECHEL, H.-Chr. TEUFEL, G.-Chr. FERNBERGER, R. LUBENAU, J. MILOÏTI, Voyages en Égypte pendant les années 1587-1588. Récits traduits de l'allemand par Ursula Castel et traduits de l'italien par Nadine Sauneron. Présentation, notes et index de Serge Sauneron, [Le Caire], Institut français d'Archéologie orientale du Caire, 1972 (16.2×19 cm; XX+266 p., 3 ill., 1 folding map) = Collection des voyageurs occidentaux en Égypte, 6.

The present volume contains parts of six travel stories, four of them originally written in German, one in Italian and one in Greek. All six travellers stayed in Cairo at about the same time, partly travelling together.
In his introduction Sauneron discusses each of the six authors. To Egyptologists the description of the pyramids, particularly the interior of the Great Pyramid and its ascent by Kiechel, is of some interest (p. 108-117). See also our number 71499.

72434 LICHTHEIM, Miriam, Have the Principles of Ancient Egyptian Metrics Been Discovered?, *JARCE* 9 (1971-1972), 103-110.

A critical examination of Fecht's metrical theory including an analysis of three applications. Concluding, the author presents a number of objections (p. 110).   *M. Heerma van Voss*

72435 LILYQUIST, Christine, Preliminary Survey at Memphis, *Newsletter ARCE* No. 80 (January 1972), 36.

Abstract of a paper.
On excavations in an area of Early Middle Kingdom Tombs at Memphis.   *L. M. J. Zonhoven*

72436 LIMME, Luc, Deux stèles inédites du Sérapeum de Memphis, *CdE* XLVII, Nos 93-94 (1972), 82-109, with 2 ill. and 1 fig.

Publication de deux stèles du Sérapéum :
1. Hildesheim 2372. Stèle généalogique, datable d'après le style et le formulaire de la fin de la 26e ou de la 27e dynastie. Le commentaire général contient une longue note sur le titre *ḥw wȝḏ* qui caractérise un sacerdoce de Mefket (Kom Abou Billou).

2. Bruxelles MRAH E.3468. Stèle rectangulaire de la première moitié de la 26e dynastie, contenant une brève généalogie.

Les deux monuments sont reproduits en photographie, les inscriptions ont été transcrites, traduites et pourvues d'un apparat critique.   *Ph. Derchain*

72437 LIMME, L., Toetanchamon. In het Britisch Museum van 30 maart tot 31 december 1972, *Spiegel Historiael*, Bussum 7, No. 12 (december 1972), 700-701, with 3 ill.

Short article about the exhibition of the Treasures of Tutankhamon in the British Museum.

72438 LINSNER, Kenneth J., Initial Technical Observations on the Shepseskaf'ankh Complex in the Western Necropolis at Giza, *Newsletter ARCE* No. 83 (October 1972), 29.

Abstract of a paper.
A short discussion of analyses of plasters, building stones and pigments, and construction techniques in the mastaba's of Iymeri and Neferbauptah (Dyn. V).   *L. M. J. Zonhoven*

72439 LIPIŃSKI, E., The Egypto-Babylonian War of the Winter 601-600 B.C., *Annali [del] Istituto Orientale di Napoli*, Napoli 32 (N.S. 22) (1972), 235-241.

The author discusses the war between Nebuchadnezzar and Necho II, in which the Babylonians were defeated and Gaza was conquered by the Pharaoh. Herodotus II, 159 refers to this war. The battle took place at Magdalos = Migdol, probably an Egyptian border fortress, to be identified with *Mktr* (Pap. Anastasi V, 20, 2-3) and [URU]Magdali (Amarna Letters and a text of Esarhaddon), which may be Tell el-Hêr near Pelusium. Other references to the war, e.g. in *Jer.* 47,1, are also discussed.

72440 LIPSCHITZ, Ora, Timn'a, *Israel Exploration Journal*, Jerusalem 22 (1972), 158, with 2 ill. on a pl.

Mention is made of a rock engraving discovered in 1972 above the Egyptian temple near Timna, representing Hathor and Ramses III (with both names in cartouches).

72441 LITTAUER, Mary Aiken, The Military Use of the Chariot in the Aegean in the Late Bronze Age, *AJA* 76 (1972), 145-157, with 10 fig.

This study of the Aegean chariot contains several references to features and representations of the chariot in Ancient Egypt.

72442 LIVCHITZ, I. G., Надписи из Ахмима, *Эпиграфика Востока,* Leningrad 21 (1972), 3-7, with 1 ill. and 1 folding pl.

'Inscriptions from Akhmim'.

Sequel to our number 71371. Three parts of the wooden coffin of a female owner *Mr.t*, once bought by Golenischev at Akhmim at the end of the last century are now registered in the Pushkin Museum (Moscow) as nos. 5308, 5311 and 5312. The outer sides contain offering formulae and the titles and name of the deceased; one of these, with a 'frise d'objets', is completely transliterated and translated.   *J. F. Borghouts*

LIVER, Jacob, see our numbers 72006 and 72690.

72443 LIVERANI, M., Elementi "irrazionali" nel commercio amarniano, *Oriens Antiquus* 11 (1972), 297-317.

Les historiens ont pris l'habitude de considérer les documents à caractère commercial de l'époque amarnienne d'un point de vue comptable théorique, abstraction faite de leur cadre. Et certains éléments isolés des échanges entre souverains leur semblent aberrants. Mais l'ensemble des cadeaux et des marchés redevient très raisonnable, quand on le replace dans le climat culturel. Il faut tenir compte des divers plans hiérarchiques des négociateurs, voire de la nature moralement différente de l'objet, qui peut inclure des échanges de princesses. Dans ce dernier cas, l'addition d'une dot est honorable, non la fixation d'un prix. De façon générale d'ailleurs, le souci d'établir et de garder de solides liens sociaux ou politiques allait tout à l'encontre des paiements immédiats en argent, d'une sèche rigueur mathématique. Les souverains fournissaient les éléments d'évaluation, sans jamais indiquer de valeur chiffrée.

J. Custers

72444 LIVERANI, Mario, Partire sul carro, per il deserto, *Annali* [*del*] *Istituto Orientale di Napoli,* Napoli 32 (N.S. 22) (1972), 403-415.

Literary analyis of the motif "departing on a chariot, through the desert", which occurs in the biographical inscription on the statue of Idrimi. The same motif is found in the *Tale of the Doomed Prince* (5,1 ff.) and, in a more or less clear form, in several other Egyptian texts, e.g. the Memphite stela of Amenophis II, the poem of the Battle of Qadesh, the Sphinx stela of Tuthmosis IV, etc.

The author discusses the function of the topos in the story, its essential elements (e.g., the desert) and those of minor importance (e.g., the speed of the journey), and the scheme of the tale as compared with historical truth, stressing that the story of Idrimi is "true", although it uses the motif.

72445 LLOBREGAT, Enrique A., In Memoriam: Roland M. de Vaux O.P., *Boletin de la Asociacion Española de Orientalistas*, Madrid-Barcelona 8 (1972), 5-6.

Obituary notice. Compare our number 71654.

72446 LLOYD, Alan B., The so-called galleys of Necho, *JEA* 58 (1972), 307-308, with 1 pl.

The golden necklace-pendants in the Louvre representing ships (E 10687), formerly dated to the Saite period are probably really Hellenistic or Roman.   *E. Uphill*

72447 LLOYD, Alan B., Triremes and the Saïte Navy, *JEA* 58 (1972), 268-279, with 5 fig.

The writer considers that the statement of Herodotus that Necho constructed triremes for his Mediterranean and Red Sea fleets implies some Greek naval assistance and argues against the view of De Meulenaere and others. Earlier examples are represented from Medinet Habu and the famous Sennacherib warship from the Nineveh reliefs. Egyptian texts of the Saite and Persian periods apply the word *kbnt* to their warships, which may have been used for ramming as well as fighting. Thucydides believed the trireme was invented in Corinth in the time of the Cypselids, but this date is almost certainly based on genealogies and a reduction from forty years to three generations per century, gives a date of 654-620 B.C. which fits very well.   *E. Uphill*

72448 LOEBENSTEIN, Helene, Die Papyrussammlung der österreichischen Nationalbibliothek. Katalog der ständigen Ausstellung. 3. umgearbeitete Auflage, Wien, Österreichische Nationalbibliothek, 1972 (14.2 × 20.4 cm; [III +] 38 p., 20 pl.) = Biblos-Schriften Herausgegeben von Josef Stummvoll, 67.

The first edition has been edited by H. Klos (1955), the second by H. Hunger (1962). In her introduction Mrs. Loebenstein deals with the significance of the papyri and the origin of the collection, the core of which consists of the papyri of Erzherzog Rainer. At present it comprises over 100,000 objects, mostly texts, but also mummy-portraits (catalogue Nos 35-36), Coptic tissues (No. 61), etc. Most of the documents are written in Greek, but some are in other languages.
The catalogue consists of 71 numbers, constituting the part of the collection permanently exhibited. Each is briefly described. We mention from the Egyptian texts: three copies of the *Book of the Dead* (Nos 15, 50 and 70), the Demotic story of Inaros (No. 9), the poetic description of Pi-Ramses in hieratic (No. 6),

the hieroglyphic map of the Faîyum from the 2nd century B.C., and several Coptic texts.
The plates show some of the more important documents.

LÖHR, Beatrix, see our numbers 72512 and 72687.

72449 LOGAN, Thomas L., The Form and Function of the *imyt-pr*, *Newsletter ARCE* No. 83 (October 1972), 29.

Abstract of a paper.
Discussion of the function and form of the *imyt-pr* document in the Middle Kingdom, it following its own precise form like all other types of Egyptian legal documents.

L. M. J. Zonhoven

72450 LOGAN, Thomas J., The *sdm.n.f* of Adjective Verbs in Old Egyptian, *Newsletter ARCE* No. 80 (January 1972), 37.

Abstract of a paper.
On the possibility of a *sdm.n.f* of adjective verbs in Old Egyptian.

L. M. J. Zonhoven

72451 LOGAN, Thomas J. and Joan Goodnick WESTENHOLZ, *Sdm.f* and *Sdm.n.f* Forms in the Piy (Piankhy) Inscription, *JARCE* 9 (1971-1972), 111-119, with 3 tables.

The *śdm.n.f* served as the morphological form for the emphatic mood (compare e.g. our number 57408). A number of the original functions in Middle Egyptian grammar had been forgotten.

M. Heerma von Voss

72452 LOPEZ, Jesus, Naufragé, col. 36-37 et 105-106, *RdE* 24 (1972), 111-115.

La phrase *in ḥt ḥḥ n.ì s(y)* qui apparaît dans les deux passages mentionnés dans le titre doit se traduire : "le mât la (= la mer) battait à ma portée". Pour donner à *ḥḥ* le sens de "battre", l'auteur rapproche ce verbe de *ḥwy* (frapper, battre) et reconstitue à cette occasion la sémantique de ce dernier verbe et de ses dérivés sous les diverses formes où on les trouve au *Wb.* : *ḥwy, ḥ3y* (3,13), *ḥw3y* (3,50), *ḥḥ* (3,151-152), *ḥwt*, la pluie.
Quant à l'étymologie suggérée sous réserve par l'auteur du mot 𓇌𓄿𓏥𓂝𓂝, "les oreilles", comme signifiant "les battantes", les exemples de ce "mot" sont tous tardifs et datent d'une époque où 𓇌 est une graphie bien attestée de 𓏏. Il faut donc lire dans ce cas *'nḥwy* et supprimer l'article du *Wb.* 3,152,8 (Cf. de Wit, *BIFAO* 55 [1955], 116-117 = notre No 4954).

Ph. Derchain

LORETZ, Oswald, see our number 72190.

72453 LORTON, David, The So-Called "Vile" Enemies of the King of Egypt (in the Middle Kingdom and Dyn. XVIII), *Newsletter ARCE* No. 80 (January 1972), 38.

Abstract of a paper.
An examination of the word *ḥsy*, "vile". See now *JARCE* 10 (1973), 65-70.   *L. M. J. Zonhoven*

LUBENAU, Reinhold, see our number 72433.

72454 LÜDDECKENS, Demotische und koptische Urkundenformeln, *Enchoria* 2 (1972), 21-31.

Verfasser vergleicht eine Anzahl demotischer und koptischer Formeln aus verschiedenen Urkundenarten. Obwohl die Rechtsvorstellungen sich im Laufe der Zeit in Folge mancherlei Einflüsse geändert haben, sind dennoch mehrere alte Rechtsvorstellungen und Sprachgut erhalten geblieben.   *R. L. Vos*

72455 LUFT, Ulrich, Das Verhältnis zur Tradition in der frühen Ramessidenzeit. Ein Vergleich zwischen dem Gefäßbuch im Papyrus Ebers und dem Berliner medizinischen Handbuch, *Forschungen und Berichte* 14 (1972), 59-71, with 4 p. of hieroglyphic texts.

Comparing the book of the vessels in Pap. Ebers (XVIIIth Dynasty) and Pap. Berlin P 3038 (XIXth Dynasty) the author particularly examines the variants of the latter in order to discover the way of transmission of texts in general. He pays special attention to the prologue which relates the find of the ancient text, by which mention its importance seems to be stressed. Apart from errors of the copyist the variants of the later version are to be explained by the difficulty to understand the Middle Egyptian.

72456 LUKE, John Tracy, Apprehensions Concerning Death in Ancient Egypt, *Michigan Academian. Papers of the Michigan Academy of Science, Arts, and Letters*, Michigan 4 (1971-1972), 371-376, with 1 ill.

The author attempts to demonstrate that Egyptian confidence in a static and secure universe in which eternal life was assured may not have been as steady as usually supposed. Actually a distinct thread of pessimism was running through their concept of death and afterlife. Pointing out some disorderly aspects of the Gîza necropolis the author suggests that the pessimism was older than the First Intermediate Period, and that the preoccupation with death arose from a deep pessimism about it.

MAHLER, Paul Emil, see our number 72032.

72457 MAKKONEN, Olli, Metsätuotteiden kauppaa muinaisessa Egyptissä, *Metsä ja puu*, Helsinki 7-8 (1972), 24-26, with 4 ill.

"The Trade of Wood Products in Ancient Egypt".

In the short, popular essay Makkonen renders examples of import of foreign species of wood and the products made of them to Egypt. He begins with a description of the find of plywood made at Saqqâra in 1933 and the use of wood products, i.a. in the process of mummification and the fabrication of incense. The trade in living trees and the unsuccessful experiment of Queen Hatshepsut to make them grow in Egypt are dealt with. At the end a discussion about birch (?) bark, found on the fowling boomerang of Tutankhamon.

The author mainly follows the opinions already expressed in Laurent-Täckholm's *Faraos Blomster* (our number 2441) and in Boerhave Beekman, *Hout in alle tijden* (our number 918).

R. Holthoer

72458 MALAISE, Michel, Les conditions de pénétration et de diffusion des cultes égyptiens en Italie, Leiden, E. J. Brill, 1972 (15.5 ×, 24 cm; XIV + 529 p., frontispiece, 3 maps [2 folded]) = Études préliminaires aux religions orientales dans l'empire romain publiées par M. J. Vermaseren, 22; rev. *AJA* 78 (1974), 315-316 (Ruth Isley Hicks); *Revue de l'Histoire des Religions* 185 (1974), 81-88 (Robert Turcan).   Pr. cloth fl. 156

The book presents important material to students of the legacy of Egypt to the Roman world. After enumerating and evaluating in the introduction earlier studies of the subject the author i.a. deals with theophorous personal names composed with the names of Egyptian divinities; the ethnic, social and economic status of the followers of Isis in Roman Italy; Isis priests and members of the community, and its belief; Egyptian divinities in Italy and their distribution, nature and cults.

The particular aim of the author is to elucidate the way in which Egyptian cults were introduced in Imperial Rome, and the historical conditions of the diffusion of the cults. An essential role in the propagation of the Isis cult have played the *negotiatores* of Delos, which appears from the importance of Anubis in Italy as on Delos.

Conclusions of the study on p. 469-481, followed by an extensive bibliography and indexes.

72459 MALAISE, Michel, Inventaire préliminaire des documents égyptiens découverts en Italie, Leiden, E. J. Brill, 1972 (15.5 × 24 cm; XVI + 400 p., frontispiece, 64 pl., 14 maps [1 folded], 4 plans [2 folded]) = Études préliminaires aux religions orientales dans l'empire romain publiées par M. J. Vermaseren, 21; rev. *AJA* 78 (1974), 315-316 (Ruth Ilsley Hicks); *Revue de l'Histoire des Religions* 185 (1974), 81-88 (Robert Turcan).

Pr.cloth fl. 156

Inventory of the literary, epigraphical and archaeological documents, genuine Egyptian or Egyptianized, found in Italy.

The documents are arranged in a geographical order, from Istria in the NE to Bruttium in the SW, after which follow chapters on Sardinia and Sicily. Within the chapters the places are followed in alphabetical order according to their Latin names. Each section contains inscriptions, a list of (partly Greek) names connected with the Isis cult, archaeological documents and literary evidence. For the large section on Rome (p. 112-246) see now too the study of Roullet (our number 72610), for the inscriptions that of Vidman (our number 70651). The inscriptions are presented with some notes, the archaeological objects briefly described, while each entry contains bibliographical notes.

Extensive indexes on p. 331-390.

The plates reproduce some of the more important objects, statues, reliefs, frescos, etc.; the maps show the distribution of documents relating to Egyptian gods such as Isis, Horus, Osiris, Ammon, Anubis, etc.

MÁLEK, Jaromír, see our number 72564.

72460 MANNICHE, Lise, Les scènes de musique sur les talatat du IXe pylône de Karnak, *Kêmi* 21 (1971), 144-164, with 10 ill.

Les ensembles musicaux, peu fréquents en Amarna, se retrouvent en dix scènes sur 15 blocs extraits du IXe pylône de Karnak. L'auteur en donne la photo et description, placée en regard. Des groupes des deux sexes y figurent, la plupart devant des offrandes accumulées, des vases. etc. Il s'agit du même motif qu'au palais et dans les banquets. La présence de la lyre géante et de la harpe angulaire retient surtout l'attention. La lyre géante apparaît aussi sur quatre "talatat" trouvées ailleurs, et semble disparaître après Akhnaton, mais ici le nombre de cordes est quasiment double. Les musiciens, qu'ils soient égyptiens ou étrangers, ne sont jamais figurés comme aveugles, mais ont tous les yeux bandés.   *J. Custers*

72461 MARAGIOGLIO, Vito e Celeste RINALDI, A preposito della costruzione della piramide di Cheope, *Atti della Accademia Nazionale dei Lincei.* Anno CCCLVIII. 1971. Serie ottava. *Rendiconti classe di scienze morali, storiche e filologiche,* Roma 24 (1971), 1972, 351-358, with 1 folding pl.

Review of our number 69480.

72462 MARCINIAK, Marek, Sur le sens de *ḏ'yt* à l'époque ramesside, *Études et Travaux*, Warszawa 6 (1972), 77-81, with 1 fig.

Facsimile, transcription and translation with commentary of one of the graffiti in the temple of Tuthmosis III at Deir el-Bahri, containing a prayer to Sobk and Horus followed by a few lines in which the writer calls himself a child of the cow (i.e., Hathor) born in her barn (i.e., the sanctuary) and dancing in her court. The author particularly discusses a word *ḏȝyt*, which may mean "room" of a temple.

See now also Marek Marciniak, Les inscriptions hiératiques du temple de Thoutmosis III (= Deir el-Bahari I), Varsovie, PWN - Éditions Scientifiques de Pologne, 1974, 71-72 (No. 12).

72463 MARTIN-ACHARD, Robert, [William Foxwell Albright], *Revue de Théologie et de Philosophie*, Lausanne IIIe série, 22 (1972), 240-241.

Obituary article. Compare our number 71650.

72464 MARTIN-ACHARD, Robert, Problèmes soulevés par l'étude de l'histoire biblique de Joseph (Genèse 37-50), *Revue de Théologie et de Philosophie*, Lausanne IIIe série, 22 (1972), 94-102.

Review article, i.a. dealing with Vergote's Joseph en Égypte (our number 59608), Redford's A Study of the Biblical Story of Joseph (our number 70453) and Ruppert's Die Josephser-zählung der Genesis (our number 65425).

72465 MARTIN-ACHARD, Robert, [Le Père Roland Guérin de Vaux], *Revue de Théologie et de Philosophie*, Lausanne IIIe série, 22 (1972), 243-244.

Obituary article. Compare our number 71654.

72466 MASALI, M., Body Size and Proportions as Revealed by Bone Measurements and their Meaning in Environmental Adaptation, *Journal of Human Evolution*, London and New York 1 (1972), 187-197, with 4 tables, 3 fig. and 1 pl.

Presentation of the results of an investigation into body size and physical constitution of 53 male and 33 female skeletons from Gebelein and Asyût preserved in the Institute of Anthro-pology at Turin. They show a fairly gracilized body both with males and females, and a morphological convergence of proportions of the two sexes.

Reprinted in : Population Biology of the Ancient Egyptians. Edited by D. R. Brothwell [and] B. A. Chiarelli, London and New York, Academic Press, 1973.

72467 MASALI, M. and B. CHIARELLI, Demographic Data on the Remains of Ancient Egyptians, *Journal of Human Evolution*, London and New York 1 (1972), 161-169, with 2 tables, 3 fig. and 1 pl.

A mortality and sex ratio survey has been done on both the osteological and the mummy collections from the Gebelein and Asyût cemeteries of Upper Egypt. The results show a fairly low average age of death for adults of about 36 years and a sex differentiation in mortality, that is, higher for young females. This fact may be correlated with childbirth.
Reprinted in : Population Biology of the Ancient Egyptians. Edited by D. R. Brothwell [and] B. A. Chiarelli, London and New York, Academic Press, 1973.   *Authors' own summary*

72468 MATTHIAE SCANDONE, G., Ricerche sui fondamenti delle relazioni tra Neith e Osiride, *Oriens Antiquus* 11 (1972), 179-192.

L'auteur relève d'abord les divers points de contact entre Osiris et Neith aux différentes époques. Puis il examine les raisons de ces affinités. Neith est avec Selkis la seule déesse extérieure à l'Ennéade héliopolitaine qui soit intégrée au système funéraire osirien dès les époques les plus reculées. Pour Selkis, cela s'explique à suffisance par ses origines dans le Delta et la protection magique qu'elle assure au roi.
Pour Neith s'y ajoutent dès la préhistoire l'existence d'édifices sacrés comme *ḥwwt Nt* et *ḥwt bìty*, des barques *sšty bìty*, de l'étape à Saïs lors du transport par eau du sarcophage royal vers Bouto, et peut-être enfin le nom de la couronne du Nord. Le royaume de Bouto pourrait avoir assimilé la couronne Rouge en même temps que Saïs et sa déesse, c-à-d. en absorbant le noyau politique le plus important du Delta. Le premier fonds commun entre les deux divinités en question, jamais figurées comme thériomorphes, serait leur symbolique royale, peut-être aussi leurs rapports avec la végétation renais-sante.   *J. Custers*

72469 MAYRHOFER, Manfred, Aus dem perserzeitlichen Ägypten. Eine namenskundliche Notiz, *Anzeiger der phil.-hist. Klasse der Österreichischen Akademie der Wissenschaften*, Wien 109, Nr. 23 (1972), 317-320.

The Persian name *Farnadāta-* occurs in a Demotic text (cfr Spiegelberg, *Sitzungsber. Pr. Akad. der Wiss.*, phil.-hist. Klasse, Jhrg. 1928, 604-622). It is the name of a satrap who wrote a letter in Demotic to the Chnum-priests of Elephantine concerning a Persian official called *štrpn* (*Ātr-bānu-).

72470 McKEON, John F.X., A Problematic Piece of Egyptian Sculpture, *Newsletter ARCE* No. 80 (January 1972), 38.

Abstract of a paper.

On the dating of a small head in the Museum of Fine Arts, Boston either to the XIIth or the XXVth Dynasty.

L. M. J. Zonhoven

72471 MEEKS, Dimitri, Le grand texte des donations au temple d'Edfou, [Le Caire], Publications de l'Institut français d'Archéologie orientale du Caire, [1972] (22.2 × 27.3 cm; XII + 186 + 87 p., 4 pl. containing maps) = Bibliothèque d'Étude, 69.

Study of the donation text at the outside of the Eastern girdle wall of the Edfu temple containing the land register of the estate of Horus, mainly situated on the left bank, between Thebes and Elephantine. Though the text appears to have been copied from a hieratic papyrus its language is purely Demotic. The text has previously been published by Brugsch (*Thesaurus*, 531-603) and Chassinat (*Le temple d'Edfou* VII, 215-251 and XIV, pl. 646-654). Meeks presents a handwritten copy arranged after the system of the *Urkunden* (p. 4*-76*), followed by textual comments.

The study consists of two parts. Part I first deals with the 8 offering scenes which are intercalated in the main text, after which follow the translation and the comments to the donation text.

Part II is devoted to the results of the study as regards history, geography, economy and metrology. The author demonstrates that the use of the name of Ptolemy Alexander I in col. I does not mean that the donation was his, but that the text has been inscribed on the wall in his reign. The register itself may date from the time of Ptolemy Soter I, and therefore has been written in Egyptian, not in Greek. The donations themselves are dated to the reigns of Darius I and II and Nectanebo II, as well as to an earlier king who may be Shabako. The second chapter discusses the geography of the region as follows from the indications of the text, e.g.: the limits of the nomes in that period, some general names for types of fields and canals, and the age of some toponyms.

In chapter 3 the author deals with royal and private donations in general, land registry and surveys, and the wealth of the Edfu temple. Chapter 4 is devoted to the formula expressing the measures of the fields, which appear to have been enumerated in the order N-S-W-E instead of N-S-E-W, which is usual in other instances. The formula for calculating the surface, $\dfrac{a+c}{2} \times \dfrac{c+d}{2} = e$ is only correct in the case of rectangular fields. At the end various terms for measures are discussed. Indexes on p. 169-186.

72472   MEEKS, Dimitri, 'Iwn-n-pt = ⲥⲁⲩⲁⲛⲙⲡⲉ = "le lin", *RdE* 24 (1972), 116-119.

L'auteur, reprenant une hypothèse de Loret, démontre grâce à quelques exemples ptolémaïques que la plante *iwn n pt* (*Wb.* 1,52,18) est le *linum humile* aux fleurs d'un bleu profond, l'espèce de lin la plus commune en Égypte, et montre la survie dans le copte d'un mot qu'on aurait pu croire, d'après les seules attestations connues, une création poétique de la langue savante de l'époque ptolémaïque.   *Ph. Derchain*

72473   MEEKS, Dimitri, Inscriptions méroïtiques dans les collections britanniques, *MNL* No 11 (Décembre 1972), 22-29.

Vorgestellt werden die Texte REM 0501-0545 aus Faras, die sich mit Ausnahme von REM 0516, 0521, 0535, 0544 im Ashmolean Museum alle im British Museum befinden. Die Transkription erfolgt nach den in *MNL* 5 (Oct. 1970), p. 3 (unsere Nummer 70261) gegebenen Richtlinien.   *Inge Hofmann*

72474   MEGUID, Bulbul Abdel, Warding off an Eclipse, *Newsletter ARCE* No. 80 (January 1972), 25-27.

Modern Egyptian customs with regard to a lunar eclipse are connected by the author with ancient Egyptian beliefs, explicitly expressed in *Book of the Dead* Chapter 80.
                                      L. M. J. Zonhoven

72475   MELTZER, Edmund S., The Field of *j3rw* Revisited, *Anthropological Linguistics*, Bloomington, Indiana 14 (1972), 23-27.

The author rejects a suggestion by Carleton Hodge (*Anthropological Linguistics* 13, 1971, 316), namely that *i3rw* in *sht-i3rw* should be read *i-3-33-w* (*33* spelled for *r*) and means "ancestors". *sht-i3rw* certainly means "marshes full of rushes". New Kingdom texts write *i-3-nr-w*, which indicates a reading *i3hw*. Perhaps the word *i3rw* may be connected with *i3rrt*, "grapes", both derived from a root concerned with plants or germination.

72476   MELTZER, Edmund S., Horus *DN* "Cutter", "Severer (of Heads)"?, *JNES* 31 (1972), 338-339.

Many interpretations have been given of the First-Dynasty Horus-name *dn*. It is here suggested that the name should be read as written and may have the meaning "Cutter" or "One who severs (heads)"; although the use of this verb is only attested from the Middle Kingdom and later. However, the form *dny* does appear in the *Pyramid Texts*.   *E. Uphill*

72477 MÉNARD, J.-E., L'Évangile de Vérité, Leiden, E. J. Brill, 1972 (15.6 × 24 cm; X + 228 p.) = Nag Hammadi Studies, 2; rev. *BiOr* 31 (1974), 263-266 (J. Helderman); *Rivista* 47 (1972), 51-53 (Tito Orlandi).

Complete French translation of the Gospel of the Truth, with an extensive commentary (p. 71-192), a bibliography (193-202) and indexes (203-228). For the edition of the text compare our numbers 4524 and 61219.
In the introduction the author i.a. discusses and rejects the suggestion of Fecht (our numbers 61229, 62179 and 63164) that the original language of the Gospel was Coptic, and that of Nagel (our number 66453) that it was Syriac. To him it has most probably been written in Greek.

72478 MENDELSSOHN, Kurt, Gedanken eines Naturwissenschaftlers zum Pyramidenbau, *Physik in unserer Zeit*, Weinheim 3 (1972), 41-47, with 7 ill. (4 in colour) and 2 fig.

See our number 71402.

72479 MÉNÉTRIER, Jacques, Origines de l'Occident (nomades et sédentaires), [Paris], Weber Éditeurs, [1972] (21 × 26 cm; 214 p., 21 maps [1 in colour], 25 pl. [15 in colour]).

The book presents the personal views of a biologist on the prehistory and protohistory of the Western world and its origins, from the beginning of the *homo sapiens* c. 35,000 B.C. to 480 B.C., centred around the contrasts between nomadic movements and sedentary stabilisation.
In part I the documentation is given, in which ancient Egypt occurs on several pages. Part II deals with ecological and ethnological correlations (on p. 141-143 a section on Egyptian art); part III offers some conclusions.
An atlas of 20 maps at the end. No indexes.

72480 MENU, Bernadette, Un contrat de prêt démotique conclu sous le règne de Ptolémée IV Philopator (P. Marseille, Inv. No 297), *RdE* 24 (1972), 120-128, with 2 pl.

Le document mentionné dans le titre de l'article est un acte authentique dressé par un notaire et revêtu de la signature de seize témoins, daté de l'an 5 de Ptolémée IV (14.7.217), fixant les modalités d'un prêt et de son remboursement, entre deux personnes apparentées. L'auteur fait suivre sa transcription et sa traduction d'un commentaire juridique, dans lequel elle envisage d'une manière générale les conditions du prêt, le problème des intérêts et celui des garanties.   *Ph. Derchain*

72481 MERRILLEES, R. S., Aegean Bronze Age Relations with Egypt [Chronologies in Old World Archaeology. Archaeological Seminar at Columbia University 1970-1971], *AJA* 76 (1972), 281-294.

Studying all available material, graphic (tomb wall representations), archaeological (mainly pottery) and textual, in connection with the relations between Egypt and the Minoan and Mycenaean world, the author draws the following tentative conclusion : the Minoans were in direct contact with Egypt during the first reigns of the XVIIIth Dynasty, until Hatshepsut; they were supplanted during this reign by the Mycenaeans, who probably came as traders; during the time of Amenophis II and Tuthmosis IV there is no evidence of any contact, and the only Mycenean pottery from later reigns comes from el-'Amarna, where it was found abundantly, as against nothing from Malkata. The reasons for this decline and resumption of pottery imports are still obscure.

72482 MERRILLEES, R. S. and J. WINTER, Bronze Age Trade between the Aegean and Egypt. Minoan and Mycenean Pottery from Egypt in The Brooklyn Museum, *Miscellanea Wilbouriana 1*, 101-133, with 34 ill. (3 in colour).

The collection of Aegean Bronze Age pottery from Egypt in The Brooklyn Museum represents in microcosm the nature and extent of the Late Minoan and Mycenean ceramic export to the Nile Valley during the second half of the 2nd mill. B.C. In connection with these Aegean vessels the first author deals extensively with the Aegean overseas trade to Egypt and its products (for the Cypriote commerce, compare our number 68405).

There is one important Late Minoan IB jug in the collection, the so-called Abbott jug (no. 37.13 E), which originally contained a liquid in which was held in suspension oleaginous matter originating from a vegetable source (cfr the appendix, p. 128-130, by the second author). Various possible materials are discussed : sesame and olive oil, perfume, saffron, lichen, purple dye and beans, all of which may have been exported to Egypt. There is also ample discussion of other vases from this period found in Egypt and their contents. The conclusion is that sesame oil and olive oil are most probable.

After a quite clear period from which no Aegean pottery is known (from Tuthmosis II to Hatshepsut) the instances from early Mycenean IIB and IIIA comprise an alabastron (no. 16.44) and several sherds of pilgrim flasks and stirrup jars. They may also have contained oil, though other products as mentioned above may not be excluded.

72483   de MEULENAERE, H., De Belgische opgravingen in Elkab en Luxor, *Spiegel Historiael* 484-488, with 6 ill., 1 map and 1 fig.

"The Belgian excavations at Elkab and Luxor".
The author describes the importance of Elkab as a centre from the Old Kingdom to the Greco-Roman Period, and its main antiquities.
During the campaigns of 1967-1969 a detailed map of the site was prepared. Important discoveries were made concerning Neolithic Elkab inside and Epipalaeolithic Elkab outside the city-wall. A temple of the XVIIIth Dynasty with blocks from the XIIIth Dynasty (Sebekhotep III), and living-quarters from Ptolemaic and Roman times have been excavated. After the transfer of the activities to Asasif the tombs from the Saite Period of Aba (Nr. 36) and of Petehorresne of the same family (Nr. 196) were investigated during the campaigns of 1970-1972.

L. M. J. Zonhoven

72484   de MEULENAERE, H., Membra dispersa van Laategyptische sculpturen, *Spiegel Historiael* 497-500, with 4 ill.

"Membra dispersa of Late Egyptian Sculptures".
The author describes how the work of Bernard V. Bothmer that resulted in a Corpus of Late Egyptian Sculpture made it possible to unite dispersed parts of statues. He discusses the criteria which may form an indication in this respect and gives examples of some 20 successful reunions.

L. M. J. Zonhoven

72485   de MEULENAERE, Herman, Scarabaeus sacer, [no place, no publisher], 1972 (20.2 × 20.7 cm; 35 p., 2 fig., 15 ill. in colour).

This is a special publication offered to the corps of physicians by Hoechst Belgium Ltd.
After an introduction the author first deals with the Scarabaeus (Ateuchus) sacer as an animal, the various uses of the scarab as an amulet, texts on scarabs, e.g. the commemorative scarabs, and the function of the scarab in pharmacy. Particular sections are devoted to the sacred-scarab and its meaning in theology and mythology, and to the connections between scarab and heart.
Throughout the book there are translations of several texts, e.g. of the *Book of the Dead*, ch. 27. The illustrations represent actual scarabs, as well as paintings and drawings from papyri and tombs.

72486   de MEULENAERE, Herman, Trois Campagnes de Fouilles dans l'Assassif, *Newsletter ARCE* No. 82 (July 1972), 8-10.

Au cours de trois campagnes dans l'Assassif ont été decouverts :

la salle d'embaumement d'Aba, haut fonctionnaire civil à Thèbes sous le règne de Psammétique I, et le tombeau de Petehorrcsne (règne de Néchao II). On s'a occupé des travaux epigraphiques et archéologiques dans quatre tombes ramessides, les nos 25 (Amonemheb), 364 (Amonemheb), 387 (Meriptah) et 406 (Piay). *L. M. J. Zonhoven*

72487 MEYER, Rudolph, Siegfried Morenz. 22.1.1914 – 14.1.1970, *Jahrbuch. Sächsische Akademie der Wissenschaften in Leipzig*, Berlin (1969-1970), 1972, 235-238, with portrait.

Obituary article. Compare our number 70619.

72488 MEYEROWITZ, Eva L. R., The Origins of the "Sudanic" Civilization, *Anthropos*, Freiburg/Schweiz 67 (1972), 161-175.

Es wird der Versuch unternommen zu zeigen, daß die "sudanische" Kultur während des ersten oder zweiten nach-christlichen Jahrhunderts vom meroitischen Reich aus in die östliche Sahara, den Fezzan und Mauretanien eindrang, in der zweiten Hälfte des 7. Jahrhunderts von dort weiter in das Tschadsee-Gebiet und den Nigerbogen und kurz nach 1000 n.Chr. an den Oberen Niger und die Gebiete im Süden des Flusses. Verantwortlich für die Diffusion sind die Zagha (Zaghawa), die in den Reichen die herrschende Aristokratie bildeten. Die Zaghawa sollen die "Äthiopen" des meroitischen Reiches gewesen sein, die aus unbekannten Gründen zu Tausenden das Niltal verließen und nach Osten flohen, nachdem sie aus Südwest-Asien eingewandert waren. Die "sudanische" Kultur wurde zum einen durch den Islam, zum anderen durch europäische Einflüsse zerstört. *Inge Hofmann*

72489 MICHAŁOWSKI, Kazimierz, Aleksandria. Zdjęcia Andrzej Dziewanowski, Warszawa, Wydawnietwo Arkady, 1972 (20.5 × 28.3 cm; 25 p., 84 pl., 1 ill., 3 plans, 3 fig., a loose p. with a second index to the pl.); rev. (of German edition) *Orientalia* 43 (1974), 145-146 (J. Leclant). Pr. cloth zł 75

Although mainly devoted to Alexandria in Graeco-Roman times some objects depicted belong to the culture of Pharaonic Egypt, e.g. the statues of Ramses II and Psammetichus I (pl. 38) and the sphinx near Pompey's Pillar (39-41). Other illustrations pertain to the Egyptian religion in the Roman Empire, e.g. the reliefs from Kom es-Shugofa depicting Osiris on his bier and Anubis as legionary (31-32).
There are also a German edition, Wien-München, Verlag Anton Schroll & Co, 1972 (Pr. DM 24.40), and a Russian edition, Варщава, Издательство Аркады, 1972 (Pr. 2 руб. 50 коп.)

72490 MICHAŁOWSKI, Kazimierz, Luxor. Aufnahmen von Andrzej Dziewanowski, Wien-München, Verlag Anton Schroll & Co, 1972 (20.5 × 28 cm; 24 p., 84 pl., 1 ill., 2 maps, 1 plan, a loose p. with a second index to the pl.).   Pr. bound DM 19.80

Like the picture book on the Karnak temple (our number 70388) the present volume contains, apart from usual pictures, some photographs of parts of the building seldom depicted. On the other hand, there is only one picture of the procession on the walls of the colonnade (pl. 65).
We did not see the original Polish edition (Warszawa, Wydawnietwo Arkady, 1972). There are other editions in various languages: Russian (Warszawa, 1972) and French (Paris, 1973).

72491 MICHAŁOWSKI, Kazimierz, Pyramidy i mastaby. Zdjęcia Andrzej Dziewanowski, Warszawa, Wydawnietwo Arkady, 1972 (20.5 × 28 cm; 30 p., 86 pl., 1 ill., 4 maps, 5 fig., 2 plans, a loose p. with a second index to the pl.); rev. (of German edition) *Antike Welt* 5, Heft 3 (1974), 56 (anonymous).

The third volume on ancient Egypt of this series (cfr our numbers 70388 and 72490) is mainly devoted to the pyramids of the Old Kingdom and their surroundings. Only a few pictures are added of the pyramids of the Middle Kingdom (see pl. 73) as well as of the pyramids of Nuri and Meroe (pl. 80-84).
Besides the usual views there are represented some less well known corners. The volume also contains several pictures of reliefs and statues.
There is also a German edition (Wien-München, 1973; pr. DM 19.80).

MIELKE, James H., see our number 72032.

72492 MILGROM, J., The Alleged Wave-Offering in Israel and in the Ancient Near East, *Israel Exploration Journal*, Jerusalem 22 (1972), 33-38, with 1 fig.

As a parallel to the *tᵉnūfa*, usually suggested to be "wave-offering" but here argued to be "elevation-offering", the author discusses an offering scene from Karnak.

72493 MILLET, Nicholas B., Egyptian, *Annual Report. Royal Ontario Museum*, Toronto 22 (1971-1972), 17-19, with 1 ill.

Report by the assistant curator on the museum's activities, mentioning among others the following recent acquisitions: a tomb relief from Memphis (Heracleopolitan Period); bronze objects from Emery's excavations at Saqqâra (a bronze baboon depicted); Nubian material from the excavations at Gebel Adda; a relief of the Steward of the Divine Votaress Harsiese (XXVIth Dynasty); two Amarna reliefs; and an "Osiris mummy" in a wooden coffin.

72494 MILLET, N. B., An Old Mortality. An Egyptian Coffin of the XXnd (sic) Dynasty, *Rotunda. The Bulletin of The Royal Ontario Museum*, Toronto Vol. 5, No. 2 (Spring, 1972), 18-27, with 11 ill. (8 in colour, 1 on cover).

After having stated that almost nothing has been written on mummy-cases and their decoration, the author examines the coffin of a Lady from the XXIInd Dynasty at Thebes, called Djemaʿetesʿankh (Inv. no. ROM 910.10), and proceeding from the object he provides information in a more general way on ancient Egyptian culture.
He discusses the name of the owner and her mother Shedtaōpe and father Pa-ʿankh-ntof, their titles, and describes the cartonnage and the subject matter of its representations, as well as the results of the X-ray examination of the mummy.

L. M. J. Zonhoven

MILOÏTI, Jacques, see our number 72433.

72495 MINK, Gerd, Die koptische Versionen des Neuen Testaments. Die sprachliche Probleme bei ihrer Bewertung für die griechische Textgeschichte, *in: Die alten Übersetzungen des Neuen Testaments, die Kirchenväterzitate und Lektionare.* Herausgegeben von Kurt Aland, Berlin-New York, Walter de Gruyter, 1972 (= Arbeiten zur neutestamentliche Textforschung 5), 160-299.

This long article discusses the present state of researches into the subject; grammatical conditions for textcritical use of Coptic readings, with examples for the way in which Greek grammatical forms and syntactical constructions have been rendered in Sahidic and Bohairic; and the problems of a text analysis as illustrated from *Joh.* 10, 1-18, comparing the Greek text with versions in various Coptic dialects.

72496 MIOSI, F. T., Hieratic Fragments in the Buffalo Museum of Natural Sciences, *Newsletter [of] The Society for the Study of Egyptian Antiquities*, Toronto 2, No. 4 (June, 1972), 3-5, with 4 pl.
The author mentions four papyrus sheets from the Buffalo Museum, New York (Cat. nos C 5186, C 12659, C 1587 and C 12661), the second from the Roman Period, the others from c. 300 B.C.
The first fragment contains parts of Spells 18 and 19 of the *Book of the Dead*.

72497 MIOSI, F. T., Methodology and the Pyramid Texts, *Newsletter [of] The Society for the Study of Egyptian Antiquities*, Toronto 2, No. 3 (February, 1972), 7-10.

The author discusses Faulkner's interpretation of *Pyr. Text* 514c (compare our number 69184), translating "Wenis is the third when he appears" (instead of "at his accession"), and connecting it with Utt. 266, where the king is said to become a "third (god) in Heliopolis", beside Re and Harakhte.

72498 MITCHELL, T. C., A Review of Acquisitions 1963-70 of Western Asiatic Antiquities (I), *The British Museum Quarterly*, London 36 (1971-1972), 131-146, with 8 pl.

On p. 143 mention of eight Amarna tablets recently acquired by the British Museum (nos 134863-134872). All have been published previously.

72499 MOCZULSKA, Krystyna and Joachim ŚLIWA, Identyfikacja zabytków egipskich ze Zbiorów Czartoryskich z wykazani zakupów z lat 1884 i 1885, *Zeszyty Naukowe Uniwersytetu Jagiellońskiego. Prace Archeologiczne* 14 (1972), 85-104, with 1 ill. and a summary in French on p. 104.

"Identification of the Egyptian Monuments of the Collection Czartoryski with the lists of Acquisitions of the Years 1884 and 1885".
In 1884 and 1885 groups of objects have been sent from Egypt to the collection Czartoryski, accompanied by detailed lists describing each object. In total 154 objects were sent, two of which are now lost, while the identification of the shawabtis proved to be impossible. From the lists the provenance of most pieces could be established.

72500 MONTEVECCHI, O., Roger Rémondon. 1923-1971, *Aegyptus* 52 (1972), 158-161.

Obituary notice, followed by a bibliography.

72501 MORENZ, Siegfried, Bōg i człowiek w starożytnym egipcie, Warszawa, Panstwowy Institut Wydawniczy, 1972 (170 p., 33 pl., 6 fig.).

Polish edition of our number 64345.

72502 MORENZ †, Siegfried, Traditionen um Menes. Beiträge zur überlieferungsgeschichtlichen Methode in der Ägyptologie II, *ZÄS* 99, 1 (1972), X-XVI.

Dieser zweite Aufsatz konnte leider nicht vollendet worden; das Anliegen findet man schon im ersten Teil, unserer Nummer 71416.

Zum Fragment sind besonders Wildungs Material und Kommentar in unserer Nummer 69676, S. 4 ff., einzusehen.

M. Heerma van Voss

MOSS, Rosalind L. B., see our number 72564.

72503 MOURSI, Mohamed I., Die Hohenpriester des Sonnengottes von der Frühzeit Ägyptens bis zum Ende des Neuen Reiches, München-Berlin, Deutscher Kunstverlag, 1972 (17 × 24 cm; 186 p., 2 fig., 2 plans, 16 pl.) = Münchner Ägyptologische Studien herausgegeben von Hans Wolfgang Müller, 26; rev. *BiOr* 30 (1973), 404-405 (David Lorton); *CdE* XLVIII, No. 95 (1973), 69-71 (Herman de Meulenaere); *JEA* 60 (1974), 281 (J. Gwyn Griffiths); *JNES* 34 (1975), 148-149 (Dieter Mueller); *ZDMG* 125 (1975), 145-147 (W. Helck).   Pr. DM 29

After an introduction the first part of the book (p. 12-146) deals with the sources. The author lists the persons called *mȝ-wr* or *wr-mȝw*, from the early dynasties until the end of the XXth Dynasty, altogether 57 persons (cfr the table on p. 138-139), fifteen of which have been high priest in Thebes (§ 40-54), one in Amarna (§ 55) and two in Thinis (§ 56-57). Of each of them the name, date, sources (which are usually discussed), titles, family relations, etc. are given. There follow seventeen sections mentioning the title without a name, including some from periods later than the New Kingdom. In § 75-79 five instances of the name *Mȝ-wr* are listed, preceded by a discussion (p. 130). In § 80-99 a survey is given of the *wrw-mȝw* from the end of the New Kingdom until the Ptolemaic Period.

The second part (147-173) contains a discussion of the material. The author argues that originally the title was *mȝ-wr*, "who sees the Great One", *wr* being first the king — hence the title was that of a prince — and later on the Heliopolitan god. Since the Middle Kingdom the title is understood as *wr-mȝw*, "Greatest of the Seers".

Then Moursi discusses costume, social position and function of the high priests of the Sun God. For the latter two periods appear to be important : that of the transition between the IVth and Vth Dynasties, and that of Amenophis IV. Two tables list the other titles of the various high priests (167-168). Little is known about their religious and cultic functions, obviously since the cult was secret. We know them, however, to have been astronomers and mediators between man and the god.

Indexes on p. 177-184. The plates depict stelae, statues, etc. of the high priests, several of them less well known.

72504 MOUSSA, Ahmed, Lintels and Lower Parts of a Leaf of a Wooden Relief-sculptured Door of the Old Kingdom from Saqqara, *MDAIK* 28 (1972), 289-291, with 1 pl.

Publication of two wooden lintels and a wooden door leaf discovered in 1970 in the vicinity of the Unas causeway. The former bear the name of the *imy-rꜣ thnt 'Ity.sn*; the door leaf, of which only the lower part is preserved, shows three rows of men and a baking scene below the figures of the tomb owner and his wife.   *Dieter Mueller*

72505 MÜLLER, Christa, Eine Grabplatte der Terenuthis-Gruppe, *GM* Heft 1 (1972), 21-22, with 1 pl. (on p. 23).

Beschreibung eines Grabreliefs im Göttinger Kunsthandel mit einer kurzen Inschrift. Das Stück gehört zu der Gruppe der Terenuthis-Stelen.

72506 MÜLLER, Christa, Kritische Bemerkungen zu Wolfgang Kosack, Historisches Kartenwerk Ägyptens, Bonn 1971, *GM* Heft 2 (1972), 23-26.

A selection of corrections and additions to Kosack's map of Coptic sites in Egypt (our number 71333).   *Dieter Mueller*

72507 MÜLLER, C. Detlef G., Jean Simon, *Oriens Christianus*, Wiesbaden 56 (1972), 210-211.

Obituary notice.

72508 MUELLER, Dieter, The Chronology of Amenemhet's Expedition to the Wadi Hammamat, *Newsletter ARCE* No. 80 (January 1972), 38.

Abstract of a paper.

72509 MUELLER, Dieter, An Early Egyptian Guide to the Hereafter, *JEA* 58 (1972), 99-125.

The two most famous examples of this type of literature are the *Book of the Hetep Field* and the *Book of the Two Ways* from el-Bersheh, to which is now added a third book from el-Bersheh, i.e. Sp. 404 (*CT* V, 181-200), which is here analyzed. The author gives a complete translation and very extensive notes on both the grammar and the content of each section, discussing the geography of the Egyptian next world which is here recounted in fuller form than anywhere else. The view is expressed that Kees was in error in assigning this text to a relatively late period, owing to its disparate and unrelated elements, and that it should in reality be dated to at least the Eleventh Dynasty and perhaps as early as the end of the First Intermediate Period.   *E. Uphill*

72510 MUELLER, Dieter, I am Isis, *OLZ* 67 (1972), 117-130.

Review article of our number 68073.

72511 MUELLER, Dieter, A Middle Egyptian word for 'measure', *JEA* 58 (1972), 301-302.

Coffin Text Sp. 404 refers to a door-keeper disguised as a corn-measurer, the word used for the measure being here discussed in detail.   *E. Uphill*

72512 MÜLLER, Hans Wolfgang and Beatrix LÖHR, Neuerwerbungen. Staatliche Sammlung ägyptischer Kunst, *Münchner Jahrbuch der bildenden Kunst*, München 23 (1972), 213-216, with 8 ill.

Among the recent acquisitions of the Egyptian collection at Munich are: two Amarna reliefs (ÄS 5890 and 5569), a granite colossal head ascribed to Ramses II (ÄS 5910), and five small papyrus rolls (ÄS 5882-5886). Most important may be a ceremonial palette with representations of animals (ÄS 5853).

MÜLLER, Hans Wolfgang, see also our number 72687.

72513 MÜLLER, Ingeborg, Zwei Neuerwerbungen aus der ehemaligen Sammlung Rudolf Mosse, *Forschungen und Berichte* 14 (1972), 104-108, with 1 fig.

Description of the former collection Rudolf Mosse in Berlin, whose owner in 1891-'92 placed funds at the disposal of Brugsch in order to buy antiquities for the Berlin Museum. Two objects from his private collection have recently been acquired, and are here published: an offering basin (Inv. Nr. 27658) from the Old Kingdom and a canopic vase (Inv. Nr. 27659), possibly from the XXVIth Dynasty.

72514 MÜLLER, Klaus E., Geschichte der antiken Ethnographie und ethnologischen Theoriebildung. Von den Anfängen bis auf die byzantinischen Historiographen. Teil I, Wiesbaden, Franz Steiner, 1972 (17 × 24 cm; XII + 386 p., 13 Abb.) = Studien zur Kulturkunde 29.

Die Entwicklungsgeschichte der antiken Ethnographie und der ethnologischen Theoriebildung wird in dem vorliegenden 1. Teil anhand von Literatur aufgezeigt für 1. Altvorderasien (Babylonien, Ägypten, Israel, Phönizien), 2. Griechenland. Hierfür werden folgende Werke untersucht: a. Homer und Hesiod, b. von Anaximander bis Aischylos, c. von Protagoras bis Poseidonios. Auf eine Verifizierung der ethnographischen Angaben und Schilderungen der antiken Autoren wurde bewußt verzichtet; es geht in dem vorliegenden Werk um eine rein wissenschaftsgeschichtliche Darstellung.   *Inge Hofmann*

72515 MÜLLER, Wolfgang, Ägyptisches Museum und Papyrus-Sammlung. Jahresbericht 1968/69, *Forschungen und Berichte* 14 (1972), 109-110.

Report on the activities of the Berlin Museum in 1968-69.

72516 MUNRO, Peter, Zu einigen ägyptischen Terrakotta-Figuren, *GM* Heft 2 (1972), 27-32, with 3 ill.

To a terra cotta figure in the Kestner Museum (No. 1935.200.39) there came to light three parallels, preserved in a private collection at London and here published. All pieces may be genuine, though their date and function are obscure. The author adds the description of what may be a Nubian woman with the hands tied on her back (Kestner Museum 1926.200), also made of terra cotta.

MUNRO, Peter, see also our number 72347.

72517 MURNANE, Jr., William J., The "King Ramesses" of the Medinet Habu Procession of Princes, *JARCE* 9 (1971-1972), 121-131, with 3 fig.

"King Ramesses" was a known son of Ramesses III and, Ramesses VI's father. In reality, he did not rule.
In an Appendix (p. 129-130), the author discusses the statue Cairo J.E. 37331; see our number 65348, p. 220-226. It represents Ramesses V together with a son and with a grandmother of the king.
Compare our number 72376.   *M. Heerma van Voss*

72518 MYŚLIWIEC, Karol, A propos des signes hiéroglyphiques "ḥr" et "tp", *ZÄS* 98, 2 (1972), 85-99, with 20 ill. and 8 fig.

Le signe ḥr (D2) est l'image d'Horus agissant comme un homme. La couleur jaune de cette face marque quelques traits féminins du dieu, comme aussi sa nature "pacifique" et lumineuse. L'hiéroglyphe tp (D1), l'opposition formelle de D2, représente Seth. La couleur rouge est celle du dieu caracterisé par sa jeunesse masculine, pleine de force et de désordre.
D'une facon plus générale, ces deux signes symbolisent deux aspects contrastants de la nature humaine.
                                      M. Heerma van Voss

72519 MYŚLIWIEC, Karol, Towards a Definition of the "Sculptor's Model" in Egyptian Art, *Études et Travaux*, Warszawa 6 (1972), 71-75.

After pointing out that some "sculptor's models" were reused as ex-votos the author adduces criteria to distinguish "sculptor's models". Indications should be sought in the details of each piece, such as an unfinished state, traces of a "proportion grid" or a "copy grid", and a fragmentary frame.

72520 NAGEL, Peter, Die Bedeutung der Nag Hammadi-Texte für die Koptische Dialektgeschichte, *in*: *Von Nag Hammadi bis Zypern*. Eine Aufsatzsammlung. Herausgegeben von Peter Nagel, Berlin, Akademie-Verlag, 1972 (= Berliner byzantinistische Arbeiten, 43), 16-27.

The author discusses first recent trends in the study of Coptic dialects, proceeding from Paul Kahle's Bala'izah (our number 3397). Against Kahle he states that Sahidic has been a local dialect until the 4th century. He also deals with Kasser's researches into the subject (see our number 66338).
The second part is devoted to the language of the Nag' Hammadi codices, particularly codices I, II and V. From these Sahidic appears to have been the local dialect of Hermopolis, from which gradually elements of other dialects were removed, first from the grammar and then from the orthography, phonology and morphology. It also appears that Subachmimic was the original language of the heretics, who later on preferred the official Sahidic language; this may be a means to date the manuscripts.

NAGEL, Peter, see also our numbers 72425 and 72426.

72521 NASTER, P., Die Zwerge als Arbeiterklasse in bestimmten Berufen im Alten Ägypten, *in*: *Gesellschaftsklassen im Alten Zweistromland und in den angrenzenden Gebieten*. XVIII. Rencontre assyriologique internationale. München, 29. Juni bis 3. Juli 1970. Herausgegeben von D.O. Edzard, München, 1972 (= Bayerische Akademie der Wissenschaften. Phil.-hist. Klasse, Abh. N.F. 75), 139-143.

L'auteur rassemble les données que l'on possède sur les trois types de nains et d'assimilés connus des Égyptiens et sur les diverses fonctions qu'ils remplissaient. Il s'agit surtout pour lui d'éclairer la situation des nains en Mésopotamie et dans les pays voisins. Seuls les nains orfèvres ou préposés au linge et aux soins de toilette pourraient se retrouver, à haute époque, de part et d'autre.   *J. Custers*

72522 NEMESKÉRI, J., Some Comparisons of Egyptian and Early Eurasian Demographic Data, *Journal of Human Evolution*, London and New York 1 (1972), 171-186, with 4 tables and 4 fig.

The author first discusses the archaeological and anthropological preconditions of palaeodemographic investigation, that is, the various requirements which have to be fulfilled in order to

allow reliable conclusions. As an illustration he discusses the analysis of a Nubian Late Paleolithic series of 51 individuals, comparing it with data from a number of other areas and drawing general conclusions.
Reprinted in : Population Biology of the Ancient Egyptians. Edited by D. R. Brothwell [and] B. A. Chiarelli, London and New York, Academic Press, 1973.

72523   NEWBY, Gordon D., The Dependent Pronoun in Semitic and Egyptian, *The Jewish Quarterly Review*, Philadelphia 62 (1971-1972), 193-198.

Whereas relationship between the independent pronouns of the Egyptian and the Semitic languages is obvious that of the dependent and suffix pronouns is less clear. The author argues that the Semitic bound form pronouns are etymologically related to Egyptian dependent pronouns, and Semitic suffix pronouns to Egyptian suffix pronouns; but Semitic suffix pronouns function as enclitics when attached to verbs, like Eg. dependent pronouns, as absence of accent shift indicates.

72524   NIBBI, Alessandra, The Sea Peoples : A Re-Examination of the Egyptian Sources, [Oxford, published by the author, 1972] (14.5 × 20.5 cm; [VI +] 73 p., 4 fig.); rev. *GM* Heft 5 (1973), 59-62 (Bernd Sledzianowski); *JARCE* 11 (1974), 104 (David Lorton).   Pr. £ 1.50

After an attempt to prove that *w3d wr* has no connection whatsoever with the sea, the author tries to derive the "Sea Peoples" from Syria and Palestine rather than from the Aegean Islands.
The book can be obtained from Blackwell's, Oxford.
Dieter Mueller

72525   Le Nil et la société égyptienne. Hommage à Champollion. Marseille, Musée Borély, 6 décembre 1972 - 1er mars 1973 (12.5 × 22 cm; 120 unnumbered p., 1 map, 7 ill., 35 pl. [7 in colour]).

Catalogue of an exhibition in the Musée Borély, Marseille, for which most objects came from the museum's own collection (the Clot-Bey collection), others from Berlin, the Louvre, and several provincial museums in France.
The preface about Champollion and the introductions to the chapters are written by Mme. Chr. Desroches-Noblecourt, apart from those to chapter 1 (The Egyptian Expedition) by Jean et Raoul Brunon and chapter 2 (the Birth of the Egyptian Civilization) by Mme. Simone Bourlard-Collin, keeper of the Museum.

In room 1 were exhibited portraits, prints, books, etc. relating to Bonaparte's expedition and to Champollion, including his bust by Eugène-Émile Thomas (see pl. nr. 23). Room 2 contained objects from the Prehistoric Period, mainly from the museum at Saint-Germain-en-Laye. There follow chapters on kingship, viziers, high officials, daily life, cult, divinities and funerary cult. For each of the 283 objects material, measures, date, provenance and present whereabouts are mentioned, while some are briefly described.

72526　NIMS, Charles Francis, Interim Report on the Work of the Epigraphic Survey. The Oriental Institute, Luxor, Egypt, for the Season 1971-1972, *Newsletter ARCE* No. 81 (April 1972), 21-25.

The documentation of the temple of Khonsu at Karnak was continued. The scenes about the doorway at the back of the pylon belong to the time of the First Prophet of Amon Paynedjem, whose costume was changed extensively, as well as his inscriptions. Much attention is paid to these changes.

L. M. J. Zonhoven

72527　NOLTE, Birgit, An Egyptian Glass Vessel in the Metropolitan Museum of Art, *Metropolitan Museum Journal*, New York 4 (1971), 1972, 167-171, with 4 ill.

Publication of a pear-shaped sand-core glass vessel now in the Metropolitan Museum of Art (Inv. No. 91.1.1365). It measures 8.11 cm in height and may have come from one of the workshops in Tell el-Amarna. The method of production is described in detail.　　　　　　　　　　　　　　　*Dieter Mueller*

72528　NORDSTRÖM, Hans-Åke, with contributions by Randi HALAND, Gun BJÖRKMAN and Torgny SÄVE-SÖDER-BERGH, Neolithic and A-Group Sites, Stockholm, Läromedels-förlagen, 1972 (24.4 × 30.8 cm; Text: XV + 259 p., 13 fig., 38 tables; Plates: 14 p., 197 pl. including maps, plans, fig. and ill.) = The Scandinavian Joint Expedition to Sudanese Nubia. Volume 3:1 (Text) and 3:2 (Plates).

Der vorliegende Band präsentiert die Funde und Ausgrabungs-daten der frühnubischen Siedlungsgebiete und Friedhöfe, die zwischen 1961-64 im Konzessionsgebiet der Scandinavian Joint Expedition gesammelt wurden. Es werden die Keramikgruppen des 5. und 4. vorchristlichen Jahrtausends beschrieben, wobei besonderen Wert auf die Analyse und Systematisierung der keramischen Kollektion und der lithischen Artefakte gelegt wurde. Die Gruppen umfassen in der Hauptsache die Khartoum-Variante, das Post-Shamarkian, das Abkan und die nubische

A-Gruppe aus den Gebieten Faras-Ost, Serra-Ost, Debeira, Ashkeit, Sahaba, Halfa Degheim, Abka und Gamai.

Inge Hofmann

72529 NOVITSKIY, G. A. and S. S. SOLOV'EVA, Всеволод Игоревич Авдиев, *Древний Восток и античный Мир* 3-7.

'Vsevolod Igorevich Avdiev'.
A short sketch of the scientific career of V. I. Avdiev; his portrait faces the title page while an anonymous bibliography of his publications will be found on p. 244-252.

J.F. Borghouts

72530 O'CONNOR, David, The Geography of Settlement in Ancient Egypt, *Man, Settlement and Urbanism* 681-698, with 7 maps and 5 tables.

The author argues (against Wilson, our number 61746) that a broadly defined type of urbanism was characteristic of historic Egypt.
There are different types of centres : the national capitals Memphis and Thebes, the capitals of the nomes, and other towns. Their roles and relations are discussed, the density of the population, etc. The author also deals with the material of the Pap. Wilbour as regards the patterns of settlement and the importance of the major towns there mentioned. He i.a. concludes to a concentration of agriculturists around the nome-capitals, partly caused by a deliberate governmental policy in order to control the population. The same pattern may have been typical for most of Upper Egypt.

72531 O'CONNOR, David, A Regional Population in Egypt to circa 600 B.C., *in* : *Population Growth : Anthropological Implications.* Edited by Brian Spooner, Cambridge, Massachusetts and London, The MIT Press, [1972], 78-100, with 13 maps.

This is a lecture given at a colloquium entitled "Population, Resources, and Technology", held at the University of Pennsylvania in March 1970.
O'Connor here studies the relations between population growth in Egypt and agricultural innovation. Proceeding from Butzer's observations on the geography of Egypt (cfr our numbers 65104 and 66108) he argues that the evidence from cemeteries may be of importance for the study of the demography. Although some calculations of the population in various periods are known the absolute size of the changes cannot yet be established. Hence the author studies the region on the West Bank between Matmar and Etmanieh, which for various reasons may be a typical area without outstanding features. The

results are presented in a table and distribution maps, and interpreted in terms of mortality rates and growth or decrease of the population during the history of pharaonic Egypt. The author i.a. points out a probable increase of the population during the Middle Kingdom, connecting it with the reclamations in the Faiyûm. At the end O'Connor enumerates the factors influencing fluctuation in the population.

72532 O'CONNOR, David, The University Museum Excavations at Malkata, 1971 : A Palace and Harbor of Amenhotep III, *Newsletter ARCE* No. 83 (October 1972), 30.

Abstract of a paper.
The results of the first season (1971) : the dating of the harbour to Amenhotep III; the revealing of unexcavated structures; the finding of the ancient beachline of the harbour; more detailed knowledge of the harbour's construction.   *L. M. J. Zonhoven*

72533 OLIVER, Jr., Andrew, Night Light, *Miscellanea Wilbouriana 1*, 135-136, with 1 colour ill.

Publication of an oval faience lamp (no. 69.117) of the early Roman Period, decorated with a woman's head in relief, with one wing.

72534 ORLANDI, Tito, Due nuove collane dedicate ai testi gnostici copti di Nag Hammadi, *Rivista* 47 (1972), 47-53.

Review article of our numbers 71335, 71516, 72214 and 72477.

72535 ORLANDI, Tito, Un encomio copto di Raffaele Arcangelo ("Relatio Theophili"), *Rivista* 47 (1972), 211-233.

Publication, with introduction and a Latin translation, of a Coptic text (In laudem Raphaelis archangeli), known as the *Relatio Theophili ad Theodosium imperatorem*, and, although ascribed to the bishop Theophilus of Alexandria (385-412 A.D.) composed in the 7th or 8th century.

72536 OTTO, Eberhard, Gedanken zu "Ägyptologie als Wissenschaft in der Gesellschaft", *GM* Heft 3 (1972), 57-59.

A reply to Horn's criticism of modern Egyptology and its methods (see our No. 72323).   *Dieter Mueller*

72537 OTTO, Eberhard, Jan ASSMANN, and R. GRIESHAMMER, Bericht über die Sitzung der Ständigen Ägyptologenkonferenz am 3. Oktober 1972 in Lübeck, *BiOr* 29 (1972), 255.

OTTO, Eberhard, see also our number 72432.

OWEN, Kipling H., see our number 72032.

72538 PADRÓ, J., El 150 aniversario del desciframiento de los jeroglíficos por J.-F. Champollion, *Ampurias*, Barcelona 33-34 (1971-72), 423-424.

Survey of the celebrations in honour of Champollion's decipherment of the hieroglyphs.

72539 PADRÓ, J., Un escarabeo de ámbar procedente de la excavaciones de Rhode, *Ampurias*, Barcelona 33-34 (1971-72), 293-295, with 1 fig.

Publication of an anepigraph scarab, made of amber and found during the excavations at Roses, with a discussion of its material.

PALMIERI, A., see our number 72579.

72540 PAOLI, G., Further Biochemical and Immunological Investigations on Early Egyptian Remains, *Journal of Human Evolution*, London and New York 1 (1972), 457-466, with 8 tables and 1 map.

The analyses as referred to in our number 72092 not being quite satisfactory the author has attempted to improve the methods. The results are here described.
Reprinted in : Population Biology of the Ancient Egyptians. Edited by D. R. Brothwell [and] B. A. Chiarelli, London and New York, Academic Press, 1973.

PAOLI, G., see also our number 72092.

72541 PARKER, Richard A., An Abstract of a Loan in Demotic from the Fayum, *RdE* 24 (1972), 129-136, with 1 pl.

Publication d'un contrat de prêt garanti par une hypothèque datable du début du 1er siècle a.C. provenant d'une momie de crocodile de Tebtynis (University of California, Berkeley, Inv. 1826), et mentionnant, entre autre, le nom du village de *Pȝ-i̓.ir-pȝ-nṯr* qui n'est autre que la forme égyptienne jusqu'ici inconnue de Theogonis voisin de Kerkeosiris.
L'intérêt du document est autant paléographique que juridique. Le commentaire s'attache surtout aux questions d'écriture.
Ph. Derchain

72542 PARKER, Richard A., Demotic Mathematical Papyri, Providence, Rhode Island, Brown University Press / London, Lund Humphries, 1972 (27 × 37.5 cm; XIV + 86 p., 25 pl.) = Brown Egyptological Studies 7; rev. *CdE* XLVIII, No. 95 (1973), 102-104 (Richard Holton Pierce); *JARCE* 10 (1973), 108 (David Lorton); *Studia Papyrologica* 12 (1973), 113 (J. Pequeroles).

Publication of a number of Demotic texts on mathematical

problems, the major ones being : Pap. Cairo J.E. 89127-130 and 89137-143, the verso of the Hermopolis legal code, dating from the 3rd century B.C., and Pap. Brit. Mus. 10520, of the early (?) Roman Period, which contains 13 exercises in 7 columns. Of the other texts Pap. Brit. Mus. 10399 bears one column and parts of two others on the recto, one column and parts of another with small fragments of three more columns on the verso, together 13 exercises. Pap. Brit. Mus. 10796 and Pap. Carlsberg 30 are very small and contain two and five problems respectively, mostly very fragmentary.

All papyri together provide us with 72 mathematical problems, which the publication numbers consecutively. Some of them pertain to arithmethical questions, among which the calculation of the square root of 10 (no. 62); others on geometrical questions, e.g. problems 42-44 (calculation of the volume of masts). No 6 even contains a general statement, while nos. 66 and 67 present multiplication tables for $\frac{1}{90}$ and $\frac{1}{150}$.

After a discussion of the physical state of the papyri and a list of the problems each contains the author makes some general remarks on mathematics of the period, pointing out the possibility of foreign influence. Special sections deal with mathematical processes as expressed in Demotic, such as addition, multiplication, etc.; with fractions, some with a numerator greater than one and some even improper and mixed fractions; with methodology, and with a few grammatical questions.

The main part of the volume (p. 13-77) consists of transliterations and translations with comments of each separate problem, always preceded by an explanation of its nature, so far as recognizable.

On p. 78-86 an index of Egyptian words with a selected palaeography. The plates contain fine photographs of all texts.

72543 P[ARROT], A[ndré], W. F. Albright (1891-1971), *Syria*, Paris 49 (1972), 499-500.

Obituary article. Compare our number 71650.

72544 P[ARROT], A[ndré], Le R.P. de Vaux (1903-1971), *Syria*, Paris 49 (1972), 277-278, with portrait.

Obituary article. Compare our number 71654.

PASQUIÉR, J.-C., see our number 72369.

72545 PAVLOV †, V. V., Голова мужчины позднеамарнского периода из собрания Государственного Музея изобразительных искусств им. А. С. Пушкина, *ВДИ* 4 (122), 1972, 90-94, with 5 ill. and an English summary on p. 94.

"A Male Head of the Late Amarna Period from the Pushkin Museum of Fine Arts".
Publication of a feldspar head (height 8.5 cm) in the collection of the Pushkin Museum at Moscow (Inv. no. 4959). Its style proves it to belong to the late stage of the Amarna Period.

72546 PECK, William H., An Eighteenth Century Traveller in Egypt, *Newsletter ARCE* No. 83 (October 1972), 30.

Abstract of a paper.
On the European traveller Sonnini de Manoncourt whose book "Voyage in Upper and Lower Egypt" is very informative.
L. M. J. Zonhoven

72547 PECK, William H., An Old Kingdom Tomb Wall, *Bulletin of the Detroit Institute of Arts*, Detroit, Michigan 51 (1972), 63-68, with 7 ill.

Description of an almost complete wall of a tomb chapel from the Vth Dynasty recently acquired by the Detroit Institute of Arts. The chapel was dedicated to a certain Mery-nesut and has been found by Reisner at Gîza (nr. G 1301). The most important part of the relief represents the owner and his wife in front of an offering table, a motif repeated in another form as part of the false door. The right hand side of the wall shows a palace façade.
For the texts, cfr our number 72231.

72548 PECK, William H., A Ramesside Ruler Offers Incense, *JNES* 31 (1972), 11-15, with 1 ill.

A relief added to the Egyptian collection of the Detroit Institute of Arts in 1965 shows a ruler offering incense. The accompanying cartouche is broken but preserves the name Ramessu and is a typical Nineteenth-Twentieth Dynasty product. From the style a date early in the former period is suggested. Compare also Kitchen, *JNES* 32 (1973), 483-484.   *E. Uphill*

72549 PECK, William H., Some Elementary Observations on the Techniques of Tomb Painting in the Theban Necropolis, *Newsletter ARCE* No. 80 (January 1972), 39.

Abstract of a paper.
The vast amount of unfinished tomb paintings is very apt to illustrate the sequence of steps of the ancient artist when making them.   *L. M. J. Zonhoven*

72550 PELTENBURG, Edgar, Some early developments of vitreous materials, *World Archaeology*, Henley-on-Thames 3 (1971-1972), 6-12.

The author discusses some of the more important stages in the development of vitreous materials (inventions of glaze, glazed pottery, glass-making and polychromy) and deals with the implications of the history of these advances. In some instances he refers to ancient Egypt, e.g. to the appearance of polychrome faiences in the reign of Amenophis III.

72551 PERNIGOTTI, Sergio, Due sacerdoti egiziani di epoca tarda, *Studi classici e orientali*, Pisa 21 (1972), 304-313, with 2 fig. and 4 pl.

Publication of two statuettes from the cachette of Karnak, Cairo JE 36743 and 37855. The former, a granite sistrophorous figure, belonged to the stolist of Thebes Besenmut, of whose family other monuments are listed. The other, a naophorous figure, belonged to Wahibre, son of Psamtik, prophet of Amun and priest of other Theban gods, who may have lived at the end of the 7th or in the early 6th century B.C.

72552 PERNIGOTTI, Sergio, Notizia preliminare su alcuni blocchi di Assuan, *Studi classici e orientali*, Pisa 21 (1972), 314-320, with 21 ill. on 4 pl.

During work in Aswân by the Papyrological Institute of the University of Milan in 1970 and 1971 in the area South of the temple of Isis several blocks with inscriptions are found, ranging from the time of Nectanebo II to that of Nero. There appeared also several blocks from a building of Tiberius, still partly *in situ*.

The author provides photographs, technical details, with transcription and translation of the texts of 3 blocks with royal names from the XXXth Dynasty and 18 from the Ptolemaic Period.

PERNIGOTTI, Sergio, see also our number 72110.

PESENTI, R., see our number 72369.

72553 PESTMAN, P. W., A note concerning the reading *ḥḏ sp-2*, *Enchoria* 2 (1972), 33-36.

The author discusses the reading of a sign occurring after words like *ḥḏ* "silver", *ḥmt* "copper" and *sw* "wheat". This sign has been variously read as *wtḥ* "refined" or *sp-2* "two times". Arguing in favour of the latter, the author explains that *sp-2* is used in order to convey to a word its proper sense : real silver (copper or wheat) is meant as opposed to something else.   *R. L. Vos*

72554 PESTMAN, P. W., Wat staat er eigenlijk op de Steen van Rosette?, *Spiegel Historiael* 462-467, with 7 ill.

"What exactly has been written on the Rosetta Stone".

Although much attention has been paid to the role of the Rosetta Stone in the decipherment of the hieroglyphs, the actual text itself is less known.

After an introduction on the social situation in Hellenistic Egypt the author deals with the scheme and the contents of the text. The central theme is the suppression of revolts by the king and the restoration of peace, though in the South with less success.

Due to the difficult position of the king he had to gain support of the priesthood, in return of which he granted them favours. As acknowledgment for this they paid honours to him. At the end the author explains why the decree was published in two languages.   *L. M. J. Zonhoven*

72555 PETERSON, Bengt J., A Tomb-Relief from the End of the First Intermediate Period, *Orientalia Suecana*, Uppsala 21 (1972), 3-8, with 1 ill. and 1 colour pl.

Publication of a tomb-relief preserved in the Medelhavsmuseet (Inv. Nr. NM 11432), originating from Saqqâra. It is the left flanking-piece of a group consisting of two such pieces placed on either side of a stela in the form of a false door. The upper register shows a girl bringing flowers to a woman, the two other registers offering-bearers. The texts (one on the left edge) indicate that the relief belonged to a lady Sat-Hathor, while the crude style points at the end of the First Intermediate Period.

72556 PETERSON, Bengt E., Eine Uschebtifigur mit modelliertem Korb, *GM* Heft 2 (1972), 49, with 2 ill.

In 1965, the author acquired in Abydos the fragment of an ushebti now in the Medelhavsmuseet in Stockholm (Inv. No. MME 1965:5). The basket carried by the ushebti is not simply indicated by black lines, but sculptored as part of the figurine.
                                                        Dieter Mueller

72557 PETRÁČEK, Karel, Die Grenzen des Semitohamitischen. Zentralsaharanische und semitohamitische Sprachen in phonologischer Hinsicht, *Archiv Orientální*, Praha 40 (1972), 6-50.

Study of the alleged relations between the phonological systems of the central-saharian and the semito-hamitic languages. On p. 35-36 a section on ancient Egyptian.

72558 PETZL, Georg, Eine Weihinschrift aus der Oase Siwa (Ammonion), *Zeitschrift für Papyrologie und Epigraphik*, Bonn 9 (1972), 68-71, with 1 ill. on a pl.

In a Greek dedicatory inscription from the Siwa Oasis appears besides Ammon the rare divine name Parammon.

L. M. J. Zonhoven

72559 PHILIPP, Hanna, Terrakotten aus Ägypten im Ägyptischen Museum Berlin, Berlin, Gebr. Mann Verlag, [1972] (17.5 × 23.3 cm; 35 p., 48 pl., 8 colour pl.); series: Bilderhefte der Staatlichen Museen, 18/19; rev. *BiOr* 30 (1973), 400 (H. Leclerq); *JARCE* 11 (1974), 108-109 (John H. Young).   Pr. DM 12

Although outside the scope of the *AEB* we mention the book because of some representations of Egyptian divinities, such as Harpocrates, Isis and Horus.

After an introduction on Graeco-Roman terra cottas from Egypt fifty-one objects are described, each represented by a fine photograph.

72560 PIERCE, Richard Holton, Three Demotic Papyri in the Brooklyn Museum. A Contribution to the Study of Contracts and their Instruments in Ptolemaic Egypt, Oslo, In Aedibus Universitetsforlaget, 1972 (16 × 24 cm; 232 p., 6 pl.) = Symbolae Osloensis fasc. suppl. 24; rev. *JEA* 60 (1974), 297-298 (W. J. Tait); *Revue d'histoire et de philosophie religieuses* 53 (1973), 442 (J. Schwarz).

This is a somewhat altered version of the author's doctoral dissertation (Brown University, 1963; compare our number 65383).

The first part contains transliterations and translations with commentary of Pap. Brooklyn 37.1796 E, Pap. Brooklyn 37.1802 E and Pap. Brooklyn 37.1803 E. All three, together with the Demotic papyrus Vatican 22, belong to the same archive and came from Saqqâra. They date from 108 B.C. and deal with sales with differed delivery.

Chapter IV attempts to indicate the place of these texts in the corpus of Demotic instruments, the latter term being distinguished from "contract" since this determines the legal relationship between parties, whereas instruments are concerned with sanctioning that relationship. The author discusses the possible reasons for the transactions and the question whether the price indeed has been paid. He argues that the Demotic instruments were modelled on their Greek counterparts and probably not a product of an Egyptian legal tradition.

Chapters V to X are devoted to details, dealing with receipts in Demotic instruments, securities, the executive clause *n ḥtr (n) iwty mn*, the paragraphs governing evidence of payment and of performance, credibility and mulet. Throughout the author compares Demotic evidence with that from the Greek texts of

the period. In the last chapter the Greek archival dockets on Demotic instruments are discussed.
Bibliography on p. 189-204; indexes on p. 205-232.

72561 PINTORE, F., Transiti di truppe e schemi epistolari nella Siria egiziana dell'età di El-Amarna, *Oriens Antiquus* 11 (1972), 101-131.

Les lettres d'El-Amarna peuvent fournir des indications quant aux effectifs et au type des troupes égyptiennes en garnison en Syrie à ce moment. L'auteur scrute d'abord les termes qui les désignent. Il s'agit surtout de compagnies de 200/250 hommes, parfois accompagnées de chars. Les textes suggèrent une nette distinction entre les garnisons stables, approvisionnées par l'Égypte, et les prestigieux corps expéditionnaires que l'on traduit souvent par "archers" (mots dérivés de *pdt*): forces mobiles nourries aux frais de l'habitant, comme les troupes en guerre. L'analyse des formules épistolaires exprime, dans des lettres émanant de princes syriens, outre l'assurance des préparatifs demandés, des offres de forces auxiliaires, voire celle de "préparation" (sur place) du tribut. L'attente mentionnée de la venue de Pharaon ne semble pas impliquer de campagne mais répond à la survivance d'une formule, ensuite transformée en "archers du Roi". Plusieurs lettres égyptiennes ajoutent d'ailleurs des développements d'allure pacifique. Seule une étude attentive permettra de préciser le rôle que jouèrent ces expéditions dans les territoires vassaux.   *J. Custers*

72562 PIRENNE, Jacques, La population égyptienne a-t-elle participé à l'administration locale?, *RdE* 24 (1972), 137-141.

En l'absence de tout document, l'auteur s'efforce d'exploiter quelques allusions des sagesses égyptiennes pour exposer la thèse qui lui est chère de l'existence de conseils d'artisans ou d'ouvriers participant démocratiquement à l'administration de ce qu'il considère comme des villes en Égypte, dont on trouverait la trace tout au long de l'histoire.   *Ph. Derchain*

72563 PORTA, Eduardo y José M.ᵃ XARRIÉ, Estudio radiografico de la momia egipcia del Museo Diocesano de Vic, *Información Arquelógica*. Boletín Informativo del Instituto de Prehistoria y Arqueología de la Diputación Provincial de Barcelona No 7 (enero-abril 1972), 17-18.

Untersucht wurde die ägyptische Mumie des Diözesanmuseums in Vich. Die etwa 16-18 Jahre alte Frau, nach der Sargaufschrift eine Amunssängerin namens *N3jw(-dgj-B3stt-rdwj)* war an Tuberkulose gestorben. Die Mumie war beraubt worden. (Vgl. Eduardo Porta Ferrés, La fisico-quimica al servicio de la arqueología, San Jorge, Barcelona 92 [1973], 3 pp., 2 ill., 1 fig.). *I. Gamer-Wallert*

72564 PORTER †, Bertha and Rosalind L. B. MOSS, Assisted by Ethel W. BURNEY, Topographical Bibliography of Ancient Egyptian Hieroglyphic Texts, Reliefs and Paintings. II. Theban Temples. Second Edition Revised and Augmented, Oxford, At the Clarendon Press, 1972 (19 × 28.2 cm; XXXVI + 586 p., 1 map, 49 p. containing maps); rev. *WZKM* 65/66 (1973/74), 275-277 (Erich Winter). Pr. cloth £ 18.

As were the two parts of Volume I (our numbers 60572 and 64402), the second edition of volume II is enormously augmented compared with the first (published in 1929). The number of pages with descriptions of texts, etc. increased from 198 (including the plans) to 541 (plans excluded). As in the second edition of volume I.1 there is added an appendix containing a classification of selected scenes (p. 542-552). The numerous plans, drawn anew by Jaromír Málek, are combined to a particular section between p. 552 and 553. The length of the indexes increased from 5 to 34 pages.
The large number of discoveries since 1929 and the wealth of publications produced so much material that almost every entry has been augmented. This particularly holds true for the Montu enclosure (1-20), the temple of Ramses III (27-34), the Shrines of Sesostris I, Amenophis I and Hatshepsut (61-74) and various other parts of the Karnak complex.
Particularly important is also a list of the statues from the Cachette (136-167). For the Luxor temple we mention the discovery of the sphinx avenue. On the West Bank the most important increases are to be found for the temple of Tuthmosis III at Deir el-Bahri (377-380), the mortuary temple of Eye and Horemheb (457-460) and that of Amenophis III (449-454), and the temples of Medînet Habu (460-527).
A list of objects from Theban temples (532-537) presents additions to the similar list in volume I.2 (782-847); compare the index to objects in museums, p. 571-584.

72565 POSENER, Georges, Catalogue des ostraca hiératiques littéraires de Deir el Médineh. Tome II (fasc. 3) - Nos 1227-1266, Le Caire, Publications de l'Institut français d'Archéologie orientale, 1972 (25 × 32 cm; X + 30 p. [= p. 29-58], 40 pl. [4 folded] [= pl. 56-79]) = Documents de Fouilles, T. 18; rev. *BiOr* 31 (1974), 69-70 (Hans Goedicke).

Sequel to our numbers 1991 and 2526 (1951-1952). With the present fascicle volume II is completed.
In his preface the author mainly discusses the ostraca containing the book *Kmyt* (cfr fascicle 1).

The ostraca of fasc. 3 contain i.a. literary texts such as the well known love song from Turin (1266), the Instruction of Hardjedef (1229-1230) and the Maxims of Any (1257-1259), as well as magical (1216 and 1263) and educational texts (1254-1256). In this fascicle are also published ostraca belonging to other collections than that of the French Institute which could be joined to the latter, namely O. Bruxelles E. 6444 (to 1248), O. Turin 6619 and 6806 + O. Gardiner 306 (to 1251), O. Florence 2617 + O. Turin 6620, 6838, 6851 (to 1252), and O. Cairo Cat. 25218 (to 1266).

Apart from the usual descriptions of each separate ostracon (p. 29-44) there are indexes to the entire volume II. In the first one the ostraca are arranged after the subject of their texts, while in some instances also other publications of the same text are mentioned. There are also indexes to characteristic words and phrases and to private names.

The plates contain facsimile and transcription of each separate text.

72566 POSENER, Georges, Champollion et le déchiffrement de l'écriture hiératique, *Comptes rendus de l'Académie des Inscriptions et Belles-Lettres*, Paris, 1972, 566-573.

Discussion of the way along which Champollion discovered the nature of the hieroglyphic writing. In §112 to 116 of his *Précis du système hiéroglyphique* he has summarized his quite correct conclusions.

72567 POSENER, G., Le nom 𓃭𓏤𓏤𓏦, *GM* Heft 2 (1972), 51-52.

The element *šny* in personal names of the New Kingdom either designates the god Amun, or stands for the king Amenophis I.

Dieter Mueller

72568 POSENER, Georges, Philologie et archéologie égyptiennes, *Annuaire du Collège de France*, Paris 72 (1971-1972), 1972, 433-439.

Sequel to the analysis of the Panégyrique Royal (our number 71466).

72569 POSENER, Georges, Sur quelques erreurs dans les calendriers des jours fastes et néfastes, *RdE* 24 (1972), 142-146.

En comparant les deux versions du calendrier du Caire et de Londres du calendrier des jours fastes et néfastes, l'auteur montre le parti que l'on peut tirer des fautes différentes commises par les deux scribes pour aider à reconstituer le texte original dont dérivent les copies actuelles. Les catégories de fautes relevées sont les suivantes : fautes de routine, provoquées par la réminiscence subconsciente de formules usuelles de la langue administrative, évoquées par un mot ou un signe, fautes purement paléographiques par confusion de signes ou de ligatures, pouvant entraîner une altération de la suite du texte "selon les réflexes conditionnés par les habitudes graphiques" menant parfois jusqu'à une réinterprétation complète (exemple choisi P. Sallier rt. 7,10 = Caire rt. 5,11).   *Ph. Derchain*

72570 POSENER-KRIÉGER, P., A propos d'une transcription erronée dans les Papyrus d'Abousir, *RdE* 24 (1972), 147-151, with 2 fig.

Correction apportée par l'auteur à sa propre transcription d'un passage des papyrus d'Abousir (notre No 68486) dans l'inventaire 23-24, où sont décrits des accessoires du rituel de l'ouverture de la bouche. Au lieu des mesures des objets, comme on l'avait cru, l'inventaire donne les dimensions des cassures constatées aux divers endroits des objets. La confusion hiératique de ⌢ avec ⌣ avait précédemment fait croire à des mesures en empans et doigts là où en réalité il faut lire seulement des fractions de doigts. Il en résulte que les objets utilisés dans le temple d'Abousir peuvent très bien avoir eu les dimensions générales des autres nécessaires de l'ouverture de la bouche, dont on connaît quelques exemplaires déposés dans des tombes.

Ph. Derchain

72571 POSNER, Ernst, Archives in the Ancient World, Cambridge, Massachusetts, Harvard University Press, 1972 (17.6 × 23 cm; XX + 283 p., 1 map, 43 ill., fig. and plans); rev. *Acta Archaeologica Academiae Scientiarum Hungaricae* 25 (1973), 420 (L. Castiglione); *Revue archéologique*. 1973, 340-341 (Y.B.); *Revue d'Assyriologie* 67 (1973), 95 (Jean Nougayrol); *ZAW* 85 (1973), 271 ([G. Fohrer]).   Pr. $10

Chapter 2 of this study is devoted to the archives in Pharaonic Egypt. After discussing the materials on which records have been written the author deals with the records themselves calling them, after Max Weber, the bureaucrat's "tools of production". Apart from the Amarna tablets hardly any archival depository is known, and even these are merely an assemblage on non-current material discarded and left behind. Consequently, storage installations and archival practices are virtually unknown.

The author discusses various problems connected with the archives in Egypt, e.g. the position of the vizier as chief archivist, the effectiveness of archival arrangements and the elimination of useless records. For his data he largely relies upon Černý's *Paper and Books* (our number 2252) and Erman-Ranke, *Ägypten und ägyptisches Leben im Altertum*,

.though more recent sources are also quoted; cfr the bibliography on p. 243-246.

72572 PRIESE, Karl-Heinz, Zur Sprache der ägyptischen Inschriften der Könige von Kusch, *ZÄS* 98,2 (1972), 99-124.

Verfasser beschäftigt sich mit den älteren historischen Inschriften. Es sind fünf napatanische, sechs aus Kawa and Fragmente aus Sanam. Die Satsformen der Erzählung werden hier von Priese erörtert.   *M. Heerma van Voss*

72573 QUAEGEBEUR, J., Contribution à la prosopographie des prêtres memphites à l'époque ptolémaïque, *Ancient Society*, Kessel-Lo 3 (1972), 77-109.

L'auteur examine essentiellement cinq stèles érigées par des grands prêtres de Memphis au 1er siècle a.C. (Brit. Mus. 147, 184, 188, 886 et une stèle de Kheredankh à University College, Londres). Une nouvelle analyse détaillée des inscriptions, dont certaines sont bilingues, lui permet de rétablir la chronologie absolue et la généalogie de cette famille.

En appendice il examine plus rapidement d'autres monuments relatifs au clergé memphite : stèle bilingue Caire 31099 (1er siècle a.C), Statue Moscou 5351, Brit. Mus. 148, 187, 383 et 387 (3e siècle a.C.) et résume les résultats de ses recherches sous forme de trois pages d'addenda et corrigenda à la Prosopographia Ptolemaica.   *Ph. Derchain*

72574 QUECKE, Hans, Eine koptische Bibelhandschrift des 5. Jahrhunderts (PPalau Rib. Inv.-Nr. 182), *Studia Papyrologica*, Barcelona 11 (1972), 77-81, with 1 folding pl.

General description of PPalau Rib. Inv.-Nr. 181/182 with a complete text of the Gospels of St. Luke and St. Mark in Sahidic. For the edition of the latter, see our following number.

72575 QUECKE, Hans, Das Markusevangelium saïdisch. Text der Handschrift PPalau Rib. Inv.-Nr. 182 mit den Varianten der Handschrift M 569, Barcelona, 1972 (16 × 22 cm; XIV + 184 p., 2 fig., 2 pl., frontispiece) = Papyrologica Castroctaviana. Studia et textus, 4; rev. *CdE* XLVIII, No. 96 (1973), 401-403 (Gérard Godron); *Enchoria* 4 (1974), 173-174 (Frederik Wisse); *Studia Papyrologica* 12 (1973), 105-109 (T. Orlandi).   Pr. DM 55.60

Publication of the ms. from the collection of the theological faculty at Barcelona (collection Palau-Ribes) containing the Gospel according to St. Mark (and that according to St. Luke = Inv. Nr. 181) in Sahidic. The text (p. 63-179) is particularly compared in the notes with ms. M 569 from the Pierpont Morgan Library.

In his introduction the editor discusses the outward appearance of the ms., its writing, the scribal errors, the language, special variants of the text, and the division into chapters.

72576 QUECKE, Hans, Eine neue koptische Bibelhandschrift (P. Palau Rib. Inv.-Nr. 182), *Orientalia* 41 (1972), 469-471.

Announcement of our preceding numbers.

72577 RABINO-MASSA, E. and B. CHIARELLI, The Histology of Naturally Desiccated and Mummified Bodies, *Journal of Human Evolution*, London and New York 1 (1972), 259-262, with 2 pl. and 1 fig.

Study of different mummified tissues, the structures of which are comparable to those of normal fresh tissues, particularly the ear cartilage. It appears to be possible to classify the mummies according to the different blood groups and to study the biochemistry of the globulins of each of them.
Reprinted in: Population Biology of the Ancient Egyptians. Edited by D. R. Brothwell [and] B. A. Chiarelli, London and New York, Academic Press, 1973.

RABINO-MASSA, Emma, see also our numbers 72150 and 72406.

72578 RACE, G. J., F. WENDORF, S. B. HUMPHREYS, E. I. FRY, Paleopathology of Ancient Nubian Human Bone Studied by Chemical and Electron Microscopic Methods, *Journal of Human Evolution*, London and New York 1 (1972), 263-279, with 1 table and 5 pl.

The definition of the discipline of paleopathology is discussed together with the theoretical bases for its study. Interrelationships between anthropology and paleopathology are considered. A discussion of methods includes macroscopic, microscopic, electron microscopic, radiographic, electron diffraction, paleoepidemiology, skeletal adaptations, serologic, paleoecologic, biochemical, and epigenetic traits. An example of study of Nubian material is as follows.
Human bone 12,000-10,000 years of age from the Egyptian Nubian Desert has shown ultrastructural preservation of collagen with periodicity of 600 Å. Intact Haversian systems and osteones were retained, but content of hydroxyproline and nitrogen was negligible. The fluorine content was markedly elevated. The complex chemical process of fossilization with retention of gross and micromorphology was examined and indicated loss of organic material with probable replacement of some hydroxyapatite with amorphous and crystalline carbonates and phosphates.

Reprinted in : Population Biology of the Ancient Egyptians. Edited by D. R. Brothwell [and] B. A. Chiarelli, London and New York, Academic Press, 1973.   *Author's own summary*

72579 RAIKES, R L. and A. PALMIERI, Environmental Conditions in the Nile Valley over the Past 10,000 Years, *Journal of Human Evolution*, London and New York 1 (1972), 147-154.

The authors argue that the Faiyûm B culture may either have preceded Faiyûm A or partly co-existed with it.
Reprinted in : Population Biology of the Ancient Egyptians. Edited by D. R. Brothwell [and] B. A. Chiarelli, London and New York, Academic Press, 1973.

72580 RAINEY, A. F., The World of Sinuhe, *in* : *Israel Oriental Studies II* (In Memoriam Samuel Miklós Stern 1920-1969), [Tel Aviv], Tel Aviv University, 1972, 369-408.

The objective of the study is to examine the written evidence concerning Syria-Palestine in the 20th century B.C. and to make certain applications to the evidence for material culture.
In three sections the author successively deals with the material culture and social structure of the period in general, the social regime as reflected in the *Story of Sinuhe*, and the two groups of *Execration Texts* (see also the table on p. 401-408). He points out the inconsistency between the social order depicted by *Sinuhe* and the *Execration Texts* and the underdeveloped nomadic communities which the archaeologists insisted to be prevalent in the period.
In the fourth section he concludes that the people of the Intermediate Bronze culture (= MB I) occupied the Levant amid the ruins of the Early Bronze civilisation, but that Egypt had actually no contacts with it. It disappeared, leaving hardly a trace in the written records. Near 2000 B.C. the Amurrites appeared and ushered in the renewal of urbanisation (Middle Bronze Age = MB II A), which is reflected in the texts. The author accordingly proposes a raised date for the Intermediate Bronze Age (from 2200 to 2050/2000 B.C.).
In an Addendum William G. Dever makes some critical remarks, to which Rainey answers in a Postscript.

72581 RAPP, Eugen Ludwig, Das Streitgespräch des Lebensmüden mit seiner Seele. Hieratischer Papyrus aus Ägypten um 2000 vor Christus. Oder : Wie übersetzt man fremde Texte?, *Pfälzisches Pfarrerblatt*, Landau 63, Nr 11 (Nov. 1972), 81-82.

The author, years ago a pupil of Ranke, discusses the problem of the reliability of translations, comparing a literal rendering of some stanzas of the text mentioned in the title with the translations by Thausing and by himself.

72582 RATIÉ, Suzanne, La Reine-Pharaon, Paris, Juillard, [1972] (13.5 × 20 cm; 269 p., 8 pl.); rev. *CdE* XLIX, No. 97 (1974), 102-103 (Agnes Rammant-Peeters).

A popular book about the life and times of Hatshepsut.
Foreword (p. 11-22): The treatment of Hatshepsut after her death. What scholars have thought about her. The position of queens in Egyptian history.
Chapter I (23-33): The Thutmoside succession (genealogical tree on p. 26).
Chapter II (35-97): Hatshepsut before she became "king". It seems that certain powers, and an official role, had been conferred upon her by Thutmose I (44). In year 2 of Thutmose III she associated her daughter Neferure (who seems not to have married Thutmose III) with the royal prerogative (61), and in the same year Hatshepsut was herself called king for the first time, though it is not until year 7 that she definitely adopted this title (65) (see now also R. Tefnin, *CdE* XLVIII, No. 96 [1973], 232-242).
Chapter III (99-166): Hatshepsut as king. The author discusses her duties, and mentions her undertakings. The young Thutmose III was not pushed aside, but was nominally respected as king (103-104). On the stela of Neferure from Sinai (now Cairo JE 38546), the year 11 is that of the princess, and corresponds to year 13 of Thutmose III (151).
Chapter IV (167-213): Wars. Festivals. Private life. Courtiers.
Chapter V (215-227): The last years and Hatshepsut's death. Senenmut seems to have fallen from favour before his disappearance (215). The persecution of the queen took place a relatively short time after her death (221). Chapter VI (229-253): Characteristics of the reign. A tendency towards archaism (230), the importance of Neferure as heiress (231), and the queen's piety, especially her profound attachment to Amonre (234).
At the end: a short glossary, bibliography and index.

Torben Holm-Rasmussen

72583 RAY, John, The *Gm* of Memphis, *JEA* 58 (1972), 308-310.

Among the Ptolemaic period deities of the Serapeum is one called *Gm* first discussed by Reich in 1933, here identified as a young steer.   *E. Uphill*

72584 RAY, J. D., The House of Osorapis, *Man, Settlement and Urbanism* 699-704, with 1 fig.

Description of the district near Saqqâra where the Serapeum, the Anubieion, and the temples of Isis Mother of Apis and of

Thoth the Ibis are situated. Here was settled a community of priests and temple personnel in a town called "House of Osorapis", of which the dromos seems to have been the main street. There was a royal residence, there were guest-houses for the pilgrims, shops, etc. The author describes a visit of a pilgrim and points out many unsolved problems concerning the town.

72585 RAY, John, Two Inscribed Objects in the Fitzwilliam Museum, Cambridge, *JEA* 58 (1972), 247-253, with 2 pl.

A drawing board with an extract from the Petubastic Cycle, 16 cm. high, 11 cm. wide and 1.9 cm. thick was presented by Major Gayer-Anderson. The object was ruled horizontally with incised lines into five equal divisions and a vertical line, showing that it was intended to divide it into squares, and has nine lines of demotic text on the recto referring to Osiris King Inaros. The text is translated and commented on. The other object — an oracular amuletic decree case of one *Šśk* — is partly of gold and invokes Khonsu in Thebes Neferhotep, suggesting a Theban origin, and being probably of Twenty-Second Dynasty date.
Compare also *JEA* 59 (1973), 231-233.   *E. Uphill*

72586 REDER, D. G., Пришельцы в Египте в XVI в. до н. э., *Древний Восток и античный Мир* 21-26.

"Immigrants in Egypt in the XVIth century B.C.".
Connecting two passages in the Karnak stela of king Aḥmose (Cairo CG 34001) where the king's mother Aḥḥotep is called "mistress of the *Ḥȝ.w-nb.wt*" (1.24 = *Urk. IV*, 21.4) resp. is praised for having collected her fugitives (*wtḫ.w*) and assembled her dissidents (*tš.w*) (l. 26 = *Urk. IV*, 21, 13-14), the author concludes that the queen, exercising some kind of sovereignty over Crete, brought Aegean immigrants into Egypt. The hebrew terms גר and תושב are compared (and the latter actually etymologically compared with *tš.w*).
Compare also our number 71580, p. 175, resp. 136-137.
                                                    J. F. Borghouts

72587 REDFORD, Donald B., Progress Report on the Work of the Akhenaten Temple Project of the University Museum, *Newsletter ARCE* No. 83 (October 1972), 31.

Abstract of a paper.
On the nature of the study of *talatat* from Luxor and Karnak by the Akhenaten Temple Project.   *L. M. J. Zonhoven*

72588 REDFORD, Donald B., Report on the Third Season of Work at the Shrine of Osiris Heqa Djet, Karnak, *Annual Report. The*

Society for the Study of Egyptian Antiquities, [Toronto], 1972, 11-20, with 8 ill. and 5 fig.

Report of the third campaign of the Canadian mission to Karnak studying the shrine of Osiris Heka Djet and its environment. This season the pottery has been dealt with by an expert, John A. Holladay. Together with the application of the modern technique of excavation this resulted in a thorough knowledge of the stratigraphical history of the site.

In the 8th century B.C. a mud-brick building was erected, which Osorkon III replaced by a stone chapel dedicated to Osiris. Shabataka replaced the mud-brick court by a stone-built antechamber. During the Kushite Period the shrine has been in constant use, but it fell into disuse under the Persians. Nectanebo I cut away much ground for the construction of a large temenos wall and renewed the decoration, whereafter the chapel enjoyed a new phase of use, apparently for domestic purposes.

72589 REDFORD, D. B., Studies in Relations between Palestine and Egypt during the First Millennium B.C. I. The Taxation System of Solomon, *in*: *Studies on the Ancient Palestinian World*. Presented to Professor F. V. Winnett on the occasion of his retirement 1 July 1971. Edited by J. W. Wevers and D. B. Redford, [Toronto], University of Toronto Press, [1972] (= Toronto Semitic Texts and Studies), 141-156.

The author rejects the theory that the court functions in Israel during the reigns of David and Solomon were modelled on offices of the pharaonic administration (cfr our number 71405). The taxation system ascribed to Solomon, however, shows close similarities to the Egyptian system. The author enumerates various Egyptian words for taxes and gives a survey of the system of taxation. He particularly discusses the verso of the Turin Royal Canon, the Chronicle of Osorkon, and a Cairo stela of Sheshonq I from Herakleopolis recording a levy for the cult of Arsaphes (JdE 39410), which particularly bears resemblance to the Solomonic provisioning system.

72590 REED, R., Ancient Skins, Parchments and Leathers, London and New York, Seminar Press, 1972 (15 × 23 cm; X + 331 p., 12 fig., 46 ill.). Series: Studies in Archaeological Science.

Pr. £ 4.90

A technical study on skins and parchment, intended for archaeologists, archivists, librarians and museum curators. The author deals, among other subjects, with methods of processing skins, methods of conservation, chemical analysis of tanning agents and physical examination of leather and parchments.

On a few pages reference is made to ancient Egypt. See

particularly the section on "Ancient Egyptian Skin Objects" (p. 260-261).

For a study of leather in ancient Egypt cfr our number 70084.

72591 REISER, Elfriede, Der königliche Harim im alten Ägypten und seine Verwaltung, Wien, Verlag Notring, 1972 (14.5× 20.6 cm; [4+] IV+134 p., 3 plans [1 folded]); series: Dissertationen der Universität Wien 77; rev. *JARCE* 11 (1974), 98-101 (David Lorton); *JNES* 34 (1975), 142-144 (Del Nord).

Pr. ÖS 75

Thesis for a doctor's degree at Vienna (1968).

In the Introduction the author gives a survey of the position of woman in Egypt, stating that only the king had a harem which is an independent institution and an important administrative unit.

Chapter I discusses the various words for harem : *ipt nswt*, the adminstrative-technical term; *pr-ḥnrt*, used in the New Kingdom as the equivalent of *ipt*; *ḥnr*, the collectivy of women in the harem; *ḥkrt-nswt*, possibly "lady in waiting" (compare our number 70409), *špst nswt*, a variant, and *imꜣt*, probably indicating the female dancers and their dwelling.

Chapter II contains the documentation for the existence of a harem, institution as well as building, in the Egyptian history, most documents dating from the New Kingdom. Chapter III describes the remains of these buildings in various palaces : those of Amenophis III at Malqata; of Akhenaton in Amarna; of Eye, represented in the tomb of Neferhotep; and of Ramses III at Medînet Habu.

In chapter IV the administration of the royal harem is discussed : its landed property and cattle, "corn-mills" (*šnʿw*), weavings-sheds, its income and expenses, based on the Pap. Petersburg 1116 A vs., the Pap. Wilbour, the Gurob Papyri and the Decree of Horemheb. The author also discusses the harem as legal body, and its officials : *imy-rꜣ* and *idnw*, the scribes, the *sš pr-ḥḏ* and the *sš wḏḥw*, the controllers and *šʿšꜣw*.

The last chapter deals with the harem as means of connecting royalty with the common world. The *ipt* is not only a harem in a narrower sense, but the totality of women at the court. There the royal children are brought up (*ḥrdw n kp*); there entered the foreign women who came to Egypt either as booty or as presents of foreign rulers — even royal princesses from Mitanni and elsewhere — so that it had a function in diplomacy, as in home policies since the pharaoh presented its inhabitants as wives to his favourites.

In an appendix the author discusses the problem whether there have been eunuchs in ancient Egypt, concluding that there is no proof for their existence.

Summary on p. 118-119; bibliography on p. 121-134.

72592 REVIV, H., Some Comments on the Maryannu, *Israel Exploration Journal*, Jerusalem 22 (1972), 218-228.

The article discusses class structure within the class of *maryannu* and its development during the second half of the second millennium B.C. The Alalakh tablets enable to distinguish between *maryannu* owning a chariot, those without a chariot, and a small number temporarily without one. In Ugarit there is a distinction between "royal *maryannu*" and others, the former probably being those without chariot; hence this seems to be a higher status. Although the rank of *maryannu* was hereditable, this possibly does not apply to the title "royal *maryannu*" nor to all advantages connected with it. Later on the class declined by absorbing socially inferior elements.
The article is published also in Hebrew in *Studies in the History of the Jewish People and the Land of Israel*, vol. 2, Haifa, 1972, 7-23.

72593 REYMOND, E. A. E., The *sꜥḥ* "Eternal Image", *ZÄS* 98,2 (1972), 132-140.

Osiris resides in this form in the necropolis and in the temple; he rejuvenates in his "Eternal Image". The same applies to the Ancestor gods who live and renew their existence in their *sꜥḥ*. The deceased, again, resides in his image thanks to the rays of the sun. The *sꜥḥ* fulfills his revivification. The ritual part played by the Children of Horus is stressed by the author.
An article inspired by our number 72595. *M. Heerma van Voss*

72594 REYMOND, E. A. E., Two Demotic Memoranda, *JEA* 58 (1972), 254-267, with 1 pl.

Papyrus Fitzhugh D.1. (20 × 7.8 cm.) is a farmer's memorandum of Ptolemaic date, with sixteen lines of text remaining, of unknown provenance but by its palaeography from the Siut or Tehne area. P. Fitzhugh D.2. (29 × 7.8 cm.) is a similar memorandum to the overseer of fields Harmenēpe, consisting of twenty lines whose writing suggests the Memphite area. Both are translated and commented on.   *E. Uphill*

72595 REYMOND, E. A. E., Two Versions of the Book of the Dead in the Royal Scottish Museum in Edinburgh, *ZÄS* 98,2 (1972), 125-132, with 2 ill. and 2 hieroglyphic transcriptions.

The author re-publishes and re-studies two hieratic documents edited by Birch, *PSBA* 7 (1885), 79-89. Pap. Edinburgh 212.113. (2) and (3). belonged to the god's father Paiōs-tjenef from (probably) the XXIst Dynasty. (2) contains a parallel of *BD* I B, (3) of *BD* 170 (Pleyte). The texts show a close interconnection. There are no vignettes.   *M. Heerma van Voss*

72596 RIEFSTAHL, Elizabeth, The Alleged Scale Armor of King Sheshonq I in the Brooklyn Museum, *Newsletter ARCE* No. 83 (October 1972), 31.

Abstract of a paper.
The fragment of the scale armour of Sheshonq I in the Brooklyn Museum dates from Roman times. *L. M. J. Zonhoven*

72597 RIEFSTAHL, Elizabeth, An Enigmatic Faience Figure, *Miscellanea Wilbouriana 1*, 137-143, with 5 ill. (1 in colour) and 3 fig.

Study of a headless and battered ithyphallic faience figure of a squatting man (Brooklyn no. 61.384), found at Lisht in a XIIth Dynasty tomb. The decoration indicating a patterned kilt would suggest that it represents a Cretan, though every element of the decoration has a prototype in Egypt. Moreover, the man wears decorated bands across the torso, pointing to the Tehenu or the Nubians. The figure thus certainly represents a foreigner. The gross obscenity, a rare feature in pre-Ptolemaic Egypt, may also point to a foreigner, while an allusion to homosexuality is not excluded.

72598 RIEFSTAHL, Elizabeth, A Figure of a Cretan in the Brooklyn Museum, *Newsletter ARCE* No. 80 (January 1972), 39.

Abstract of a paper. See our preceding number.

72599 RIEFSTAHL, Elizabeth, The Recent History of King Sety's Model with Bibliography, *Miscellanea Wilbouriana 1*, 20-23.

Appendix to our number 72047.
The author relates how William J. Shaw visited Tell el-Yahûdîya shortly before 1875 and there acquired the model. It was brought to the U.S.A. and bought from Shaw's collection by Lieutenant-Commander Gorringe. The model has been published by Émile Brugsch (*Rec. Trav.* 8 [1886], 1-9), but has since been almost forgotten.

72600 RIEFSTAHL, Elizabeth, A Unique Fish-Shaped Glass Vial in the Brooklyn Museum, *Journal of Glass Studies*, Corning, New York 14 (1972), 10-14, with 3 ill. (1 in colour).

Publication of a yellowish glass vessel (Brookl. Mus. Acc. No. 37.316 E) in the form of a *bolti* (*Tilapia nilotica*). The author mentions other fish-shaped glass vessels, stating the present one to be almost unique since it is made of transparent glass and spots and lines of blue glass forming a pattern on the body are applied directly to the core before it was covered with the clear glass. The piece may come from Saqqâra and is to

be dated to the XVIIIth Dynasty. Its function may have been purely magical.
In an appendix Robert H. Brill gives a chemical analysis of the glass.

72601 RIES, J., La Religion de l'Égypte préhistorique. Un état de la question, *Bollettino del Centro Camuno di Studi Preistorici*, Capo di Ponte, Brescia 9 (1972), 103-104.

Report of a lecture.

RINALDI, Celeste, see our number 72461.

72602 ROBE, E. [and] A. BELMANE, Музей зарубежного искусства ЛССР. Путеводитель по отделу искусства древнего Востока, Рига, 1972 (12 × 17 cm; 30 p., ill.   Pr. коп. 20

"Museum für die ausländische Kunst der Lettischen Sovjetischen Sozialistischen Republik. Führer durch die Abteilung des alten Orients" (in Riga).
Ägypten : S. 3-20. Vordynastische Keramik, eine Mumie, Kanopen, ein Sarkophag (Spätzeit), Skarabäen, Shawabtis, Bronzen, Skulptur, Statue von *Mry-rˁ* (veröff. W. Wreszinski, *ZÄS* 67, 1931, 132-133, Abb. IX-X).
Ehemalige Sammlung in Mitau.   *E. S. Bogoslovsky*

ROBICHON, James M., see our numbers 72214 and 72215.

72603 ROCCATI, Alessandro, Une légende égyptienne d'Anat, *RdE* 24 (1972), 152-159, with 1 pl.

Publication d'un fragment de papyrus de Turin (sans numéro) sur lequel sont conservées quelques lignes de la légende d'Anat et de Seth, dont des débris sont connus par le P. Chester Beatty VII, vs 1,5 - 2,3. Les deux documents se complètent et le texte reconstitué permet de conclure que l'aventure se situe dans le Delta oriental et qu'Anat n'est pas la protagoniste de l'histoire comme on l'avait cru. L'auteur fournit une transcription des deux sources et une traduction du texte reconstitué.

Ph. Derchain

72604 ROCCATI, Alessandro, Note lessicali sulle biografie egiziane, *Rivista* 47 (1972), 149-159.

The author examines the auxiliary use of the participle of *ìì* "to come" in phrases such as *ìw ḥꜣy* "who has come naked". This participle corresponds to the relative particles *nty* and *iwty* used in other versions of the same phrase *(ìw dì.n.ì ḥbsw n nty ḥꜣw, dì.n.ì ... tbw n iwty sw)*; similar substitutes are formed with the help of *gmì* "to find".
As clothes (*ḥbsw*) and sandals (*ṯbw*) are the essential parts of

any attire, they are often listed together, and the lacuna in Pap. Chester Beatty V rt. 7,1 can be restored *iw.f [dgȝy] nn wn t(b)wy*.   *Dieter Mueller*

ROCCATI, Alessandro, see also our number 72710.

72605   ROQUET, Gérard, Sur l'origine d'un hapax en vieux-Nubien :

ⲧⲟϧⲟⲛⲁⲉ < Copte : (ⲧ +)ϧⲉⲛⲉⲧⲉ < Égyptien : *ḥwt-nṯr* 𓉐 ?, *BIFAO* 71 (1972), 97-118, with 1 chart.

Das im altnubischen Kreuzeshymnus vorkommende Wort ⲧⲟϧⲟⲛⲁⲉ, bisher versuchsweise als "Tempel", "(heidn.) Altar" übersetzt, leitet sich vielleicht über das Koptische vom altägyptischen *ḥwt-nṯr* her, während das altnubische Synonym ⲁⲣⲫⲁⲉ, "Tempel", über das koptische ⲉⲣⲫⲉⲓ vom alt-ägyptischen 𓉐 abgeleitet wird.   *Inge Hofmann*

ROQUET, Gérard, see also our number 72399.

72606   ROSENVASSER, A., The Stela Aksha 505 and the Cult of Ramesses II as a God in the Army, *Revista del Instituto de Historia Antigua Oriental*, Buenos Aires 1 (1972), 99-114, with 1 pl. and 8 fig.

(Referat, gehalten auf dem XXVII. Internationalen Orienta-listenkongreß von Ann Arbor, Michigan 1967). Die kleine Sandsteinstele (45×33 cm) wurde 1962 von der Franco-Argentinischen Expedition in Akscha gefunden, im Vorhof des Tempels. Ein in Soldatentracht einmal als Standar-tenträger, das andere Mal als Wedelträger abgebildeter Mann namens *Wp-wȝwt* hatte sie dem falkenköpfigen, mit der Sonnen-scheibe gekrönten *Rʿ-mssw mrj-Jmn* und dem rein menschen-gestaltigen, ebenfalls mit Sonnenscheibe dargestellten *Jmn n Wsr-mȝʿt-Rʿ Stp-n-Rʿ* geweiht. *Wp-wȝwt* oblag es allem Anschein, als Standartenträger in der Garnison von Akscha zugleich beim lokalen Kult Ramses' II. als Wedelträger zu fungieren.
                                                    I. Gamer-Wallert

72607   ROSENVASSER, A. and P. FUSCALDO, Las piezas egipcias del Museo Etnográfico de Buenos Aires [Primera parte]. I. El Papiro Buenos Aires Sinuhe B 251-6. II. Las aventuras de Sinuhe : el pasaje B. 251-257 y el papiro Buenos Aires. A propósito de H. Grapow, "Der stilistische Bau der Geschichte des Sinuhe", 1952. III. El papiro funerario de Khonsu-Thot (Frags. 2 y 3). IV. El papiro funerario de Khonsu-Thot (Frag. 1). V. El ataúd de Amenardis, *Revista del Instituto de Historia Antigua Oriental*, Buenos Aires 1 (1972), 5-97, with 5 fig. and 3 pl.

Die Völkerkundliche Sammlung der Philosophischen Fakultät der Universität von Buenos Aires besitzt mehrere Aegyptiaca, darunter einen Sarg sowie Reste von zwei weiteren, 5 Ushebti, 7 Statuetten, eine Totenmaske, Tiermumien und Reste von zwei Papyri. Letztere und der wohlerhaltene Sarg werden ausführlich behandelt.

Der bekanntere der beiden Papyri, der sog. Papyrus Buenos Aires, enthält einige Zeilen der Audienz des heimkehrenden Sinuhe im kgl. Palast (B 251-256), nach Meinung des Verf.s eine etwas ältere Fassung als Papyrus Berlin 3022. Bei dem zweiten Papyrus handelt es sich um drei Fragmente des Totenbuches eines *Ḫnsw-Dḥwtj*, Teile von Kap. 18 und 117 sowie von der Vignette zu Kap. 148. Der hölzerne Sarg anthropoider Form war für eine *Jmn-jr-djs*, Tochter des *Ns-pꜣ-hꜣ* und der *Jrt-rw* bestimmt. Die Herkunft der Stücke ist unbekannt.

I. Gamer-Wallert

72608 ROSSINI, Lucia, Un frammento di un gruppo statuario rappresentante la dea Mut, *Rivista* 47 (1972), 161-169, with 2 pl. and 1 fig.

Le Musée de Turin conserve la partie supérieure droite d'un groupe de calcaire. Un dieu momiforme à coiffure lunaire y figurait en bas-relief, entre la déesse debout, portant une perruque tripartite et un pschent, et le dieu disparu à sa gauche. Il doit donc s'agir de la triade thébaine. Le buste de Mout donne une impression de vérité et d'élégance. Le revers du groupe portait une stèle à sommet arrondi. Le tableau qui la surmonte représentait au milieu la scarabée ailé tenant le soleil, et sur les deux côtés le "Père divin Mosé" en adoration. Le texte disposé en colonnes est de nature funéraire, et montre nombre de parallèles avec une grande stèle d'Abydos. L'analyse de la pièce engage à dater celle-ci de la XIXe dynastie; le style permet peut-être de la situer plus précisément sous le règne de Séthi Ier.

J. Custers

72609 ROTHENBERG, Beno, Timna. Valley of the Biblical Copper Mines, [London], Thames and Hudson, [1972] (18.5 × 24.5 cm; 248 p., 77 fig. [including maps and plans], 72 pl. [8 in colour] containing 153 ill. [25 in colour]; series: New Aspects of Antiquity; rev. (American edition) *AJA* 78 (1974), 299-300 (Prentiss S. de Jesus); (German edition) *Antike Welt* 5, Heft 2 (1974), 55 (anonymous); *BiOr* 30 (1973), 338 (anonymous); (English edition) *Man* 8 (1973), 643-644 (M. C. Quinnell); *Palestine Exploration Quarterly* 105 (1973), 174-175 (Crystal-

M. Bennett); *Phoenix* 19 (1973), 268-271 (K. R. Veenhof); *Qadmoniot* 6 (1973), 131-132 (A. Kempinski).   Pr. cloth £6

After a preface by Sir Mortimer Wheeler and the author's introduction chapter I describes the Timna valley and the excavation campaigns. Chapter 2 discusses the chalcolithic copper industry of the 4th mill. B.C., while chapter 3 is devoted to the mines, smelting places and settlements of the Ramesside Period. All kinds of remains have been discovered, slag heaps, water reservoirs, magazines, furnaces, houses and burial places. The excavations of one site (site 2, N.W. of Har Timna) are extensively described. Among the finds, apart from some camel bones, particularly the ceramics are of importance. Three different kinds occur in the same period, one of which now called Midianite. They are connected with the sanctuaries and rock drawings discussed in chapter 4, and with the Hathor temple dealt with in chapter 5.

The temple, built of a white sandstone not found in this region, was first erected under Sethi I, possibly on the place of a preceding sanctuary. The naos, leaning against the wall of the "Pillar of Solomon", may have contained a Hathor statue and a small sphinx, remains of which were discovered in the neighbourhood. There were also Hathor pillars in the temple, and incense altars. The building is quite similar to that in Serabît el-Khadîm. At an unknown moment it was destroyed, and rebuilt under Ramses III, while an earthquake put an end to this second building. Afterwards the place was used for a tent sanctuary by the Midianites.

Among the over 10,000 small finds there are : a hoard of iron and copper ornaments, faience objects, etc., and a faience mask of Hathor. Inscriptions are found of almost every ruler of the XIXth and XXth Dynasties down to Ramses V.

In chapter 6 the author discusses the meaning of the discoveries for the archaeology and history of the Negev. The Egyptian name of Timna may have been Atika (cfr Pap. Harris I, 78, 2). The existence of the sea-route here mentioned is possibly confirmed by a recently discovered inscription of the name of Ramses III near Elath, and the discovery of a harbour on Gezîret el-Fara'ûn, an island in the neighbourhood of Elath.

Chapters 7 and 8 deal with Roman and Arabian mining activities, and chapter 9 presents a survey of 6000 years copper metallurgy in the Arabah.

The volume is lavishly illustrated by maps and plans, drawings and photographs. Bibliography on p. 240-242; indexes p. 246-248. There is also a German edition : Timna. Das Tal der biblischen Kupferminen, [Bergisch Gladbach], Gustav Lübbe Verlag, [1973].

72610 ROULLET, Anne, The Egyptian and Egyptianizing Monuments
of Imperial Rome, Leiden, E. J. Brill, 1972 (15.7 × 23.8 cm;
XVI + 184 p., 230 pl. containing 346 maps, fig. and ill., 3 folding
plans) = Études préliminaires aux religions orientales dans
l'empire romain publiées par M. J. Vermaseren, 20; rev. *Acta
Archaeologica Academiae Scientiarum Hungaricae* 25 (1973),
424 (L. Castiglione); *Aegyptus* 52 (1972), 207-208 (S. Curto).
Pr. cloth fl. 160

The main part of the book consists of a catalogue of 333 Egyptian
and Egyptianized objects known to have been present at Rome
in the time of the Empire, though of some the present
whereabouts are unknown. Each of them is described with the
technical data, if available, and a bibliography, while the
majority of them is represented on the plates either by
photographs or by old drawings or engravings.
The objects consist of several categories : architectural elements,
obelisks and pyramids, statues of divinities, of kings and queens,
and of private individuals, zoomorphic sculpture (Apis bulls,
baboons, crocodiles, falcons, etc.) and various objects such as
canopic jars and cippi.
To this material the author presents an introduction in the first
three chapters. Chapter 1 deals with the historical conditions
under which the objects came to Rome or were there made,
the influence of Egyptian cults, the destruction of the city by
which the sight of the monuments was lost, as well as their
later history through the Renaissance, until the early
19th century.
Chapter 2 discusses the style and type of the monuments. Most
genuine objects came from the Delta and are relatively
contemporary objects, though some obelisks date from the
New Kingdom. Part of the imports was taken at random or
from famous sites, but others may have been selected by
Isis priests. The copies seem to have been made in Rome itself
by Egyptian craftsmen, while in Hadrian's time the second
generation has lost the skill and style of their fathers.
Chapter 3 is devoted to the setting of the monuments in
imperial Rome : the Iseums, particularly the Iseum Campense,
other temples, tombs with pyramids, obelisks in circuses and
elsewhere, gardens and villas, e.g. the Gardens of Sallust and
Hadrian's villa at Tivoli.
At the end (p. 149-158) four appendixes listing : I. Egyptian
monuments visible at Rome in the Middle Ages; II. Egyptian
antiquities in Rome in the 15th/16th century; III. the monuments
exported from Egypt; and IV. those created in Rome itself.
There follow (p. 159-174) important captions to the figures on
the plates, and indexes (175-184).

72611 RUBINSHTEIN, R.J., Выставка памятников письменности древнего Египта. К 150-летию дешифровки египетских иероглифов франсуа Шампольоном, Москва, Главная редакция восточной литературы издательства "Наука", 1972 (14.4 × 21.4 cm; 8 p., 4 pl.). At head of title: Государственный музей изобразительных искусств имени А. С. Пушкина.
Pr. коп. 20

"Ausstellung der Denkmäler des alten Ägyptens. Zum 150. Geburtstag der Entzifferung der ägyptischen Hieroglyphen von François Champollion". (nicht gesehen).

72612 RUFFLE, John, "Out of the Land of Egypt..." and into the City of Birmingham, *Warwickshire & Worcestershire Life*, Leamington Spa-Manchester 19, No. 1 (March 1972), 39, with 4 ill.

Recent acquisitions of the Birmingham City and Art Gallery which came from the excavations at Saqqâra.

72613 RYDER, M.L., Wool of the 14th Century B.C. from Tell el-Amarna, Egypt, *Nature*, London/Washington 240 (1972), 355-356, with 1 fig. and 1 table.

The author has examined samples of wool from the temple stores of el-'Amarna, offering a highly technical description of their characteristics. The wool appears to have been cut off with a knife, shears not yet having been invented.

SA'AD, Ramadan, see our numbers 72030, 72405 and 72629.

SÄVE-SÖDERBERGH, Torgny, see our number 72528.

72614 SAFFIRIO, Luigi, L'alimentazione umana nell'antico Egitto, IV. Età storica o dinastica, *Aegyptus* 52 (1972), 19-66.

Suite de nos nᵒˢ 65426 et 66515. Un préambule rend compte des derniers enrichissements de nos connaissances pour l'époque préhistorique. Cette fois l'étude englobe les dynasties thinites, l'Ancien Empire et la 1ère Période Intermédiaire.
L'unification administrative permet d'agir sur la crue : digues et canaux se sont développés en un réseau d'irrigation. La productivité agricole s'accroît fortement. D'autres facteurs la favorisent, notamment les techniques d'agriculture intensive et les larges disponibilités de main d'œuvre. Les céréales principales demeurent le blé et l'orge. Parmi les résidus végétaux retrouvés figurent les fruits du mimusops, du sycomore, du jujubier et du dattier. Les conditions favorables à l'élevage se situaient dans le Delta, ainsi que le gros de ce patrimoine. Mais la viande ne pouvait constituer un aliment courant. Le lait et le fromage apparaissent très tôt. On conservait aussi la graisse animale

fondue; les huiles végétales restaient d'un usage limité. L'industrie boulangère était variée et le brassage de bière non amère, à base de pain, dépaissait de loin l'activité qui produisait, dans les grands domaines, des vins de raisin, de palme et de datte. La chasse était devenue un sport, mais la pêche en eau douce se pratiquait à grande échelle; l'aviculture est bien attestée. Le commerce extérieur, très florissant lors de l'apogée memphite, laisse supposer une forte exportation de céréales, dirigée surtout vers la Méditerranée. Mais des investissements improductifs, comme ceux destinés aux immenses nécropoles, entraînaient un important gaspillage. La décadence proviendrait de la crise des finances publiques. Les *Admonitions* reflètent la perte de terres cultivables, la famine généralisée, bref une régression par rapport à l'époque prédynastique.
Voir depuis: (alimentation) Henry de Morant, *Archeologia* No 61 (1973), 64-71. *J. Custers*

72615 SAFFIRIO, L., Food and Dietary Habits in Ancient Egypt, *Journal of Human Evolution*, London and New York 1 (1972), 297-305.

The first part, dealing with the Prehistoric Period, summarizes the results of the author's study published before (see our numbers 65426 and 66515).
The second part, on the dynastic times, discusses the diet of the Old Kingdom; of the upper classes in the New Kingdom as it can be reconstructed from the contents of the tomb of Kha; food in the workmen's village of Deir el-Medîna; military rations, and those of a body of quarrymen. The investigation is exclusively based on actual remains of food and containers and on representations, not on texts.
Reprinted in: Population Biology of the Ancient Egyptians. Edited by D. R. Brothwell [and] B. A. Chiarelli, London and New York, Academic Press, 1973.

72616 SALAMÉ-SARKIS, Hassan, Ardata — Ardé dans le Liban-Nord. Une nouvelle cité cananéenne identifiée, *Mélanges de l'Université Saint-Joseph*, Beyrouth 47 (1972), 121-145, with 1 map, 1 plan, 11 fig., 8 pl. (one folding).

The author deals with the history and archaeology of Ardeh (Ardata), an important city in Northern Lebanon during the second half of the second millennium B.C., situated 16 km S.E. of Tripolis. On p. 127-132 a survey of its role during the XVIIIth Dynasty and the Amarna Period. It also occurs in the "letter of the general" (cfr our number 71115).

72617 SALEH, Abdel-Aziz, The *Gnbtyw* of Tuthmosis III's Annals
and the South Arabian *Geb(b)anitae* of the Classical Writers,
BIFAO 72 (1972), 245-262.

Proceeding from a sentence in the annals of Tuthmosis III
(*Urk.* IV, 659, 5-7) the author discusses earlier identifications
of the *Gnbtyw* and the theories concerning the localisation of
the aromatic-producing countries. He also points out the
information of classical authors on the Gebbanitae, a South
Arabian people the relations of which with the historical
Qatabians is still obscure, as is also the origin of the Qataban
state. Hence the author cannot offer more than hypotheses
about the *Gnbtyw* delegation to Tuthmosis III.
In an appendix Saleh deals with some tomb-pictures of the
delegations from the South-Eastern incense-producing countries
to Egypt, and makes remarks on the well known passage of
Pap. Harris I, 77,8.

72618 SALEH, Abdel-Aziz, Some Problems Relating to the Pwenet
Reliefs at Deir el-Baḥari, *JEA* 58 (1972), 140-158.

An analysis of certain problems connected with the Hatshepsut
scenes and inscriptions, and the possible connections with the
Gebbanitic Qatabanian Arabs in Egypt during the reign of
Tuthmosis III. In the annals of year 31-32 the coming of the
Gnbtyw envoys (?) with rich gifts is recorded. Under Flora the
writer suggests that it and all the fauna shown in these scenes
is almost entirely tropical and to be located on the Red Sea
between the Eritreas and Somalia, *snṯr* being incense, *'ntyw*
resin (?) and *ihmt* perhaps balsam. Following Vycichl *iwdnb* can
be equated with South Arabian laudan-um. The population of
Punt had gold and Parehu the chief of the country had a dagger
possibly suggesting the Yemen area, but the Puntites may have
had cause to fear Egyptian penetration of S. Arabia as a threat
to their own trade relations.   *E. Uphill*

72619 SAMSON, Julia, Amarna. City of Akhenaten and Nefertiti.
Key Pieces from the Petrie Collection. With an Introduction
by Professor H. S. Smith, London, Published for the Depart-
ment of Egyptology, University College [by Aris and Phillips
Ltd], [1972] (21.5 × 30.5 cm; X + 110 p., 2 maps, 1 plan, 5 fig.,
72 ill., 8 colour ill. [on p. 64 and 69]); rev. *BiOr* 30 (1973), 231
(Bengt J. Peterson); *CdE* XLVIII, No. 95 (1973), 92-95 (Pierre
Gilbert); *The Connoisseur* 183, No. 738 (August 1973), 316-317
(R. J. L. Wynne-Thomas); *JEA* 60 (1974), 267-268 (Geoffrey
Martin).   Pr. cloth £ 8

The purpose of this book is to illustrate and discuss the finest works from Amarna in the Petrie Museum in the Department of Egyptology at University College London.

In the Introduction H. S. Smith discusses the history of the Amarna Period, pointing out the various unsolved questions, and presents a description of the site of el-Amarna.

Miss Samson first discusses the significance of the collection, the great majority of the objects being from Petrie's excavation in 1891-1892 in and around the Great Palace and the Great Temple. She mentions various features of the Amarna art, quoting pieces of the collection.

The catalogue itself begins with the statues and statuettes, among which a "Royal Trio" and a famous female statuette (Nefertiti or a princess?). There follows a note on monkey statuettes. Then successively are studied the reliefs, arranged in chronological order according to the style; the inlays; glass; faience and moulds; and a few inscriptions. Each piece is carefully discussed with full reference to the data such as provenance, material, etc. There are clear photographs for every object as well as some from other collections for reason of comparison. At the end a chronological table and an index.

72620 SANDARS, N. K., Thirty Seasons at Ras Shamra in Syria, *Levant*, London 4 (1972), 139-146.

This article, a review of *Ugaritica*, Paris 6 (1969) discusses among other articles our numbers 69139 (Galling) and 69552 (Schachermeyr).

72621 SANDISON, A. T., Evidence of Infective Disease, *Journal of Human Evolution*, London and New York 1 (1972), 213-224.

Critical discussion of the possibilities to discover evidence of infective diseases in ancient Egypt.

Reprinted in : Population Biology of the Ancient Egyptians. Edited by D. R. Brothwell [and] B.A. Chiarelli, London and New York, Academic Press, 1973.

72622 SATINOFF, Merton Ian, The Medical Biology of the Early Egyptian Populations from Asswan, Assyut and Gebelen, *Journal of Human Evolution*, London and New York 1 (1972), 247-257, with 10 pl. and 2 tables.

Survey of the palaeopathology of the ancient Egyptian skeletal collection in the Institute of Anthropology at Turin. The material, 1300 skulls and 650 skeletons from dynastic times and 59 skeletons from the Predynastic Period, came from Aswân, Asyût and Gebelein. The author i.a. stresses the need to correlate the results of the investigation with certain environmental data such as the daily food.

Reprinted in : Population Biology of the Ancient Egyptians. Edited by D. R. Brothwell [and] B. A. Chiarelli, London and New York, Academic Press, 1973.

72623 SATINOFF, Merton I., Study of the Squatting Facets of the Talus and Tibia in Ancient Egyptians, *Journal of Human Evolution*, London and New York 1 (1972), 209-212, with 2 pl. and 1 fig.

Description of the results of a study of squatting facets of the talus and tibia of 300 male and female skeletons preserved in the Institute of Anthropology at Turin.
Reprinted in : Population Biology of the Ancient Egyptians. Edited by D. R. Brothwell [and] B. A. Chiarelli, London and New York, Academic Press, 1973.

72624 SATZINGER, Helmut, Koptische Papyrus-Fragmente des Wiener Kunsthistorischen Museums, *CdE* XLVII, Nos 93-94 (1972), 343-350.

Among the Coptic fragments recently acquired by the Wiener Kunsthistorisches Museum are : a Greek-Coptic glossary, a list of personal and topographical names; a list of numbers and dates; and an amulet. They are here transcribed, with brief comments.

72625 SATZINGER, Helmut, Zu den koptischen Menander-Sentenzen, *CdE* XLVII, Nos 93-94 (1972), 351-354.

Some remarks and notes to the text published in our number 68259.

72626 SATZINGER, Helmut, Zur Phonetik des Bohairischen und des Ägyptisch-Arabischen im Mittelalter, *WZKM* 63/64 (1972), 40-65.

From the study of two texts from the 13th century A.D., one written in the Arabic language but in the Coptic script, the other in the Bohairic dialect and in Arabic script, the author draws some conclusions as to the sounds of both Bohairic and Arabic in that period.

72627 SAUNERON, Serge, Une description égyptienne du caméléon, *RdE* 24 (1972), 160-164, with 1 fig.

Dans le P. Brooklyn 47.218.48 + .85,2,15-16, figure une description très précise d'un animal nommé ⊔ı⟨⟩ı𓏘, inconnu jusqu'ici, qui n'est autre que le caméléon.
L'auteur rassemble à son sujet une série d'observations d'anciens voyageurs qui montrent l'intérêt suscité par ce curieux saurien.
Ph. Derchain

72628 SAUNERON, Serge, Les travaux de l'Institut français
d'Archéologie orientale en 1971-1972, *BIFAO* 71 (1972), 189-230,
with 18 pl.

Report of the director of the French Institute at Cairo
offering a survey of the activities. We mention : excavations at
Karnak North (cfr our number 72335); work by Miss Letellier
on the blocks in the open air museum at Karnak; various
activities at Deir el-Medîna (taking photographs of the tomb
walls; publication of the papyri; study on various kinds of
objects); work on the temple of Dendera; publication of the
Demotic codex of Tûna el-Gebel, prepared by Girgis Mattha;
various studies regarding Coptic and Islamic Egypt, as well as
publications of the Institute, particularly the series "Voyageurs
occidentaux en Égypte".

72629 SAUNERON, Serge et Ramadan SA'AD, Travaux au IXe pylône
de Karnak en 1968-1970, *Kêmi* 21 (1971), 145-150, with 2 fig.
and 3 folding plans.

Suite de notre No 69547. D'octobre 1968 à juin 1970, on a
procédé au démontage des assises 12 à 15. Au fur et à mesure
on a exécuté le relevé horizontal de chaque assise, la
numérotation des pierres, le dessin des faces principales, enfin
le lavage, la photographie et l'empreinte des faces décorées.
La 12e assise, seule encore divisée en caissons, comprenait de
gros blocs de contre-parement. Plus bas, le poids accru des
blocs a accentué les différences de niveau. La remontée des
eaux par capillarité a fort dégradé la 15e assise. Un tableau
donne les nombres totaux de blocs des assises 11 à 15 et
ceux des blocs décorés, avec leurs numéros respectifs.
Voir aussi Daniel et Manniche, notres nos 72166 et 72460.

J. Custers

SAUNERON, Serge, see also our numbers 72405 and 72433.

72630 SAVEL'EVA, T.N. and K.F. SMIRNOFF, Ближневосточные
древности на Южном Урале, *ВДИ* 3 (121), 1972, 106-123,
with 10 ill., 3 fig., 1 map and an English summary on p. 122-123.

"Near Eastern Antiquities in the South Urals".
Among the objects dealt with there is the Egyptian alabaster
vessel found near Orsk (from the 5th or early 4th century B.C.)
with cuneiform inscriptions and in hieroglyphs the words
"Artaxerxes the Great King" (p. 106-113, with fig. 2 and 3).

72631 el-SAYED, Ramadan, Documents relatifs à Sais et ses divinités.
Recherches complémentaires, *Annuaire. École Pratique des*

Hautes Études. Vᵉ section - sciences religieuses, Paris 79 (1971-1972), 447.

Additions to our number 69549.

72632 SCANLON, George T., Excavations at Kasr el-Wizz. A Preliminary Report. II, *JEA* 58 (1972), 7-42, with 26 fig., a plan and 18 pl.

Sequel to our number 70487.
A plan is given of the enlarged church and early monastery whose architectural history is discussed between the years A.D. 850-950, and it is now certain that there were at least two building periods. As enlarged the early buildings measured about 54.5 m × 28.5 m and detailed descriptions are given of some of the parts. One significant difference between Wizz and the normal Nubia-Egyptian monastery entrances was the lack of a 'tower-keep' or a 'windlass' leading to upper levels, thus showing the lack of need for fortified constructions. Photographs and drawings are included of pottery and many important objects including pages (illuminated) from a fine prayer book discovered in one cell. *E. Uphill*

72633 SCHADEN, Otto, Tutankhamon and Ay Blocks from Karnak, *Newsletter ARCE* No. 80 (January 1972), 39-40.

Abstract of a paper.
On 70 blocks from a temple or shrine of Tutankhamon and Ay at Karnak. *L. M. J. Zonhoven*

72634 SCHENKEL, Wolfgang, Meroitisches und Barya-Verb : Versuch einer Bestimmung der Tempusbildung des Meroitischen, *MNL* No 11 (Décembre 1972), 1-16.

Anhand von drei meroitischen historischen Texten wurde mit Hilfe einer experimentellen Segmentierung versucht, die Texte derart in Sätze zu zerlegen, daß die Wortformen in Satzendposition in wenige Klassen mit möglichst vielen Mitgliedern vergleichbar strukturierter Segmente zerfielen. Die so gewonnenen, vermutlich verbalen Morpheme wurden mit Morphemen der Barya-Verbalflexion gleichgesetzt und auf diese Weise (wiederum vermutliche) Tempussuffixe herausgearbeitet. *Inge Hofmann*

72635 SCHENKEL, Wolfgang, Zur Fortführung des Projektes M.A.A.T. in Göttingen, *GM* Heft 2 (1972), 33-36.

The computer program for the analysis of Egyptian texts, formerly located in Darmstadt, will be continued in Göttingen and adjusted to the more modern technical equipment now available. *Dieter Mueller*

72636 SCHENKEL, Wolfgang, Zur Relevanz der altägyptischen "Metrik", *MDAIK* 28 (1972), 103-107.

The author briefly describes the principles and main elements of ancient Egyptian metrics, and raises the question whether this term is applicable to the prosodic structure of Egyptian literature. *Dieter Mueller*

72637 SCHENKEL, Wolfgang and Bernd SLEDZIANOWSKI, Ein chronologischer Fixpunkt für die Kunstgeschichte der zweiten Zwischenzeit Ägyptens : *Sbk-m-zꜣw=f*, *GM* Heft 3 (1972), 21-24.

The famous statue of Sobekemzaf in Vienna (Kunsthistorisches Museum Inv. No. 5801) must belong to the XVIIth Dynasty, because his sister Nebukhais (Louvre Stela C. 13) was the wife of King Sekhem-re-shedy-tawy Sobekemzaf II.
Compare also : Helmut Satzinger, *GM* Heft 5 (1973), 17-20, and Günther Vittmann, *GM* Heft 5 (1973), 39-42 and *GM* Heft 10 (1974), 41-44. *Dieter Mueller*

72638 SCHENKEL, Wolfgang and Bernd SLEDZIANOWSKI, Horus "Flügelsonne", der Superheld, *GM* Heft 3 (1972), 25-30.

The authors discover a profound similarity between the Horus myth of Edfou and modern Comic Strips. *Dieter Mueller*

SCHENKEL, Wolfgang, see also our numbers 72355 and 72396.

72639 SCHIFF GIORGINI, Michela, Storia e scavi del Tempio di Soleb, *Studi classici e orientali*, Pisa 21 (1972), 7-22.

Der Vortrag ist eine Art Rechenschaftsbericht über die vierzehn-jährige Ausgrabungstätigkeit der Verf. im Sudan. Seit 1957 wurde in Soleb und seit 1963 in Sedeinga, 15 km von Soleb entfernt, gearbeitet. Es wird nicht nur über den Sedfesttempel Amenophis' III. ausführlich berichtet, in dem Amun von Theben und der König selbst (*Nb mꜣꜥt Rꜥ*, Herr von Nubien, großer Gott, Herr des Himmels) verehrt wurden, sondern auch über die Gräber, so über das berühmte Taharqa-Grab sowie die meroitischen Funde in Soleb und Sedeinga. Die Methoden der Ausgrabung und Dokumentation werden dargelegt; die Publikation von Soleb ist in sechs Bänden geplant (zu den bereits erschienenen Werken vgl. unsere Nr. 65444 und 71510). *Inge Hofmann*

72640 [SCHLÖGL, E.], Aegyptische Kunstwerke aus Zürcher Privat-besitz, *in* : *Antike und Orient. Eine Literaturauswahl*, Zürich, Buchhandlung Libresso, [1972], 41-50, with 17 ill.

In this catalogue of a book-shop there are represented and described seventeen Egyptian objects of art, some of which are unpublished. We mention a bronze statuette of a queen from the Late Period (XXIInd Dynasty) and a wooden statuette of a standing man from the late Old Kingdom.

72641 SCHMIDT, Gerd, De Aegypto : Ezra Pound und das ägyptische Totenbuch, *Arcadia*. Zeitschrift für vergleichende Literatur-wissenschaft, Berlin 6 (1971), 297-301.

Verfasser weist nach, daß Pound beim Schreiben des Gedichtes "De Aegypto" ganze Passagen wörtlich von Budge, *The Book of the Dead*. The Chapters on Coming Forth by Day (ed. 1898) übernommen hat. Jedoch, mit der "Substanz" des Totenbuches hat Pounds Gedicht kaum etwas gemein.   *Erhart Graefe*

72642 SCHNEIDER, Hans D., Egyptische Kunst, *Vista*, Driehuis (N.H.) 3 (1972), 8-15 and 4 (1972), 12-18, with 7 ill.

The author briefly describes the most important factors which have defined the Egyptian art, such as the landscape, the role of Maat, the negation of the death, art as a craft, and he characterizes the Egyptian style.
Vista is the two-monthly paper of the "Stichting van Amateur Beeldende Kunstenaars Verenigingen in Nederland (F.A.B.K.)"; address : Van Lenneplaan 10, Driehuis (N.H.).

72643 [SCHNEIDER, Hans D.], Je tiens l'affaire! 14 september 1822. 150 jaar geleden ontcijferde Champollion le Jeune de Egyptische Hiëroglyphen, [Leiden, Rijksmuseum van Oudheden, 1972] (21.2 × 29.7 cm.; 24 p., 1 pl., ill. on cover).

Explanatory text in Dutch to an exhibition on account of the 150th anniversary of Champollion's decipherment of the hieroglyphs.
In three chapters the author presents a survey of Champollion's life, the decipherment itself, and the contents of the Stone of Rosetta, while a fourth chapter deals with the relations between Champollion and the Netherlands, particularly Reuvens, the founder of the Leiden Museum.
Bibliography on p. 24.

72644 SCHNEIDER, H. D., Jonge wetenschap in oud museum, *De Ibis*, Amsterdam 3 (1972), 80-86 and 120-122, with 8 fig.

"Young science in Old Museum".
A description of the history of the Egyptian collection in the Museum of Antiquities at Leiden for the general public.
Continued in vol. 4 (1973), 16-24.

72645 SCHNEIDER, H. D., Nederlandse opgravingen in Egypte, *Spiegel Historiael* 479-483, with 6 ill. and 1 fig.

"Dutch excavations in Egypt".

The author shortly sketches the history of Egyptian archaeology, new trends in methodology and present activities of several countries. He describes the results of Dutch excavations during several campaigns : those at Abu Roash, which were concerned with Early Dynastic tombs and yielded rich material, those at Shokan near Abu Simbel, where a Meroitic village was discovered, and those at Coptic Abdallah Nirqi.
At the end a few words are devoted to the Dutch Institute, opened in 1971, and the excavations in Sakkara in cooperation with the Egypt Exploration Society.   *L. M. J. Zonhoven*

SCHOONOVER, Kermit, see our number 72124.

72646 SCHOTT, Erika, Bücher und Bibliotheken im alten Ägypten, *GM* Heft 1 (1972), 24-26.

The author provides information about a book under this title prepared by her late husband, Prof. Siegfried Schott.

72647 SCHOTT, Erika, Das Goldhaus in der ägyptischen Frühzeit, *GM* Heft 2 (1972), 37-41.

The examination of several seals and tablets of the Early Dynastic Period suggests that the so-called "Gold House" was an administrative agency of the royal palace in Buto, controlling the expenditure of beverages, cattle, and especially oil. The author concludes that the Egyptian word for "gold" was originally not confined to a specific precious metal, but had a more general meaning such as "valuables" or even "legal tender".
See our following number.   *Dieter Mueller*

72648 SCHOTT, Erika, Das Goldhaus unter König Snofru, *GM* Heft 3 (1972), 31-36, with 5 fig.

The author proposes a new restoration of a fragmentary scene from Snofru's Valley Temple at Dahshur, showing a procession around the Gold House. The references to religious ceremonies on various fragments of the Palermo Stone suggest that this procession was connected with the Apis bull, and not yet part of the Opening of the Mouth which appears under King Cheops.   *Dieter Mueller*

72649 SCHOTT †, Siegfried, Thoth als Verfasser heiliger Schriften, *ZÄS* 99,1 (1972), 20-25.

Als Autor heiliger Schriften hat man Thoth bisher nur an

Quellen griechisch-römischer Zeit nachgewiesen. Vielleicht kennt schon das Neue Reich diesen Gott als Verfasser.

M. Heerma van Voss

72650 SCHWAB-SCHLOTT, Adelheid, Altägyptische Texte über die Ausmaße Ägyptens, *MDAIK* 28 (1972), 109-113, with 6 pl.

The author supplements her dissertation about the dimensions of Egypt (our No. 69555) with the publication of photos of six of the cubit rods used there, and adds another text referring to the distance between Elephantine and the Fifteenth Upper Egyptian nome (Theb. Tomb No. 196). The latter presupposes a length of 12.8 km for the *itrw*, confirming the data supplied by P. dem. Heidelberg 1289.   *Dieter Mueller*

72651 SEGER, Joe D., Shechem Field XIII, 1969, *BASOR* No. 205 (February, 1972), 20-35, with 3 plans, 3 ill. and 1 fig.

That the city of Shechem was in the hands of the Egyptians around 1550 B.C., is reconfirmed on account of the finds of scarabs and scarab impressions, and the pottery repertoire.

L.M.J. Zonhoven

72652 SEGER, Joe D., Tomb Offerings from Gezer, [Jerusalem], The Rockefeller Museum, 1972 (18 × 21 cm.; 11 + 6 p., 26 pl. [3 in colour], 1 map, 1 loose plan in colour, fig. on endpapers and cover).

Catalogue in English and Hebrew of an exhibition of the finds made during the Hebrew Union College Excavations at Gezer. We mention a number of scarabs and an Egyptian glass vessel as well as objects in Egyptian style such as a knife blade and an ivory comb. Some of these are depicted on the plates.

SEIDEL, Mathias, see our number 72687.

72653 SEIDL, Erwin, Die Verrechnung und die Kompensation in den juristischen demotischen Papyri, *RdE* 24 (1972), 165-168.

Le terme démotique *'p* que l'on rencontre fréquemment dans des documents fiscaux (A) et des contrats (B) signifie exactement :
en A, "porter en compte, enregister un payement";
en B, "compenser, i.e. déduire d'une dette une autre dette du créancier envers le débiteur".   *Ph. Derchain*

72654 SELEM, Petar, Egipatski bogovi u rimskom Iliriku, *Akademija nauka i umjetnosti Bosne i Hercegovine, Godišnjak IX, Centar za balkanološka ispitivanja*, Sarajevo 7 (1972), 5-95, with a French summary on p. 95-104.

"Egyptian Gods in Roman Illyricum".

Plastic arts and epigraphic monuments, which indicate the spreading of deities of Egyptian origin in Illyricum from the 1st to the 4th century A.D., have been collected and interpreted. For the statuettes in Egyptian style compare our numbers 66542 and 71524. The inscriptions and their syncretistic character, first of all concerning Isis, Serapis and Jupiter-Amon have been studied. The Isis cult was first to appear; it was the most widespread up to the line of Severus, when the leading role was taken over by Serapis. According to the presented hypotheses, Isis' early appearance among the Liburni was due to democratization and similarity of her cult to autochthonous cults. The main transmitters were custom-house officers, then Roman functionaries, citizens etc. Aquileia was the most significant centre, through which these beliefs were penetrating into the Western parts of Illyricum. Special attention has been given to coexistence with Mithra and Magna Mater.   *S. P. Tutundžić*

72655 SETTGAST, Jürgen, Ein anthropoider Sarkophagdeckel der 19. Dynastie, *Jahrbuch Preussischer Kulturbesitz*, Berlin 10 (1972), 245-248, with 2 pl.

Publication of the anthropoid lid of a sarcophagus, made of rose granite and found at Asyût (Berlin, Inv. no. 1/72). The anepigraph sarcophagus itself is lost. The inscription on the lid mentions the overseer of the granaries of Upper and Lower Egypt Sa-Iset, who was the son of Keni and is known to have lived in the time of Ramses II.

72656 SEVERAL, Michael W., Reconsidering the Egyptian Empire in Palestine during the Amarna Period, *Palestine Exploration Quarterly*, London 104 (1972), 123-133.

The author reconsiders the situation in Palestine during the Amarna Period, alleged to be disastrous. The Amarna Letters state four problems: *a.* intercity conflict; *b.* Hapiru/SA.GAZ conflict, though the word Hapiru may have been used as a synonym for one's foes; *c.* disruption of trade and communications; *d.* disregard of imperial orders and bureaucratic incompetence and corruption — but no loss of legitimacy of the power.

Of these four points only *c.* is unique to the letters, the others being recurrent problems in the Near East. The author argues that there was in fact no collapse of the Egyptian empire in this period (compare our number 70206), and that it was only afterwards that the decline began.

72657 SHEIKHOLESLAMI, Cynthia May, A New Chronology for Dynasties XXII and XXIII and its Consequences for Egyptian History, *Newsletter ARCE* No. 80 (January 1972), 40.

Abstract of a paper.
A proposal for a new co-regency in the middle of the XXIInd Dynasty (rival kings Takelot II and Pedubast) and rival Theban High Priests (Osorkon and Harsiese II), with chronological consequences for the later reigns of Dyn. XXII and XXIII.

L. M. J. Zonhoven

72658 SHORE, A. F., A Drinking-Cup with Demotic Inscription, *The British Museum Quarterly*, London 36 (1971-1972), 16-19, with 1 pl.

Study of a bronze bowl in the British Museum (No. 57370) and its Demotic inscription, dated in year 6 of Vespasianus (= A.D. 73). According to the text the cup was dedicated to Isis by members of a guild who used to carry the statue of the goddess on their shoulders during their ceremonies.

72659 SHORE, A. F., Fragment of a Decorated Leather Binding from Egypt, *The British Museum Quarterly*, London 36 (1971-1972), 19-23, with 1 fig. and 1 pl.

The author studies the fragments of a detached back cover of a binding in the Department of Egyptian Antiquities, The British Museum No. 67080.

72660 SHORE, A. F., Portrait Painting from Roman Egypt, London, The Trustees of the British Museum, 1972 (14.1 × 21.7 cm; 32 p., 20 pl. [4 in colour], ill. on cover).

This is a second edition of a handbook to the mummy portraits in the British Museum; for the first edition cfr our abstract no. 61776.
The text discusses the recovery and provenance of the portraits, their date, the hairstyle, jewellery and dress, the people depicted, as well as style, technique and purpose of the objects. As regards the latter, the author agrees with Petrie's suggestion that they had been placed around the open court of a house, their use for funerary purposes probably being only secondary; in this respect they may have been quite different from the mummy masks.

SHORE, A. F., see also our number 72257.

SHURINOVA, R. D., see our number 72332.

72661 SIJPESTEIJN, P. J., Gynaecologische aspecten van de Papyrus Ebers, Amsterdam, Philips-Duphar Nederland n.v., [1972] (21.8 × 31 cm.; 100 p., [in box], 1 map, 3 fig., 84 ill. [47 in colour]).

In the first section the author deals with Egyptian medicine in general, mainly as it was known to classical authors.
There follows in 8 sections a study of the gynaecological part of Pap. Ebers, each passage with a representation of the hieratic text, a (very bad) transcription, and a translation with some comments. Moreover, each section gives some information concerning the papyrus. This is completed in section 10 and followed by short notes on other medical papyri.
The illustrations, mainly depicting objects from the Leiden Museum, in general have no connection with the subject of the text.

72662 SILVERMAN, David P., An Old Kingdom Statue in the Oriental Institute, *Newsletter ARCE* No. 83 (October 1972), 31.

Abstract of a paper.
A seated male statue in the Oriental Institute Chicago assigned to the Middle Kingdom is redated to the Old Kingdom.

L. M. J. Zonhoven

72663 SIMPSON, William Kelly, Acquisitions in Egyptian and Ancient Near Eastern Art in the Boston Museum of Fine Arts, 1970-71, *The Connoisseur*, London 179, No. 720 (February 1972), 113-122, with 14 ill. (2 in colour; 1 on cover).

Recent acquisitions of the Boston Museum of Fine Arts include a predynastic amulet in the shape of a bull's head (Acc. No. 1971.133); a private head of the Middle Kingdom (Acc. No. 1970.441) and the stela of a police captain named Ameny (XIIth Dyn.; Acc. No. 1970.630); a bronze doorbolt with an ibex head (Acc. No. 1970.442); a painted limestone ostracon with the representation of a feline (Acc. No. 1970.599; almost certainly not a cheetah!); a block statue of the XXVth Dyn. (Acc. No. 1971.21); a Saite cosmetic box (Acc. No. 1970.571); and the footcase of a mummy with the representation of two bound enemies (Acc. No. 1971.217; Roman Period).

Dieter Mueller

72664 S[IMPSON], W. K., Ah-mose, called Pa-tjenna, *Boston Museum Bulletin*, Boston 70, Nos 361-362 (1972), 116-117, with 1 ill.

Among the museum's recent acquisitions the author briefly describes the upper part of a pair statue of an XVIIIth Dynasty official.

72665 SIMPSON, William Kelly, Department of Egyptian and Ancient Near Eastern Art, *Annual Report of the Museum of Fine Arts*, Boston 96 (1971-72), 50-55, with 6 ill.

Report of the curator of the Department of Egyptian and Ancient Near Eastern Art, mentioning the activities of the department and some recent acquisitions (see a list on p. 51-53).

72666 SIMPSON, William Kelly, Egyptian and Ancient Near Eastern Art in Boston, 1970-71, *The Burlington Magazine*, London 114, No. 829 (April, 1972), 237-242, with 14 ill.

Among recent acquisitions of the Boston Museum of Fine Arts are a seated alabaster statue of the First Intermediate Period (Acc. No. 1971.20); a steatite figure of Amenophis III (Acc. No. 1970.636); a bronze statuette of a Kushite king (Acc. No. 1970.443; perhaps Taharqa); a kneeling bronze statue of King Nekho II (Acc. No. 1970.637); and two private statues of the XXVIth Dyn. (Acc. No. 1970.495 and 1970.509). For these statues, see our number 72672.   *Dieter Mueller*

72667 SIMPSON, William Kelly, The Lintels of Si-Hathor-Nehy in Boston and Cairo, *RdE* 24 (1972), 169-175, with 1 pl.

Les deux fragments du Caire (1.6.24.11) et de Boston (1972.17) appartiennent au même linteau. Le style, qui a parfois fait penser à l'époque saïte doit pourtant plutôt faire dater le monument du Moyen Empire. On en rapprochera un autre linteau brisé du Caire (JE 26437) au nom d'un certain Nehy, identique vraisemblablement avec Si-Hathor-Nehy. Les deux pièces ne paraissent cependant pas pouvoir provenir du même ensemble.
                                                 Ph. Derchain

72668 SIMPSON, William Kelly, The Literature of Ancient Egypt. An Anthology of Stories, Instructions and Poetry. With Translations by R. O. Faulkner, Edward F. Wente, Jr., William Kelly Simpson, New Haven and London, Yale University Press, 1972 (13 × 20.3 cm.; VIII + 328 p., 4 pl., fig. on wrapper); rev. *BASOR* No. 206 (April, 1972), 58 ([Delbert R. Hillers]); *CdE* XLIX, No. 97 (1974), 87-89 (Michel Dewachter); *JEA* 59 (1973), 255-256 (J. Gwyn Griffiths); *JNES* 33 (1974), 166-167 (K. A. Kitchen); *OLZ* 70 (1975), 19-20 (H. Brunner); *Phoenix* 18 (1972), 204-205 (K. R. Veenhof).   Pr. bound $10

After an introduction dealing with Egyptian literature in general and the techniques of translating there follow four parts. Part 1 is devoted to the narratives and tales of the Middle Egyptian literature; part 2 to Late-Egyptian stories; part 3 to instructions, lamentations and dialogues; part 4 to songs, poetry and hymns.

Each section consisting of a single story, instruction, type of poetry, or suchlike, begins with a short introduction, mentioning earlier editions and translations and signed by one of the three authors. The translations themselves are accompanied by explanatory notes, but only rarely by philological comments, though some notes refer to different translations or comments by other scholars. The lines of the Egyptian texts are indicated in the margin.

On p. 327-328 a selected bibliography to ancient Egypt.

In 1973 there has appeared at the Yale University Press an enlarged edition, paperback (pr. $2.95) as well as bound, called "New Edition".

72669 SIMPSON, William Kelly, Recent Acquisitions in Egyptian and Ancient Near Eastern Art at the Museum of Fine Arts, Boston, *AJA* 76 (1972), 220.

Summary of a paper.

72670 SIMPSON, William Kelly, A Relief of the Royal Cup-Bearer Tja-wy, *Boston Museum Bulletin*, Boston 70, No. 360 (1972), 68-82, with 9 ill., 1 fig. and 1 plan.

Publication of a relief recently acquired by the Boston Museum of Fine Arts (No. 1972.657). One side consists of five registers with various scenes, the other bears 15 lines of text. The part missing seems to be small.

The relief came from the tomb of the royal cup-bearer Tjawy and may date from the late XVIIIth or the early XIXth Dynasty. From Tjawy two statues (one Cat. Gén. 632, the other Brit. Mus. 1459) and a relief in Cairo are known; the latter may be from the same tomb. The relief is carefully described, with translation of all texts. The second register has a scene of a storehouse with a shrine of Weret-Hekau, registers three and four contain banquet scenes, while the text on the verso consists of an address of Tjawy to the living.

72671 SIMPSON, William Kelly, A Relief of the Royal Cup-Bearer *Tja-wy* in the Museum of Fine Arts, Boston, *Newsletter ARCE* No. 83 (October 1972), 32.

Abstract of a paper.
Compare our preceding number.

72672 SIMPSON, William Kelly, Three Egyptian statues of the Seventh and Sixth Centuries B.C. in the Boston Museum of Fine Arts, *Kêmi* 21 (1971), 17-33, with 10 ill. and 4 pl.

Le Musée de Boston a acquis en 1970 et 1971 trois pièces inscrites de même période. La statue-cube de *Djed-Ptah-iouf-ankh* fils d'*Ankh-pa-khred* (Acc. No. 1971.21), en quartzite rouge, a des traits rudes; les pieds et les bras sont cachés sous le vêtement; le pendentif *bȝt* figure entre les mains.

La statue de schiste vert montrerait le vizir de Psamétik Ier, *Bakenrenef* (Acc. No. 1970.495), en marche et les bras pendants. C'est une œuvre de type conventionnel mais de qualité, avec modelé appuyé des muscles et des clavicules.

La partie supérieure d'une statuette de travail très soigné, en schiste métamorphe vert (Acc. No. 1970.509), représente un personnage naophore debout, et proviendrait du Delta ou de Memphis. Sur la poitrine apparaît une boucle de vêtement et entre les sourcils une légère protubérance. *J. Custers*

72673 SIMPSON, William Kelly, A Tomb Chapel Relief of the Reign of Amunemhet III and Some Observations on the Length of the Reign of Sesostris III, *CdE* XLVII, Nos 93-94 (1972), 45-54, with 1 ill.

Publication en photographie d'un fragment de bas relief du Museum of Fine Arts à Boston (Inv. 71403), provenant probablement du Fayoum. Le texte rendu seulement en transcription phonétique, la photographie en permettant la lecture, contient un fragment d'autobiographie traditionnelle ainsi que les noms et titres du propriétaire de la tombe, *ʿnḫw* et de sa mère *Mr.s-tḫ*.

Dans une note complémentaire, l'auteur réexamine les données relatives à la durée du règne de Sésostris III, sans aboutir à une conclusion nouvelle (plus haute date attestée, an 19; nécessité de lui attribuer 36 ans pour des raisons astronomiques selon Parker).

A comparer Hans Goedicke, Remarks about a Recent Acquisition, *GM* Heft 17 (1975), 27-30. *Ph. Derchain*

72674 SIMPSON, William Kelly, Two Egyptian Bas Reliefs of the Late Old Kingdom, *North Carolina Museum of Art. Bulletin*, [Winston-Salem] 11, Number 3 (December 1972), 2-13, with 1 plan and 12 ill.

Publication of two reliefs recently acquired by the North Carolina Museum of Arts (nrs G 72.2.1 and 72.2.2), both representing the owner, Khnumti, whose good name was Khnumhesuf, sitting in front of an offering table. The right panel is unfinished and, though its scene is almost completely a parallel to the other one, its workmanship is of less quality.

The author describes the scenes, comparing with them those of other stela-chapels. The quality of the better panel may point to a date at the end of the VIth Dynasty.

SLEDZIANOWSKI, Bernd, see our numbers 72637 and 72638.

72675 ŚLIWA, Joachim, Egipskie plakietki fajansowe z przedstawie-niami obcokrajowców, *Meander*, Warszawa 27 (1972), 487-503, with 12 ill.
"Egyptian Faience Tiles with Representations of Foreign Peoples".
The author deals with faience tiles with representations of foreigners, coming from the palace edifices of Ramses III. The objects of this kind from Medînet Habu have been described mainly on account of materials from the Egyptian Museum in Cairo, but also referring to plaquettes from the Ägyptisches Museum in Berlin. Mention has been made of the only object of this type in the Polish collections (the National Museum in Cracow, the Czartoryski Collection), of which the origin may be very likely traced back to Medînet Habu (see our number 72499). The complex from the palace in Tell el-Yahûdîya, on the other hand, has been illustrated with the fragments from the Ägyptisches Museum in Berlin and the fragments of tiles from the Kunsthistorisches Museum in Vienna.   *J. Śliwa*

72676 ŚLIWA, Joachim, Egipskie "świątynie słońca", *Filomata*, Kraków 255 (luty 1972), 262-274, with 4 ill. including 3 plans.
"Egyptian Sun Temples".
Article for the general reader.

72677 ŚLIWA, Joachim, Przedstawienia tzw. "ludów libijskich" w zabytkach egipskich, *Zeszyty Naukowe UJ* t. CCLXXXII, *Prace Archeologiczne* 14, *Studia z Archeologii Śródziemnomorskiej* 1, Kraków (1972), 7-43, with 5 fig. and 11 ill., and a French summary (p. 41-43).
"Representations of the so-called Libyan Peoples on Egyptian Monuments".
The present paper deals with the *Ṯhnw* people and *Ṯmḥw*, *Mšwš* and *Rb* tribal groups, who lived west of the Nile valley. The author has based his investigations on written and iconographic Egyptian sources. Like his predecessors, he has attempted to establish the origin of these tribal groups, their interrelations, the region they inhabited, the character of their contacts with Egypt and to give some aspects of their history. In addition, much attention has been devoted to the verification of main iconographic features and the reconstruction of some aspects of their economic and religious life (e.g. remarks concerning God Ash; the practice of "putting on his belt").
J. Śliwa

ŚLIWA, Joachim, see also our number 72499.

SMIRNOFF, K. F., see our number 72630.

72678   SMITH, H. S., Dates of the Obsequies of the Mothers of Apis, *RdE* 24 (1972), 176-187, with 8 tables.

Le souterrain appelé Iséum à Saqqara exploré par Emery, qui abritait des sépultures des mères d'Apis, a fourni de nombreuses stèles qui permettent de reconstituer le rituel des funérailles des vaches sacrées (semblable à celui des taureaux) et de comprendre comment étaient exécutés et retribuées les travaux requis.

En appendice, huit tableaux fournissent un résumé des données essentielles des stèles, telles que dates, noms des vaches, événements mentionnés, etc.   *Ph. Derchain*

72679   SMITH, H. S., The Rock Inscriptions of Buhen, *JEA* 58 (1972), 43-82, with 7 pl., 2 tables and 23 fig.

A corpus of two of the four groups of ancient Egyptian rock inscriptions copied within the E.E.S. archaeological concession at Buhen. Air photographs provide the location of these in relation to the Middle Kingdom fort, and brief descriptions are given of about 50 Middle Kingdom inscriptions at Hill A and Gebel Turob. Their palaeography and the titles of the carvers are discussed, and a complete name list with owner's ancestors given where known. It is suggested that the Eleventh Dynasty names here more probably reflect either ancestors of the inscribers, or else belong to men born about the beginning of the Twelfth Dynasty, and thus do not constitute real proof of the presence of the earlier dynasty. The shelters at the top of the hills round Buhen are seen as watch-posts as against Vercoutter's earlier idea of roughly made fortified outposts.

                                            E. Uphill

72680   SMITH, H. S., Society and Settlement in Ancient Egypt, *Man, Settlement and Urbanism* 705-719.

After stressing the point that at present excavations have not yet unearthed any complete settlement on the alluvial flood plain the author turns to the documentary sources illuminating life in towns and villages. From legal documents of the 4th and 3rd centuries B.C. he sketches a picture of a settlement of casual appearance, regulated by a legally defined and jealously guarded pattern of ownership. The houses of the lower and middle classes cluster around the sources of income of their inhabitants, in contrast to the quarters laid out by the government and those settlements which it provided for the artisans, such as Deir el-Medîna.

Section II discusses the power of the pharaohs, who built temples, palaces, new settlements and frontier towns. Section III deals with the Egyptian ideas of the nature of their world as reflected in the temple, the pyramid complex and the towns.

SMITH, Harry S., see also our number 72619.

72681 SMITH, Marian Robertson, The Kinds of Coptic Loan-Words Yet Remaining in Colloquial Egyptian, *Newsletter ARCE* No. 83 (October 1972), 32-33.

Abstract of a paper.
On Coptic loan-words in colloquial Egyptian, divided into categories : household expressions, agricultural words, words on sailing on the Nile, obscene words.   *L. M. J. Zonhoven*

72682 SMITH, R. W., Computers en de Egyptologie, *Spiegel Historiael* 493-496, with 6 ill.

"Computers and Egyptology".
The author describes how with the help of the computer 35,000 blocks origating from buildings of the Amarna Period and reused in the foundations of the Hypostyle Hall and the 2nd and 9th pylons at Karnak can be arranged.
He discusses the data on basis of which the computer provides the information needed.   *L. M. J. Zonhoven*

72683 SOLA, Francisco de P., Roger Rémondon (1923-1971), *Studia Papyrologica*, Roma 11 (1972), 113-116.

Obituary article, with a bibliography.

72684 SOLÉ, Jacques, Un exemple d'archéologie des sciences humaines : L'étude de l'Égyptomanie du XVIe au XVIIIe siècle, *Annales. Économies-Sociétés-Civilisations*, Paris 27 (1972), 473-482.

Article inspiré par notre No 67050.

SOLOV'EVA, S. S., see our number 72529.

72685 SPALINGER, Anthony J., A Preliminary Report on Epigraphic Work at Gizeh, *Newsletter ARCE* No. 83 (October 1972), 33.

Abstract of a paper.
Discussion of the palaeography of the signs, the discovery of new texts, the correction of Lepsius' copies, and the colours used by the scribes in the Vth Dynasty mastabas of *Špss-k3.f-ꜥnḥ, ꜣy-mry, ꜣtì* and *Nfr-b3w-Ptḥ.*   *L. M. J. Zonhoven*

72686 SPALINGER, Anthony, The Year 712 B.C. and Its Importance for Egyptian History, *Newsletter ARCE* No. 80 (January 1972), 41.

Abstract of a paper.
An attempt is made to place the Kushite conquest of the Delta in 712 B.C. by relying on Sargon II's annals, and a new chronology for the XXVth Dynasty is proposed.
See now *JARCE* 10 (1973), 95-101.   *L. M. J. Zonhoven*

SPOONER, Brian, see our number 72531.

72687 Staatliche Sammlung ägyptischer Kunst, München, Residenz Hofgartenstraße, 1972 (19.5×21 cm.; X + 170 (+ 12) p., 1 + 100 pl. containing 147 ill., 10 colour pl., colour ill. on cover); rev. *CdE* XLVIII, No. 95 (1973), 73-75 (Agnes Peeters); *JARCE* 10 (1973), 118 (Earl L. Ertman).

Catalogue of the Collection of Egyptian Antiquities in Munich, edited by Beatrix Löhr and Hans Wolfgang Müller, with collaboration of W. Barta, Dietrich Wildung, Arne Eggebrecht, Mathias Seidel and Christine Strauss.
For an earlier exhibition catalogue, compare our number 66006. After an introduction, a brief survey of the history of the collection, and a bibliography there first follows a description of the obelisk erected in front of the building (p. 1-2) and of some Assyrian and Egyptian reliefs and sculptures exhibited in the entrance hall (3-6). All other objects are dealt with in the chronological order, from the Palaeolithic to the Coptic Period. Each period begins with an introduction, while special sections with an introduction are devoted to sarcophagi and tomb equipment (90-95) and to Nubia (134-150).
There are enumerated all together 148 numbers, several of which indicate a show-case containing various objects. All objects are carefully described with all relevant data, including a bibliography, while many of them are depicted on the plates.
At the end a concordance between the exhibition and the inventory numbers, with indications which objects are depicted in the volume.

72688 STADELMANN, Rainer, Der Tempel Sethos I. in Gurna (Erster Grabungsbericht), *MDAIK* 28 (1972), 293-299, with 1 plan and 3 pl.

A preliminary report on the work of the German Archaeological Institute in the funerary temple of Seti I at Qurnah 1969-1972. The remnants south of the First Court belong to a palace very similar to those attested at the Ramesseum and the temple of Ramses III at Medînet Habu.   *Dieter Mueller*

STADELMANN, Rainer, see also our number 72357.

72689 STAMBAUGH, John E., Sarapis under the Early Ptolemies, Leiden, E. J. Brill, 1972 (15.5 × 24 cm.; XII + 102 p., 3 pl.) = Études préliminaires aux religions orientales dans l'Empire romain publiées par M. J. Vermaseren, 25; rev. *Acta Archaeologica Academiae Scientiarum Hungaricae* 25 (1973), 422-424 (L. Castiglione); *BiOr* 31 (1974), 79-80 (Anna Świderek).

Pr. cloth fl. 64

Although outside the scope of the *AEB* the book is of importance for the knowledge of the Egyptian legacy to the Hellenistic world. Moreover, it contains references to Egyptian divinities, particularly Osiris and Apis.

72690 STERN, Ephraim, אספקטים ארכיאולוגיים לתולדות השפלה וחוף הים בראשית קאה ד' לפסה"נ, in : המקרא ותולדות ישראל / Bible and Jewish History. Studies in Bible and Jewish History Dedicated to the Memory of Jacob Liver, Tel-Aviv, Tel-Aviv University, Faculty of Humanities, 1971, 207-221, with a map and an English summary on p. XXII.

"Archaeological Aspects of the History of the Coastal Regions of Palestine during the Fourth Century B.C.E.".
Recent excavations in nine sites along the coast of Palestine i.a. show a general destruction in this region c. 380 B.C. The author connects this with the Egyptian struggle for independence. The assumption is strengthened by the finds of an inscription of pharaoh Nepherites I at Gezer and inscriptions of pharaoh Achoris at Akko and Sidon.

STERN, Samuel Miklós, see our number 72580.

STIER, Hans Erich, see our numbers 72190, 72329 and 72779.

STRAUSS, Christine, see our number 72687.

STRONACH, David, see our number 72794.

72691 STROUHAL, Evžen, Kdo stavěl pyrimidy?, *Nový Orient*, Praha 27 (1972), 39-44, with 8 ill., 1 plan and 2 pl.
"Who has built the pyramids?".
Article for the general public.

72692 STROUHAL, Evžen, Rostliny oe starém Egyptě, *Nový Orient*, Praha 27 (1927), 8-10, with 2 colour ill. on cover, 5 ill. (2 on inner side of cover), and 2 pl.
"Plants in Ancient Egypt".
Article for the general public.

72693 STRUGNELL, John, In Memoriam — Roland Guérin de Vaux, O.P., *BASOR* No. 207 (October, 1972), 3-6, with portrait (on cover).

Obituary article. See our number 71654.

72694 STUCHEVSKIY, I. A., Коллективность зернового производства в древнем Египте эпохи Нового царства, *Древний Восток и античный Мир* 37-45.

"The collective character of grain production in Ancient Egypt during the New Kingdom Period".
Remarks on collective labour during ploughing and sowing.

72695 SZCZUDŁOWSKA, Albertyna, Pyramid Texts Preserved on Sękowski Papyrus, *ZÄS* 99,1 (1972), 25-29, with 1 pl.

Full edition of a spell from the late papyrus Kd; compare our numbers 4367 and 63492. The text combines *Pyr.* 269-275 with 266.   *M. Heerma van Voss*

72696 TAYLOR, F., The Oriental Manuscript Collections in the John Rylands Library, *Bulletin of the John Rylands Library*, Manchester 54 (1971-72), 449-478.

See p. 454-455 for Egyptian hieroglyphic, hieratic and Demotic ostraca and papyri, and p. 458-460 for Coptic ostraca, papyrus, paper, parchment, and papyri not described by Crum.

72697 TEIXIDOR, Javier, On the Authenticity of the Madrid Papyrus, *JNES* 31 (1972), 340-342.

The authenticity of an Aramaic papyrus dated to Year 7 of Darius II and published by the writer in *Sefarad* 24 (1964), 325-326 (see our number 64480) was questioned by J. Naveh in *JNES* 27 (1968); see our number 68434. The papyrus in question was acquired from an antique dealer in Nov. 1963 at a low price, and seemed authentic. The writer here discusses five points in Naveh's article and repeats his belief in the genuine nature of the document.   *E. Uphill*

TEUFEL, Hans Christoph, see our number 72433.

72698 THAUSING, G., Österreichische Ausgrabungen in Ägypten, *Österreichische Hochschulzeitung*, Wien, 15.7.1972, 4, with 4 ill.

Preliminary report of the Austrian campaign of 1972 in 'Asâsîf, during which i.a. parts of the tomb of vizier Ankhhor (tomb X) and of the causeway of Tuthmosis III have been excavated.

72699 THÉODORIDÈS, Aristide, Considérations sur le testament dans l'Égypte pharaonique, *in* : *Atti del seminario romanistico internationale* (Perugia-Spoleto-Todi, 11-14 ottobre 1971), Perugia, Libreria editrice universitaria, 1972, 264-276.

The article summarizes the contents of our number 70528. The author discusses and rejects six arguments brought forward to deny the occurrence of actual testaments in ancient Egypt and argues that the *imyt-pr* could contain such a deed.

72700 THÉODORIDÈS, Aristide, In Memoriam Jacques Pirenne (1891-1972), *Revue internationale des droits de l'antiquité*, Bruxelles 19 (1972), I-XVII, with a portrait.

Obituary article. Compare our number 72814.

72701 THÉODORIDÈS, A., Mettre des biens sous les pieds de quelqu'un, *RdE* 24 (1972), 188-192.

L'expression égyptienne *rdy ḥr rd.wy* (var. *ꜥ.wy*) *n*, "placer un bien sous les pieds (var. les bras) de quelqu'un", que l'on trouve dans certains textes juridiques, signifie exactement "procurer à quelqu'un l'usufruit d'un bien". L'auteur examine rapidement à cette occasion le mécanisme juridique en question.
Ph. Derchain

72702 THÉODORIDÈS, Aristide, La révocation d'un acte testamentaire dans le Pap. Kahoun VII,1, *Revue internationale des droits de l'antiquité*, Bruxelles 19 (1972), 129-148.

The author once more studies Pap. Kahun VII, 1 (compare our number 70528), this time concentrating his attention on the problem of cancelling a previous decision. Against Mrsich (see our number 68419) he argues that an *imyt-pr* is indeed a document with the value of a testament. The first *imyt-pr* mentioned in the text cannot have been a donation since it was never executed. In this context he particularly discusses the expression *rdî sꜣ r*, which reflects a wilful action.

72703 THIRION, Michelle et Jean YOYOTTE, Les extraits du Journal d'Entrée du Musée du Caire reproduits en annexe de "Bulletin de l'Institut d'Égypte" (1885-1899), *Kêmi* 21 (1971), 239-241.

Durant quinze ans, l'usage avait été pris de donner en annexe au volume du *BIE* l'inventaire quasi complet des objets entrés au Musée du Caire pendant l'année. Cet inventaire recouvre les nos 26.416 et suivants du JE, volume 4; le vol. 5 en entier et le vol. 6 jusqu'au no 34.049. La présente table de concordance fixe les numéros d'objets année par année avec leur référence bibliographique, permettant ainsi un dépouillement systématique immédiat.
J. Custers

72704 THISSEN, Heinz-Josef, Zu den demotischen Graffiti von Medinet Habu, *Enchoria* 2 (1972), 37-54, with 1 pl.

Verfasser versucht, insofern möglich, die von W. F. Edgerton in facsimile publizierten demotischen graffiti (Chicago, 1937 = Oriental Institute. Publications vol. 36) von Medinet Habu zu bearbeiten und die Informationen die sich diesen Graffiti entnehmen lassen, vorzulegen.
Einige Graffiti sind datiert. Die Graffiti Nos. 86 und 235 werden eingehend besprochen.   *R. L. Vos*

72705 THISSEN, Heinz-Josef, Zum Namen "Bothor" im koptischen Kambyses-Roman, *Enchoria* 2 (1972), 137-139.

Verfasser versucht den im koptischen Kambyses-Roman vorkommenden Namen ⲃⲟⲑⲟⲣ auf den Namen *Wḏȝ-Ḥr*, "Horus ist heil", zurückzuführen.   *R. L. Vos*

72706 TÖRÖK, L., On the State of Nubiology, *Acta Archaeologica Academiae Scientiarum Hungaricae*, Budapest 24 (1972), 305-319.

Es handelt sich im wesentlichen um eine ausführliche Besprechung von DINKLER, E. (Hrg.), Kunst und Geschichte Nubiens in christlicher Zeit, Recklinghausen, 1970. Für die Meroitistik kommt dabei S. 306 f. über die Ausgrabungen von Musawwarat es Sufra in Frage (vgl. unsere Nr. 70265).
                          Inge Hofmann

72707 TÖRÖK, L., A Special Group of Meroitic Property Marks from the 1st to 2nd Centuries A.D., *MNL* No. 10 (Juillet 1972), 35-44, with 3 pl.

Die hier behandelte Gruppe von "Eigentumsmarken" findet sich auf Gegenständen aus 1. königlichen Begräbnisstätten, als königliche Zeichen; 2. nicht-königlichen Begräbnisstätten, als königliche Zeichen; 3. nicht-königlichen Begräbnisstätten, als nicht-königliche Zeichen. Die Gegenstände aus 1. und 2. stammen aus dem königlichen Besitz und sind bei 2. als Geschenke zu werten, da zudem die meisten Zeichen auf Amphoren angebracht sind. Die 3. Gruppe verwendet die Zeichen ohne die königlichen Attribute (Königsring, *wȝś*-Szepter). Die "Eigentumsmarken" sind nur für eine kurze Periode belegt, und zwar auf Gegenständen, die hellenistischen Einfluß verraten.   *Inge Hofmann*

72708 TOSI, Mario, La cappella di Maia, Torino, Edizioni d'Arte Fratelli Pozzo, 1972 (22 × 28 cm.; 41 p., frontispiece, 1 plan, 29 ill. [3 in colour], colour ill. on cover) = Quaderno n. 4 del Museo Egizio di Torino (2a edizione).

Second, slightly revised edition of our number 69607. Particularly the illustration has been renewed and enlarged.

72709 TOSI, Mario, Una stirpe di pittori a Tebe, [Torino], Edizione d'Arte Fratelli Pozzo, [1972] (22 × 28 cm.; 39 p., frontispiece, 25 ill. [5 in colour], 2 colour ill. on cover) = Quaderno n. 7 del Museo Egizio di Torino.

After a description of the village of the necropolis workmen at Deir el-Medîneh and its population the author discusses a family of painters of which the first known member was Apy (c. 1330 B.C.). The family is attested by stelae and other sources and consists of Apy's son Pay, the grandsons Parahotep, Paraemheb and Nebre, and several members of the following generations. The author discusses the technique of wall painting, describes "a working day", and deals with the tomb of Nakhtamon, son of Nebre (no. 335) in which relatives of the owner are depicted. All this is illustrated from objects in the Turin Museum.
The last section describes the decline of the village, while two appendixes discuss the genealogy of the family and translate the hymn to Shu of stela Turin CGT no. 50042.

72710 TOSI, Mario and Alessandro ROCCATI, Stela e altre epigrafi di Deir el Medina n. 50001 – n. 50262, Torina, Edizioni d'Arte Fratelli Pozzo, [1972] (24.6 × 33 cm.; 364 p., 1 map, 1 plan and 280 ill.); series: Catalogo del Museo Egizio di Torino. Serie Seconda - Collezioni. Volume I; rev. *BiOr* 31 (1974), 251-252 (Dominique Valbelle); *CdE* XLVIII, No 95 (1973), 97-99 (Herman de Meulenaere); *Studi Piemontesi* 1 (1972), 211-213 (Enrichetta Leospo).   Pr. L. 20,000

In their introduction to this catalogue of stelae etc. from Deir el-Medîna the authors describe the valley, the village and its inhabitants, its houses and its necropolis, the organisation of the work in the tombs, school and culture in the village; all together constituting the surroundings from where the stelae and other inscribed material here published originated. They also discuss the fire in most of the tombs, which cannot be ascribed to a particular period. After some remarks about history and abandonment of the village the authors deal with the excavations in the valley and the way in which the objects came to the Turin Museum — partly through the collection Drovetti and partly by the excavations of Schiaparelli. At the end a list of the principal tombs in the valley (cfr the map on p. 28-29).
The catalogue itself contains a careful description with all data such as provenance, material, colour, etc., of each of the

262 stelae and other inscribed material, mostly fragments. All texts are given in hieroglyphs and translation, while important prosopographical notes are added. Each object is represented by a clear photograph.

In an appendix (211-240) the authors discuss the classification of the stelae according to various principles; the religious meaning of the inscriptions and representations; the contents of the inscriptions: adorations, offering formulae, prosopography, language and writing (cfr a list of signs on p. 235); a concordance between the museum numbers according to various systems and those of the present publication; a list of the tombs of Deir el-Medîna with their dates; and a chronological table of the pharaohs of the New Kingdom.

There are indexes to pharaohs and viziers, to private persons, to titles and to toponyms.

72711 T[OURNAY], R., In Memoriam. Le Père Roland de Vaux, *Revue Biblique*, Paris 79 (1972), 5-6, with portrait.

Obituary article. Compare our number 71654.

72712 TRAN TAM TINH, V., Le culte des divinités orientales en Campanie en dehors de Pompéi, de Stabies et d'Herculanum,' Leiden, E. J. Brill, 1972 (15.5 × 24 cm; XXII + 261 p., 2 plans, 1 map, 73 pl.) = Études préliminaires aux religions orientales dans l'empire romain publiées par M. J. Vermaseren, 27.

Pr. cloth fl. 120

Sequel to our numbers 64492 and 71570.

From this volume chapter I may be mentioned since it discusses the cult of Isis and Serapis in the various centres of Campania. The catalogue of documents on p. 49-84.

72713 TRAUNECKER, Claude, Données d'hydrogéologie et de climatologie du site de Karnak, *Kêmi* 21 (1971), 177-196, with 9 fig.

Suite de notre No 70533.

Un graphique enregistre les niveaux de la nappe phréatique, de juin 1969 à juin 1970; il confirme l'indépendance de la zone du temple par rapport au Nil, l'influence qu'exerce la rive Est irriguée et le "retard" des eaux du Lac sacré. Le relief de ce dernier varie beaucoup et influence la morphologie du site, remarquablement constante néanmoins. Un autre graphique éclaire les différences de régime, pouvant se réduire à quatre types, entre le Lac et ses environs. Des manuscrits de Legrain permettent la comparaison entre le mouvement actuel de la nappe et celui de 1900. L'irrigation pérenne réduit l'amplitude et a ramené la cote maximum de 74 à 72,6, asséchant certaines fondations. Les caractères chimiques des eaux, relativement réguliers, se précisent. Relevons, parmi les observations climatologiques, que les variations de température se manifestent jusqu'à 50 cm de profondeur. 　　　　　　　　*J. Custers*

72714　TRAUNECKER, Claude, Observations sur la dégradation des grès des temples de Karnak, *Kêmi* 21 (1971), 197-215, with 9 ill. and 5 fig.

Les observations climatologiques et hydrologiques ainsi que des travaux de fouilles ont fourni l'occasion d'étudier la dégradation des grès de Karnak. On distingue trois groupes de zones, d'ailleurs très irrégulières : le sous-sol, une bande brune, encore mal connue, dans les parties hautes, enfin et surtout la base des murs. Seules certaines pierres montrent des cristallisations. Le véritable danger semble provenir moins de la nappe phréatique que du contact avec la frange capillaire. Il suffit à l'humidité, pour se propager, d'un contact partiel avec un bloc exposé par une surface à l'évaporation diurne. Le sol battu et stabilisé à la chaux par les Anciens, ou couvert d'une pellicule d'argile, présentent à la remontée de l'eau un obstacle réel. Ce dernier doit pourtant être total pour isoler efficacement. Les recherches de cet ordre devront être poursuivies. On envisagerait l'étanchement des bases de murs par électro-osmose, et même par endroits un nettoyage aux ultra-sons. 　　　　　　　　*J. Custers*

72715　TRAUNECKER, Claude, Les rites de l'eau à Karnak d'après les textes de la rampe de Taharqa, *BIFAO* 72 (1972), 195-236, with 8 fig. (2 folded) and 2 pl.

The author publishes the texts on the stone walls along the slope recently discovered in front of the 1st pylon of Karnak (cfr our number 72404), in which the name of the builder, Taharqa, has been replaced by that of Psammetichus II. Taharqa's buildings here may be connected with the exceptionally high inundation of his year 6.
After a translation with comments of the texts the author discusses the provenance of the water used for libations and offerings, suggesting that it was drawn from the quay and carried in *nmst*-vessels with theomorphic lids (the heads of a ram, a woman and a falcon). The type of vessel is amply discussed.
Scenes of the procession carrying the water vessels of the god are rare; those in the temples give a symbolic representation of the ritual, while in some Theban tombs there occurs a more realistic picture (cfr our number 70489). Descriptions of water processions are preserved in classical sources; the ritual itself

is mentioned in the Edfu temple. It may have been connected with the New Year festival, while Plutarchus mentions the Theban tradition in an Osirian context.

72716   Treasures of Tutankhamun. Sponsored by the Trustees of the British Museum, The Times and the Sunday Times. Held at the British Museum 1972, [London, 1972] (21 × 24 cm.; 144 p., 1 map, 1 plan, 5 fig., 101 ill., 16 colour ill. on cover); rev. *Times Literary Supplement*, October 18, 1974, 1170 (T. G. H. James).

Catalogue of the exhibition of 50 objects from the tomb of Tutankhamun, with a foreword by Lord Trevelyan and an introduction by I. E. S. Edwards, the author.
There are two general chapters, one containing a survey of the history of the period and, particularly, the reign of Tutankhamun himself, the other a description of the tomb and its discovery. The second part contains the catalogue itself. Each of the 50 objects is depicted, sometimes also in detail, and extensively discussed, while the measures and bibliographical notes have been added.
The same work, under the author's own name, has been published by The Viking Press in 1973 (Pr. cloth $14) and by Michael Joseph (£3).

72717   TRIGGER, B. G. — J. LECLANT, In Memoriam André Heyler. 1924-1971, *MNL* No. 9 (June 1972), 1-3.

Obituary notice, with list of publications on p. 4-5. Compare our number 72813.

72718   TUFNELL, Olga, William Foxwell Albright. 1891-1971, *Palestine Exploration Quarterly*, London 104 (1972), 75.

Obituary article. Compare our number 71650.

72719   UPHILL, E. P., The Bibliography of Walter Bryan Emery (1903-1971), *JEA* 58 (1972), 296-299.

A list of all the works published in Professor Emery's lifetime, numbering 82 items, and consisting of 11 books, 1 lecture, 65 articles and preliminary archaeological reports, 4 reviews and 1 obituary. It is emphasized, however, that in view of the vast corpus of unpublished work that he left, the list of publications will eventually be much longer, particularly in the section of large works.   *E. Uphill*

72720   UPHILL, Eric P., A Bibliography of Sir William Matthew Flinders Petrie (1853-1942), *JNES* 31 (1972), 356-379.

A complete list of the published works of Flinders Petrie numbering 102 books, 7 parts of other books, 14 exhibition catalogues, 11 miscellaneous works, 3 printed lectures, 9 sets of encyclopaedia articles, 410 articles on Near Eastern and European archaeology etc., 388 reviews, 3 editorial forewords, 5 obituaries, 49 bibliographies, 6 notes and news; total 1024 items. Indications are also given of where to find unpublished material as well. *E. Uphill*

72721 UPHILL, Eric, The Concept of the Egyptian Palace as a "Ruling Machine", *Man, Settlement and Urbanism* 721-734, with 1 plan, 1 fig. and 3 pl.

Although the pharaohs, being not only the absolute rulers of the country but also divinities on earth, had enormous palaces, as its stone replica within Djeser's enclosure wall demonstrates, relatively little is known of them. The author presents a vivid description of the only well known residence, the complex of Medînet Habu with its palaces, houses, roads and temples, in order to show how the architecture created a feeling of awe in the mind of the subjects through its architectural illusions.

UPHILL, Eric P., see also our number 72172.

72722 VALBELLE, Dominique, Le naos de Kasa au Musée de Turin, *BIFAO* 72 (1972), 179-194, with 1 ill., 5 fig. (2 folded) and 4 pl.

Study of the well known painted wooden naos of the necropolis workman Kasa in the Turin Museum.
After listing previous publications the author presents a description of the naos and its scenes, followed by the translations of the texts with comments. The exact provenance of the object, one of the few wooden naoi preserved, is unknown; it may have been from the house of the owner or one of the chapels of Deir el-Medîna. Its original contents are equally unknown. The naos is dedicated to Anukis and to the entire triad of Elephantine, but it is uncertain whether this means that Kasa came from that city.

72723 VALBELLE, Dominique, Ouchebtis de Deir el-Médineh, [Le Caire], Publications de l'Institut français d'Archéologie orientale, 1972 (24.5 × 31.7 cm.; VI + 87 p., 31 pl. [one folded] containing a map, drawings and photographs) = Documents de Fouilles, 15.

The author publishes the shawabtis found at Deir el-Medîna by the French excavators, excluding those which then already were in the museums and collections since their provenance is mostly uncertain.
The catalogue consists of two groups of shawabtis, 72 from the New Kingdom and 86 from the Third Intermediate Period.

Several of them are known in more than one copy, in some cases even hundreds, which the author calls a "troop". The objects of the first group are arranged in an alphabetical order, while 6 instances at present in the Louvre Museum are added at the end (nos 67-72); those of the second group are again arranged alphabetically after the name of the owner. Each statuette is carefully described, with mention of its type, material, size, technique, provenance, etc., as well as its inscription and references to the bibliography. Moreover, the plates contain a photograph and/or a facsimile of the text.

In the introduction the author discusses types of shawabtis, material (either wood, terra cotta or faience), fabrication and epigraphy. In a separate section (p. 17-25) she deals with the historical and topographical context, indicating i.a. that the necropolis was intensively used during the Third Intermediate Period by people from the middle classes, lower priests and scribes, who are hardly identifiable from elsewhere.

Indexes of names and titles on p. 81-84.

VALLAT, François, see our number 72794.

72724 VALLOGGIA, Michel, Une stèle égyptienne du Musée d'art et d'histoire de Genève, *Genava*, Genève 20 (1972), 55-60, with 1 ill.

Publication of a stela recently acquired (No. inv. 19583), of unknown provenance. The quite common text mentions Hathor of *Tp-iḥw* (Atfîḥ), The stela is to be dated between the mid XIIth and the early XIIIth Dynasties.

72725 VANDERLIP, Vera Frederika, The Four Greek Hymns of Isidorus and the Cult of Isis, Toronto, A. M. Hakkert Ltd., 1972 (23 × 30.5 cm.; XVI + 108 p., 15 pl.) = American Studies in Papyrology, 12; rev. *JEA* 60 (1974), 284-285 (J. Gwyn Griffiths).

Study on the four Greek Isis hymns of Isidorus found by the Italian excavators on the temple of Medinet Madi in 1935. For an abstract, compare our number 66590.

Although mainly a discussion of the Greek texts and thus outside the scope of the *AEB*, chapters 3 and 5, on the spread of the Isis cult under the early Ptolemies and Isis' characterization in the aretologies, are of importance to the study of the later development of Egyptian religion.

72726 VANDIER, Jacques, Champollion et le Louvre. A propos du cent cinquantième anniversaire du déchiffrement des hiéro-glyphes, *La Revue du Louvre et des Musées de France*, Paris 22 (1972), 419-422, with 3 ill.

Lecture held at the occasion of the inauguration of the renewed Egyptian gallery in the Louvre Museum, in which the author describes the role of Champollion for the Egyptian collection.

72727 VANDIER, Jacques, L'intronisation de Nitocris, ZÄS 99,1 (1972), 29-33, with 2 fig. and 1 pl.

Publication intégrale du bas-relief Louvre E. 26905; grès, hauteur 27 cm, largeur 105 cm, originaire de Karnak (?). Ce qui reste des scènes nous montre le "baptème", et l'accueil par Amon. L'auteur rapproche le relief de la *stèle de l'adoption*, voir notre No 64076.   *M. Heerma van Voss*

72728 VANDIER, Jacques, Nouvelles acquisitions. Musée du Louvre. Département des Antiquités Égyptiennes, *La Revue du Louvre et des Musées de France*, Paris 22 (1922), 89-102, with 30 ill. and 185-192, with 15 ill.

Description of recent acquisitions by the Louvre Museum, among which we mention (in part 1): objects from the excavations on the Isle of Sai; a talisman of wax representing a dog trampling a man who is lying on his back (E. 27079); a "soul house" (E. 26927), representing a courtyard with an offering table and what may be a false door (First Intermediate Period or XIth Dynasty); the large wooden statue of Hapidjefa (cfr our number 71587).
In the second part are described : a relief representing Ramses II offering to Horus, shaped as a falcon-headed sphinx (E. 26918); a vessel in the form of an ibex (E. 26924), from the New Kingdom; twelve terra cotta figurines, from the collection Fouquet; the limestone statue of a female follower of Isis, from the early 4th century A. D. (E. 26928).
For other acquisitions, see p. 539.

72729 VANDIER, Jacques, La statuette-bloc de Padikhonsou, *RdE* 24 (1972), 193-200, with 1 pl. and 1 ill.

Publication d'une statue bloc en stéatite émaillée de 0,055 m de hauteur (Louvre E 27070) du *wr ḥmww mdḥw Nḥn* Padikhonsou, datable selon toute vraisemblance de la fin de l'époque éthiopienne. Les deux titres du dédicant mentionnés ici font l'objet chacun d'une note de commentaire où sont rassemblés les exemples connus.   *Ph. Derchain*

72730 VANDIER D'ABBADIE, J., Catalogue des objets de toilette égyptien, Paris, Éditions des musées nationaux, 1972 (22× 27.8 cm; VIII+183 p., 4+831 ill., 11 ill. in colour [on 2 pl.]); at head of title : Musée du Louvre. Département des antiquités égyptiennes; rev. *BiOr* 30 (1973), 218-219 (Birgit Nolte); *JARCE*

11 (1974), 104-106 (James Weinstein); *La Revue du Louvre et des Musées de France* 24 (1974), 76 (Ch. Desroches-Noble-court).

In the introduction the author explains why some kinds of objects have been omitted, such as slate palettes, and others included. She also discusses the use of cosmetic spoons, the occurrence of kohol-jars and kohol-tubes, and the types of mirrors.

The catalogue itself contains 831 numbers, divided into the following categories: cosmetic spoons, toilet boxes and their lids, kohol-tubes and -jars, aryballes, unguent vessels and their lids, unguent or oil horns, mortars to pulverize ointments, combs, hair-pins, kohol-sticks, razors, mirrors and perfume flasks.

Each object is carefully described, with all technical details including bibliography, and all are represented in photograph.

72731 VANTINI, Giovanni, Il nuova Museo Nazionale del Sudan. La più grande galleria di pittura paleocristiana, *Levante*, Roma 19, N. 3-4 (Dicembre 1972), 11-25, with 1 map and 4 ill.

General article about the national Museum of Khartûm, with sections on the salvation of monuments in the Sudân and on the Egyptian monuments in this country.

72732 VATTIONI, F., Studi sul libro dei Proverbi, *Augustinianum.* Periodicum quadrimestre Instituti Patristici "Augustinianum", Roma 12 (1972), 121-168.

Extensive bibliography to the *Book of Proverbs*. On p. 129-137 relevant articles concerning Egyptian Wisdom Literature, on p. 137-138 articles on "Egypt and the Bible".

72733 te VELDE, H., The Swallow as Herald of the Dawn in Ancient Egypt, *Ex Orbe Religionum* 26-31.

English version of our number 71593 (without the ill.).

72734 VERCOUTTER, Jean, Une campagne militaire de Séti I en Haute Nubie. Stèle de Saï S. 579, *RdE* 24 (1972), 201-208, with 1 pl.

Les fragments de la stèle de Saï S. 579 portent encore neuf lignes d'un texte historique parallèle à celui de la stèle inédite d'Amara No 101. Il y est question d'une campagne en l'an 8 ou 9 de Séti Ier contre le pays d'Irem révolté, que l'auteur, d'après les indications du texte, inclinerait à situer dans le désert oriental entre le Nil et la Mer Rouge au nord de la zone des pluies annuelles. L'article livre une photographie, la transcription, la traduction et un commentaire de l'inscription.

Ph. Derchain

72735 VERCOUTTER, Jean, L'Ile de Sai. Exploration archéologique au Soudan Nilotique, *Archeologia*, Paris No 50 (septembre 1972), 62-70, with 21 ill. and 1 map.

Bericht über die Ausgrabungen der Mission archéologique française au Soudan auf der Insel Sai, auf der Relikte fast aller Kulturepochen gefunden wurden : prähistorische, besonders paläolithische Funde auf der Inselmitte, einen Friedhof der Kerma-Kultur mit mehreren Tausend Tumuli und eine Siedlung aus derselben Zeit. An ägyptischen Überresten aus dem Neuen Reich (18. bis 20. Dynastie) fanden sich ein Militärlager, ein Fort, Tempel, eine Stadt und wenigstens zwei Friedhöfe. Aus der meroitischen Epoche stammt ein großer Friedhof, desgleichen aus der Zeit der X-Kultur; während der christlichen Zeit spielte Sai als Bischofssitz eine große Rolle, war vielleicht sogar zeitweise Hauptstadt des Reiches Makuria, so daß die vielen Relikte aus dieser Zeit (ein Fort, Kirchen, Siedlungen, Friedhöfe) nicht verwunderlich sind. Die jüngsten Überreste stammen aus der türkischen Zeit, als Selim I. 1520 n.Chr. die Insel besetzte.

Inge Hofmann

72736 VERNER, Miroslav, Periodical Water-Volume Fluctuations of the Nile, *Archiv Orientální*, Praha 40 (1972), 105-123, with 3 diagrams and 1 loose folding fig.

A mathematical and statistical analysis of data concerning the water level of the Nile between AD. 612 and AD. 1470 suggests a periodical fluctuation of the flood volume. If this pattern is applied to the history of ancient Egypt, it would seem that the periods of high floods coincided with the Middle and New Kingdoms, the Saite, Ptolemaic and Christian Periods, while the Second and Third Intermediate and the Roman Periods were times of drought. *Dieter Mueller*

72737 VERNER, M., Professor Zbyněk Zába. * 19th June 1917, † 15th August 1971, *Archiv Orientální*, Praha 40 (1972), 1-5.

Obituary notice, followed by a bibliography. Compare our number 71655.

72738 VERNUS, Pascal, Contributions à l'étude de la géographie et de la religion d'Athribis et sa région, *Annuaire. École Pratique des Hautes Études*. V^e section-sciences religieuses, Paris 79 (1971-1972), 487-489.

Summary of the author's doctoral thesis dealing with Athribis and its principal divinity *Ḥnty-ḥty*.
Compare P. Vernus, Athribis, in : Lexikon der Ägyptologie. I, Lieferung 4 (1973), col. 519-524, and Chentechtai, op. cit., Lieferung 6 (1974), col. 923-926.

72739 VERNUS, Pascal, Encore une fois le titre *w'b ḥrt, Kêmi* 21 (1971), 7-9.

Il convient d'ajouter, aux témoins de ce titre groupés dans notre No 69630, trois documents fournis par la statuaire du Moyen Empire. Cela permet d'attribuer à la même période le fragment de relief "de Tanis" déjà cité : la statue de Brooklyn pourrait représenter le même personnage. Trois autres documents, n'impliquant ceux-là aucun lien avec Ptah ni Memphis, présenteraient un titre *w'b ḥrt* différent.   *J. Custers*

72740 VINNICOMBE, Patricia, Motivation in African rock art, *Antiquity* 46 (1972), 124-133, with 1 table.

A review article of books on the rock art of Africa, among which our number 65083.

de VIRVILLE, M., see our number 72142.

72741 VITTMANN, Günther, Ein Beitrag zur altägyptischen Namensforschung, *WZKM* 63/64 (1972), 66-68.

The author argues that the name on the stela Leiden V 125, usually read as *Ḥw(j)*, in fact is to be connected with the preceding *ḥtp* to *Ḥtp-ḥw.ì*, "My protector may be gracious". In this type of names *ḥtp* is an optative *sḏm.f.*, in contrast to the common type "the god NN + *ḥtp*", where it is a pseudo-participle.

72742 VOLKOFF, Oleg V., Voyageurs russes en Égypte, Le Caire, Publications de l'Institut français d'Archéologie orientale, 1972 (16 × 24.2 cm.; VIII + 387 p., 17 pl.) = Recherches d'Archéologie, de philologie et d'histoire, 32.

The author discusses nineteen Russian travellers to Egypt, from the archimandrite Grethenios who visited the country in A.D. 1400 to Mme Gavrilov who did the same in 1950, 1951 and 1953. Each chapter consists of an introduction and more or less extensive extracts from the diaries and books of the travellers. The first chapters are very short, later ones far longer. None of the visitors was an egyptologist proper, though Lukianov (chapter 18) has published on ancient Egypt; his journey, however, went to the Sinai.
The appendix deals with the description of Alexandria by the archimandrite Constantin (A.D. 1795). Among the illustrations we mention the caricature of an egyptologist (pl. 12).
Extensive indexes on p. 347-384.

72743 VOS, R. L., Einige eventuelle Fälle der Kontamination, *Enchoria* 2 (1972), 141-142.

Die Form ⲧⲉⲣⲛⲁ wird vom Verfasser als eine Kontamination des Fut. I und des Fut. II gedeutet.

72744 VOS, R. L., ⲙⲟⲩ ⲛⲧⲛ "dahinsterben (weg) von", *Enchoria* 2 (1972), 143-144.

Der in W. E. Crum, *A Coptic Dictionary*, S. 159 b belegte Ausdruck ⲙⲟⲩ ⲛⲧⲛ wird vom Verfasser behandelt und übersetzt.

72745 VYCICHL, Werner, Die ägyptische Bezeichnung für den "Kriegsgefangenen" , *GM* Heft 2 (1972), 43-45.

The Egyptian term for "prisoner of war" consists of two elements — the passive participle *sqr* and a word *ꜥnḫ* meaning "to bind". *Dieter Mueller*

72746 VYCICHL, Werner, Berberisch *Tinĕlli* "Faden, Schnur" und seine semitische Etymologie, *Muséon* 85 (1972), 275-279.

The author connects Berberic *tinĕlli* i.a. with Egyptian *nwt* and Coptic ⲗⲟⲟⲩ.

72747 VYCICHL, Werner, L'origine du nom du Nil, *Aegyptus* 52 (1972), 8-18.

L'auteur réfute l'étymologie assyrienne du Nil (*nâru*) proposée dans notre No 68582. La raison décisive est l'apparition de la forme "Néylos" chez Hésiode, au milieu du 8e siècle. Vycichl dit quelques mots des Libyens du Delta, et s'occupe surtout de l'alternance *n : l*, en donnant nombre d'exemples en berbère, en copte et en arabe égyptien. Au Nil, *līl(u)*, s'apparenteraient les mots pharaoniques *nnw* : "eau primordiale" et *nyny* : "verser de l'eau (sur les mains)", outre le tardif *nn* : "inondation" et probablement le bohairique ⲥⲛⲏⲓⲛⲓ : "sâqieh". L'accadien *nīlu(m)* : "inondation", sans doute apparenté à Neilos, et phonétiquement plus proche que *nâru*, pourrait cacher un ancien nom verbal **naylu*(*m*). Le libyen "λίλυ : eau" d'Hésychius serait une forme secondaire d'assimilation progressive.

J. Custers

72748 VYCICHL, Werner, Sur les noms des parties du corps en égyptien, *CdE* XLVII, Nos 93-94 (1972), 173-182.

Article de recension critique de l'ouvrage posthume de P. Lacau, *Les noms des parties du corps en Égyptien et en Sémitique* (= notre No. 70332). L'auteur discute en particulier les étymologies de *ḏꜣḏꜣ* (tête), *ỉb* et *ḥꜣty* (cœur), *ḥwn.t ỉmy.t ỉr.t* (pupille), *ns* (langue), *ḏbꜥ* (doigt), *nfr* (trachée), *ḳs* (os), *wꜥr.t* (jambe) et *rd* (pied), les termes *wnm* et *ỉnm* (droite) et *ỉꜣb* (gauche) et la négation symbolisée par les bras étendus. *Ph. Derchain*

72749 VYCICHL, Werner, Ushebti. Die Vokalisation des ägyptischen Verbaladjektivs, *Muséon* 85 (1972), 533-534.

The author argues that *wšb.t-y* has been pronounced as **wašb-i.t-îy*, in Late Eg. **wašbēti*, with parallel form **šawbēti*.

72750 van der WAERDEN, B. L., Aegyptische Planetenrechnung, *Centaurus*, Copenhagen 16 (1972), 65-91, with 4 fig.

The author mainly deals with the Stobart Tablets (Liverpool Museum), defending his earlier theories against the criticism of Neugebauer and Parker (our number 69445). His main thesis is that according to the Egyptian theories the speed of a planet is constant over a certain distance, and on certain points suddenly changes; this theory is, according to van der Waerden, derived from Babylonian astronomy.

72751 WAGNER, Guy, Inscriptions grecques d'Égypte, *BIFAO* 72 (1972), 139-167, with 14 pl.

The author publishes 24 inscriptions from Kom Abu Bellu, Tell el-Yahûdîya, Heliopolis and elsewhere. There occur Egyptian names, while no. 16 (pl. XLI) bears two lines of hieroglyphs and a third one half in hieroglyphs, as well as two small Demotic inscriptions.

72752 van de WALLE, B., Une base de statue-guérisseuse avec une nouvelle mention de la déesse-scorpion Ta-Bithet, *JNES* 31 (1972), 67-82, with 3 ill. and 5 fig.

For several years a dossier has been compiled on the goddess *Tȝ-Biṭ.t* in order to show her role in Egyptian mythology, using such material as ostrakon E 3209 of Mus. Roy. d'Art etc., and following Drioton's notable study showing this Scorpion deity was connected with the birth of Horus and was the patron of doctors. An important late period black basalt statue base in the O.I.C. collections, no. 9379, is here treated. The person originally represented is not named, being only called the "patient" (*ḥry-dm*). The inscriptions on the top, side and back are all magical, translations and commentaries being provided, and invoke both Horus and Hapi who brings the Inundation (*Nwn wr*) on behalf of the patient. Much of this is cryptic, using a formula consisting of narrative phrases and fragments of discourse, but is incomplete. An addendum refers the reader to J. F. Borghouts' study *The Magical Texts of Papyrus Leiden*, our number 71075, which appeared too late for comment in the above.   *E. Uphill*

72753 van de WALLE, B., Egypte en de Westerse beschaving, *Spiegel Historiael* 501-508, with 10 ill. and 1 fig.

"Egypt and Western civilization".
After an introduction on the power of attraction of the Egyptian civilization to Europe the author deals with the admiration of the Greeks for Egypt and the Egyptian background of parts of the Bible. He further discusses the role of Egyptian religion, art, literature (especially wisdom literature), mathematics and medicine in the Greek and Biblical worlds which formed the basis of our civilization.   *L. M. J. Zonhoven*

72754   van de WALLE, B., *Rś-wḏ* comme épithète et comme entité divines, *ZÄS* 98,2 (1972), 140-149.

The term *rs-wḏ*, first attested *Pyr.* 331 as an epithet of Osiris, becomes increasingly frequent after the XVIIIth Dynasty, when it is also applied to Amun and especially to Ptah-Sokar. The available evidence suggests that several cults of (Osiris) *rs-wḏ* existed in the Delta, and the frequent association with Ptah-Sokar-Osiris seems to have led to the establishment of a cult center of some importance in the necropolis of Memphis.
     Dieter Mueller

72755   van de WALLE, Baudouin, Voyageurs occidentaux en Égypte (1400-1700), *CdE* XLVII, Nos 93-94 (1972), 183-184.

Article de présentation de la nouvelle collection publiée sous le même titre par S. Sauneron et qui comprend jusqu'ici quatre volumes.
A comparer nos numéros 72296 et 72433.   *Ph. Derchain*

72756   WALTERS, C.C., An Elementary Coptic Grammar of the Sahidic Dialect, Oxford, B.H. Blackwell, 1972 (20.3 × 25.9 cm.; [X +] 84 p.); rev. *Muséon* 85 (1972), 558-559 (Gérard Garitte); *Orientalia* 42 (1973), 460-462 (H. Quecke).

This elementary grammar intends more or less to replace the *Introductory Coptic Grammar* of Plumley (our number 603), taking into account the principal advances in our knowledge that have occurred since 1948. This appears not only from a more modern terminology (e.g., Potential Future for the older IVth Future or Finalis), but also from references to recent literature throughout the text. For more detailed information the section headings refer to Till's *Koptische Grammatik*.
Discussion of alphabeth and phonology is very restricted (p. 1-3). There follow the noun, the non-verbal sentence, the verb and the various types of verbal sentences. The author has added nine exercises, translations into English as well as into Coptic, each preceded by a vocabulary.
As regards the outer form, the English text is printed, while the Coptic is written in a clear and regular hand.

72757 WARD, W. A., Middle Egyptian *nhrhr*, "Self-satisfaction", *ZÄS* 98,2 (1972), 155-156.

The author discusses Egyptian verbs of the type *n-abab*, and arrives at the conclusion that they frequently have an intensive-reflexive meaning. The verb *nhrhr* (*Wb*. II, 287,2), derived from the root *hr* "to be content", must therefore mean something like "self-satisfaction". *Dieter Mueller*

72758 WARD, William A., The Shasu "Bedouin". Notes on a Recent Publication, *Journal of the Economic and Social History of the Orient*, Leiden 15 (1972), 35-60.

Review article of our number 71204.
The author first points to a possible occurrence of the Shasu in a scene from the causeway of the Unas complex, which, if correct, would alter our whole view on the people. He then contests Giveon's conclusions in our number 70209, and, defending a possible connection between *šsȝw* and *ȝȝsw* (cfr our number 68237), he argues that Shasu was a general description of the people the Egyptians encountered in Africa as well as SW Asia. Giveon's statements concerning mass deportation of conquered peoples is also contested.
After providing reasons for his doubting the possibility to recognize representations of the Shasu by their dress Ward discusses the meaning and etymology of the word *ȝȝsw*. In the Egyptian view they are a group of mercenaries and robber-bands, originating from Transjordan and similar to the Ḥapiru further north; thus a social class typified by a military character. Whether their name is a loan-word or originally Egyptian remains uncertain.

72759 WARD, William A., A Unique Beset Figurine, *Orientalia* 41 (1972), 149-159, with 3 pl.

Publication of a bronze statuette discovered with several others around 1955 near Heracleopolis and now in the collection of Mr. Fouad Matouk (Beirut). The small figurine represents Bes suckling a baboon, and depicts either a male deity with female attributes, or Beset, the female counterpart of Bes. The author re-examines the evidence for the Egyptian belief in bi-sexual deities, and concludes that it rests on very weak foundations. The figurine from Heracleopolis represents undoubtedly Beset with the head of a male Bes. *Dieter Mueller*

72760 WEBER, Ein koptischer Zaubertext aus der Kölner Papyrus-sammlung, *Enchoria* 2 (1972), 55-63, with 3 pl.

Der Verfasser publiziert in Übersetzung mit ausführlichem Kommentar den fragmentarisch erhaltenen Papyrus 10.235 aus der Kölner Papyrussammlung. Der Text könnte aus Aschmunein stammen und die Schrift weist auf eine Datierung im 6. Jh. hin. Ausser Anlehnungen an das Johannes-Evangelium enthält der Text jüdisch-christliche Elemente.   *R. L. Vos*

72761   WEEKS, Kent R., Preliminary Report on the First Two Seasons at Hierakonpolis. Part II. The Early Dynastic Palace, *JARCE* 9 (1971-1972), 29-33, with 1 plan on 2 pl.

Compare our number 72218.
The palace was discovered within the townsite. Most of its facade is well-preserved. The gateway consists of two niched walls. The author offers a discussion of the term "palace facade" on p. 32-33.   *M. Heerma van Voss*

WEIDMANN, Denis, see our number 72369.

72762   WEINSTEIN, James, A Foundation Deposit Tablet from Hierakonpolis, *JARCE* 9 (1971-1972), 133-135, with 2 ill. on a pl.

Publication of a rectangular glazed faience plaque (8.4 × 4.8 × 1.2 cm.) in University College, London, No. 16248. Quibell and Green found it in a scattered Hatshepsut-Tuthmosis III deposit.
                    M. Heerma van Voss

72763   WEINSTEIN, James, The Introduction of Bronze in Ancient Egypt, *Newsletter ARCE* No. 80 (January 1972), 41.

Abstract of a paper.
It is likely that a copper-arsenic alloy was employed from the late Old Kingdom down into the Middle Kingdom and then was supplanted by tin-bronze.   *L. M. J. Zonhoven*

WENDORF, Fred, see our number 72578.

72764   WENIG, Steffen, Das Grab des Prinzen Cha-em-Wast Sohn Ramses' II und Hohenpriester des Ptah von Memphis, *Forschungen und Berichte* 14 (1972), 39-44, with 2 pl.

The statement of Maspero that prince Khaemwaset had a tomb near the great pyramid is certainly not correct; Mariette rightly thought that he was buried near the Serapeum.
The author discusses four reliefs from the tomb (Louvre N 518 and E 25497, Brooklyn Inv. No. 37513 and Berlin Inv. No. 12410). The first three bear inscriptions with Khaemwast's name, the second, as an old photograph shows, in its original state, the upper portion being now lost. The Berlin relief, acquired together with Inv. No. 12411 ("Trauerrelief"), i.a. shows a high priest of Ptah, and its style agrees with that of Louvre N 518. Two of these four pieces certainly come from Saqqâra, where the offering chapel of Khaemwast's tomb may have been above the Serapeum.

WENTE, Edward F., see our number 72668.

72765 Werke ägyptischer Kunst von der Frühzeit bis zur Spätantike. Ägyptische Münzen. Auktion 46. 28. April 1972, Basel, Münzen und Medaillen A.G. — Monnaies et Médailles S.A., [1972] (20.5 × 29 cm.; 102 p., 43 pl., frontispiece in colour, ill. on cover).

Catalogue of an auction of Egyptian antiquities at Basel, the text of which has been written by Michael Atzler, except that on the Hellenistic objects and the coins.
144 objects, dating from the Prehistoric Period to the end of the Ptolemaic Period, are amply described, with references to parallels and bibliographical notes, and well depicted in the photographs. The collection consists of the following objects:
9 from the Predynastic Periods, i.a. palettes and pottery;
18 from the Old Kingdom, i.a. a relief and a false door of Djati (late VIth Dynasty) and two wooden statues from the late Old Kingdom or slightly later;
10 from the Middle Kingdom, i.a. heads of statuettes, a headless sphinx of Sesostris III, and a wooden model boat;
21 from the New Kingdom, i.a. a fragmentary head of a statuette of Amenophis III, reliefs from the Amarna and the Ramesside Periods, and a fragmentary head of Amon with the features of Tutankhamun;
61 from the Late Period, i.a. bronzes, stone vases, wooden figures, parts of coffins, a relief from the 4th century B.C., statuettes and amulets;
23 from the Ptolemaic Age, i.a. a mummy mask and reliefs.

72766 WESSETZKY, V., 150 évez az egyiptologia, *Élet és Tudomány*, Budapest 27 (1972), 2162 and 2187, with 2 ill.

"150 Jahre alt ist die Ägyptologie".
Bericht über das 150-jährige Jubiläum der Ägyptologie.

Vilmos Wessetzky

WESSETZKY, Vilmos, see also our number 72193.

72767 WESTENDORF, Wolfhart, Die Göttinger Ägyptologie und der Göttinger Sonderforschungsbereich 13, *GM* Heft 1 (1972), 52-55.

Als Teilprojekt des Sonderforschungsbereiches Synkretismus untersuchen Göttinger und mit ihnen zusammenarbeitenden Ägyptologen besonders synkretistische Erscheinungen in den altägyptischen religiösen Texten als Produkt einer Sammlung und Auswertung religiöser Begriffe. Verfasser gibt eine Überblick über diese Studien und äußert einige Bedenkungen gegen die Situation der Mitarbeiter.

72768 WESTENDORF, Wolfhart, Koptisches Handwörterbuch. Bearbeitet auf Grund des Koptischen Handwörterbuchs Wilhelm Spiegelbergs. Lieferung 4, Heidelberg, Carl Winter Universitätsverlag, 1972 (17.8 × 25 cm.; 80 p. [= p. 241-320]); rev. *Deutsche Literaturzeitung* 95 (1974), 18-19 (Hans-Friedrich Weiß); *Orientalia* 42 (1973), 471-472 (H. Quecke); *Revue de l'histoire des religions* 183 (1973), 212 (A. Guillaumont); *WZKM* 65/66 (1973/74), 253-255 (Helmut Satzinger).

Sequel to our number 70589.
This fascicle contains the words ⲧⲡ̅ⲣⲟ — ϣϥⲓⲧ.

72769 WESTENDORF, Wolfhart, Siegfried Schott (1897-1971), *ZDMG* 122 (1972), 19-21, with portrait.

Obituary article. See our number 71652.

WESTENHOLZ, Joan Goodnick, see our number 72451.

WEVERS, J. W., see our number 72589.

72770 WILD, Henri, Champollion à Genève, *BIFAO* 72 (1972), 1-46, with 14 pl.

In 1826 during a short visit to Geneva Champollion composed a catalogue of the Egyptian antiquities in the Musée d'Art et d'Histoire, which has been lost, and is rediscovered by the author among the papers of Naville.
The author describes the visit of October 1826 at the end of the Italian journey of Champollion and publishes letters by Champollion and others, including one written from Toulon after the return from Egypt.
In the addenda Wild discusses another document of Champollion and the analysis by a graphologist made for Naville.
Annexe I amply discusses the objects mentioned in this "Catalogue manuscrit des antiquités égyptiennes de Genève", which describes 9 stelae, 15 bronzes and 4 papyri. Annexes II and III present the document of Champollion and the graphological analysis.

72771 WILD, Henri, Une statue de la XIIe dynastie utilisée par le roi hermopolitain Thot-em-hat de la XXIIIe, *RdE* 24 (1972), 209-215, with 1 pl. and 2 fig.

Le fragment de statue d'homme assis vu dans le commerce au Caire provient apparemment d'un atelier thébain dans la tradition dite de l'"école du Fayoum" et est datable du règne de Sésostris III. On y lit les restes d'une inscription au nom du roi Thot-em-hat, connu par un petit nombre d'autres monuments, notamment la statue de *Ṯȝ-n-ḥsrt* (*CGC* 42212) dont l'auteur réexamine la généalogie, dans l'espoir de dater ce roi obscur. Il propose finalement ± 730.

On verra maintenant à ce sujet Kitchen, *Third Interm. Period* (voir notre numéro 72379), 485 qui propose de son côté une datation 725/710.   *Ph. Derchain*

72772 WILDUNG, Dietrich, Description et analyse d'antiquités égyptiennes par l'informatique, *BSFE* No. 63 (Mars 1972), 19-31, with 2 fig. and 2 tables.

Survey of the aims and methods of the "Dokumentation Ägyptischer Altertümer". Cfr our numbers 71233 and 71621.

72773 WILDUNG, Dietrich, Ramses, die große Sonne Ägyptens, *ZÄS* 99,1 (1972), 33-41, with 1 fig. and 1 ill.

Veröffentlichung einer Triade in Marseille (Borély 1089); Höhe 10,2 cm. Breite 6,2 cm, Tiefe 3,2 cm, Chalzedon. Die Gruppe zeigt in Hochrelief drei stehende Figuren : Re-Harachte, Amon-Re und zwischen ihnen Ramses II. Die beiden Götter verkünden die Geburt einer neuen Gottheit in der Person des Könings als "die große Sonne (*šw*) Ägyptens".
Verfasser erörtert Ikonographie und Aussage.
                                           M. Heerma van Voss

72774 WILDUNG, Dietrich, Two Representations of Gods from the Early Old Kingdom, *Miscellanea Wilbouriana 1*, 146-160, with 1 fig. and 14 ill.

The pieces here studied are : a head broken off an anorthosite gneiss (so-called "Chephren diorite") figure, now in the Musées d'Art et d'Histoire in Brussels (no. E. 7039), formerly in the collection Scheurleer in The Hague, and a statue of the same material, broken off below the knees, of a striding figure in The Brooklyn Museum (no. 58192). The two heads are very close parallels. The total height of the Brooklyn statue will have been just over 29 cm, that of the Brussels head being 8.3 cm. Proportionally the measures are too large to conform to the classical canon.
The stone of the sculptures is almost exclusively used in the region of Memphis, which provides an indication as to their provenance, while the rather frequent use in the Old Kingdom points to that period, as does the deviation of the usual proportions. The round-topped back slab, which may be connected with the "stèle cintrée" used until the early IVth Dynasty — afterwards again in the Middle Kingdom — and the shape of the wig point to the IIIrd or early IVth Dynasty, while the style of the face narrows this down to Dynasty III, more exactly to the time of Djeser. From the beard, the penis

sheath and the knife in the right hand of the Brooklyn statuette it may be concluded that a god is represented, possibly either Onuris or Ha, and the same may hold true for the Brussels head.

WILDUNG, Dietrich, see also our number 72687.

72775 WILLIAMS, Ronald J., Scribal Training in Ancient Egypt, *JAOS* 92 (1972), 214-221.

Since the role of the scribe in Egypt became vital with the development of a complex state at the beginning of the Old Kingdom it is of importance to know the evidence concerning scribal training. The author has assembled the documents, proceeding from two passages by Diodorus. He deals with various aspects of the subject such as the Instructions, school texts, the contents of the training, the existence of schools ('*t n sb*ȝ), the House of Life as scriptorium, the theory of education, etc., illustrating his survey with several translated passages from a number of texts.

72776 WILSON, John A., Thousands of years. An Archaeologist's Search for Ancient Egypt, New York, Charles Scribner's Sons, 1972 (15.5 × 23.4 cm.; 218 p., 18 pl.); rev. *JEA* 59 (1973), 264 (E. P. Uphill); *JNES* 32 (1973), 349-351 (Miriam Lichtheim).
Pr. cloth $9.95

In this vividly written autobiography the author relates his career, from his early childhood at New York, through his first position at the University of Beirut and his studies under Breasted at Chicago to his work as an epigrapher at Luxor and his professorship at the Oriental Institute. Chapters are devoted to his contacts with colleagues, to congresses, to his administrative and his scientific work, to his government service during the war, to the Nubian campaign in which he played a significant part, and to the recent excavations at Hieraconpolis and the Akhenaten Temple Project. The last chapter contains a summary of the author's creed as an Egyptologist.

WINNETT, F. V., see our number 72589.

WINTER, J., see our number 72482.

72777 WISEMAN, D. J., William Foxwell Albright, *Bulletin of the School of Oriental and African Studies University of London*, London 35 (1972), 346-348, with portrait.

Obituary article. See our number 71650.

72778 de WIT, Constant, La circoncision chez les anciens Égyptiens, *ZÄS* 99,1 (1972), 41-48, with 4 ill.

A reconsideration of the entire literary and archaeological evidence leads the author to the conclusion that the Egyptians have practiced both partial and total circumcision from prehistoric times onward down to the present time.

Dieter Mueller

72779 WOLF, Walther, Vom Wesen der ägyptischen Kunst, *in* : *Antike und Universalgeschichte*. Festschrift Hans Erich Stier zum 70. Geburtstag am 25. Mai 1972, Münster, Verlag Aschendorf, [1972] (= Fontes et Commentationes. Schriftenreihe des Institutes für Epigraphik an der Universität Münster. Supplementband 1), 1-16, with 3 fig. and 20 ill. on 11 pl.

The fundamental concepts of Egyptian art are described and compared with the basic principles of art in Classical Greece and the Western World (see already our No. 2109).

Dieter Mueller

72780 WOOD, Wendy, A Reconstruction of the Triads of King Mycerinus, *Newsletter ARCE* No. 83 (October 1972), 33-34.

Abstract of a paper.
On a reconstruction of the triads of Mycerinus (probably eight) in his valley temple.   *L. M. J. Zonhoven*

72781 WRIGHT, G. R. H., Kalabsha. The Preserving of the Temple, Berlin, Gebr. Mann Verlag, 1972 (27 × 37.2 cm.; 91 p., 24 fig., including maps and plans, 171 ill. on 38 pl., 19 folding sheets including maps and plans) = Deutsches Archäologisches Institut. Abteilung Kairo. Archäologische Veröffentlichungen, 2.

Es handelt sich um eine Darlegung des Transfers des Tempels von seinem ursprünglichen Standort nahe Khor Kalabsha in Nubia zu der jetzigen Stelle seiner Wiederaufrichtung oberhalb von Khor Ingi. Die Arbeit bezweckt "to make as clear as possible the organisation and mechanics of dismantling, transporting, consolidating and re-erecting some 13 000 blocks of an ancient monument, together with a detailed recital of the technical difficulties and the measures adopted to deal with them" (p. 9).
Eine kurze Bibliographie bringt die frühen Beschreibungen des Tempels, die Surveys, Reports und Studien sowie die späteren Arbeiten, die sich mit Kalabsha befassen. Ein Index schließt die Arbeit ab.   *Inge Hofmann*

72782 Writing and Lettering in Antiquity, London, Charles Ede Ltd, [1972] (11.5 × 22.5 cm.; 28 unnumbered p., 37 ill.).

Sales catalogue of an antiquities dealer, containing i.a. descriptions of 14 Egyptian items (all represented by photographs). They are fragments of inscriptions and coffins, a wooden stela, funerary cones, a heart scarab, etc.

Nos 46 to 69 are fragments of Coptic papyri from the former collection of Sir Thomas Phillips. They probably came from the archives of Pesenthius, bishop of Coptes, and date from between A.D. 550 and 650.

72783   WYNNE, Barry, Behind the Mask of Tutankhamen, London, Souvenir Press, 1972 (14 × 21.5 cm.; 205 p., frontispiece, 25 ill.); rev. *BiOr* 31 (1974), 356 (anonymous).   Pr. bound £ 2.50

This is the story of the discovery and clearing of Tutankhamon's tomb written in the style of a novel. The author obtained information from some of the persons involved, particularly Sergeant Adamson who for several years guarded the tomb, and from Lord Carnarvon's son. The occult "occurrences" around the discovery are related but no definite judgement is expressed.

72784   XELLA, Paolo, Per una riconsiderazione della morfologia del dio Horon, *Annali [del] Istituto Orientale di Napoli*, Napoli 32 (N.S. 22) (1972), 271-286.

Survey of the role and character of the god Hurun, mainly based on new material from Ugarit, but also on Egyptian evidence.

72785   YORKOFF, Hildreth, A Mold from Mari and its Relations, *Journal of the Ancient Near Eastern Society of Columbia University*, New York 4 (1972), 20-32 and 81-84, with 2 ill. and 2 fig.

A terra cotta mould found in the palace at Mari i.a. depicts a man leading a stag by one of its antlers. The motif is clearly Egyptian, through it seems not to occur after the Old Kingdom. The style of the antlers is also Egyptian.

The author adds some remarks on the domestication of deer in the ancient Near East and Egypt. Although the ritual usage of the stag is known from the Near East there are no remains of deer from Egypt in contexts which imply sacrifice.

On p. 81-84 a note concerning the concept of domestication and concerning the stag.

72786   YOUNG, William J., The Fabulous Gold of the Pactolus Valley, *Boston Museum Bulletin*, Boston 70, No. 359 (1972), 4-13, with a colour pl. on cover, 2 maps and 11 ill. [5 in colour].

After discovering that the natural gold of the Pactolus Valley near Sardes in Central Anatolia contains small inclusions of platiridium the origin of various gold objects from the Bronze Age could be traced. Among them are most of the objects recently acquired by the Boston Museum (see our number 70556), although not the cylinder seal with the names of Menkauhor and Djedkare, which consists of a gold-silver alloy.

72787 YOYOTTE, Jean, Les Adoratrices de la Troisième Période Intermédiaire. A propos d'un chef-d'œuvre rapporté d'Égypte par Champollion, *BSFE* No 64 (Juin 1972), 31-52, with 4 ill.

Proceeding from a discussion of the famous bronze statuette of Karomana brought from Thebes by Champollion (Louvre Inv. No. 500; cfr our number 67282) the author deals with the Divine Adoratrices during the Third Intermediate Period. After the XXth Dynasty they became sovereigns of Thebes and were virgins. The author relates the story of the alleged baby of Maatkare. He suggests that the tombs of these women were situated within the enclosure of the Ramesseum, and draws up a list of them from the shawabtis which came from these tombs. The series at present known is: Maatkare-Henuttawi-Mehytenusekht-Karomana-Kedemerut-Shepenupet, but some more names may become known in future. Of these Mehytenusekht, also called Mutemhat, is possibly a near relative of Sheshonq I, while Kedemerut may have to be dated to the period of Libyan anarchy (c. 800 B.C.).

72788 YOYOTTE, Jean, Champollion, *Archeologia*, Paris No 52 (novembre 1972), 8-9, with 2 ill
Brief biography of Champollion for the general public.

72789 YOYOTTE, Jean, La localisation de Ouenkhem, *BIFAO* 71 (1972), 1-10.

Wnḥm, a place-name known from Demotic texts and from two hieroglyphic inscriptions of the Ptolemaic Period, is to be sought in the northern part of the Memphite nome, somewhere between Abûsîr and Tirsâ. This follows from the data derived from Pap. Louvre E 3268 and Pap. Innsbruck as well as from Brit. Mus. stela 378.

72790 YOYOTTE, Jean, Notes et documents pour servir à l'histoire de Tanis. I. Bocchoris à Tanis et l'expansion des premiers rois saïtes vers l'Orient, *Kêmi* 21 (1971), 35-45, with 2 ill. and 1 fig.

Trois données suggèrent par leur rapprochement que Tefnakht a étendu sa domination jusqu'aux confins orientaux du Delta.
I. Une stèle de donation le représente en roi et porterait le toponyme *T3-šnwt-n-'Inb-ḥd*, chef-lieu du futur nome Arabia.
II. *Diodore* I 45,2 pourrait garder le souvenir d'une campagne difficile de Tefnakht en Arabie.

III. Ne plus voir en *II Rois* 17,3-4 la désignation d'un roi inconnu "So" mais, comme le fait Goedicke, une allusion à la ville de Saïs, présente le dynaste saïte comme chef effectif en Égypte, du point de vue hébreu. De plus, un fragment de cartouche en *...rn.f*, jadis trouvé à San, attesterait la présence de Bocchoris à Tanis comme pharaon, tout au moins pour un moment.

J. Custers

72791   YOYOTTE, Jean, Petits monuments de l'époque libyenne, *Kêmi* 21 (1971), 47-52, with 11 ill. on 3 pl., 2 ill. and 3 fig.

Un torse royal de bronze, collection R.M., Paris, représente un roi Osorkon : le IIe du nom, d'après le groupement des signes dans le cartouche. Une pièce de faïence aux noms d'Osorkon II "aimé de Bastet", coll. M. Yoyotte, fait pendant au no 8180 du Musée de Berlin. "Une statuette à l'ancienne d'époque libyenne", en quartzite brun, dont il reste aujourd'hui le buste, vu à Paris, montrait un dignitaire enveloppé dans un manteau ; elle portait les cartouches d'Osorkon II ou III. "Encore un exemple de l'étrange titre **mk*" apparaîtrait sur une statuette de faïence (fiche du Wörterbuch) avec le vocable libyen *Šrkn*.   *J. Custers*

72792   YOYOTTE, Jean, Pétoubastis III, *RdE* 24 (1972), 216-223, with 1 pl., 2 fig. and 1 ill.

Examinant le court dossier du roi *Shr ỉb Rˁ* Pétoubast fils de Bastet en même qu'une série de sceaux de forme et de composition analogues à celles d'un des documents au nom de ce pharaon éphémère, tous au nom d'Amasis, l'auteur pense pouvoir dater son règne de la révolte égyptienne contre le satrape Aryandès en 522-520 plutôt que de l'époque libyenne (Gauthier) où de la fin du règne de Darius, comme il l'avait proposé lui-même. Il semblerait que *Shr ỉb Rˁ* Pétoubast fils de Bastet ait pendant un certain temps possédé Memphis.   *Ph. Derchain*

72793   YOYOTTE, Jean, Religion de l'Égypte Ancienne. Année[s] 1969-1970 et 1970-1971, *Annuaire. École Pratique des Hautes Études. Ve section* - sciences religieuses, Paris 79 (1971-1972), 157-195.

Sequel to our number 69690.
Survey of the scientific work of the section during two courses. We mention i.a. studies to the origins of the subversion and retreat of Re after the "Book of the Divine Cow" (p. 162-165) and to the primordial revolt and retreat of Re after the "Book of the Faiyûm" (Pap. Faiyûm, Pap. Bulaq 1 and 2, Pap. Hood, etc.; 165-167); researches into the historical and religious

geography of Lower Egypt, particularly to Pi-Ramses and Tanis (167-173); into some titles of provincial priests (175-178), the cults of Thoth in Lower Egypt (178-182), the hymn to Sukhos of Pap. Ramess. VI (187), etc.

For a report about the activities of the section, see p. 429-434.

72794 YOYOTTE, Jean, [Une statue de Darius découverte à Suse.] Les inscriptions hieroglyphiques. Darius et l'Égypte, *Journal Asiatique*, Paris 260 (1972), 253-266.

The article deals with the hieroglyphic inscriptions on a statue of Darius, in Egyptian style and certainly of Egyptian manufacture, though clad in a Persian costume, recently found at Susa.

For the discovery, see the preceding section by Monique Kervan (p. 237-239), with a plan, a section and 4 pl.; for a description with comment, i.a. stressing the importance of the role that Egyptian sculptors played in Iran, see the section by David Stronach (241-246); for the inscriptions in Old Persian, Elamite and Accadian, see the section by François Vallat (247-251).

Yoyotte presents the Egyptian texts in transcription and translation with comments to their contents. The texts occur on the girdle (titles), the pleats of the garment (extensive titulary) and the base (dedication and a list of names of 24 regions, each in a fortress-cartouche under a seated figure). Yoyotte suggests that the statue is a copy of one that already stood in the temple of Atum at Heliopolis, and dates it on various arguments to c. 495 B.C.

YOYOTTE, Jean, see also our number 72703.

72795 ŽABKAR, Louis V., The Egyptian Name of the Fortress of Semna South, *JEA* 58 (1972), 83-90, with 1 pl. and 4 fig.

The Oriental Institute Expedition excavated at the fortress of Semna South and the adjacent Meroitic cemetery, 1966-68. A dump outside the fort on the north-west yielded informative Twelfth Dynasty material, while some pits proved to be clay quarries. Of special interest was a large quantity of seal impressions from scarabs and other seals naming various forts, from which it was deduced that the name of this fort was *ḏȝir Stĭ* (not *ḫȝst* as previously thought), to be translated as "Subduing the Setui-Nubians".   *E. Uphill*

72796 ZANDEE, J., L'exemplarisme du monde transcendant par rapport au monde visible dans le Tractatus Tripartitus du Codex Jung (pages 51-140), *RdE* 24 (1972), 224-228.

Dans le traité mentionné dans le titre, nettement marqué par la gnose valentinienne, l'auteur montre qu'il existe une étroite relation entre les première et troisième parties, la première décrivant en somme le modèle idéal, dans le monde transcendant, de ce qui se passe sur terre, objet de la troisième partie. Des trois classes d'hommes, l'auteur examine plus spécialement les deux dernières, celles des psychiques et des hyliques, et montre comment leur correspondent dans l'univers transcendant respectivement les catégories du Démiurge et du Cosmocrator (diable). Il insiste également sur le caractère platonicien originel de la théorie. Il n'entrait pas dans les intentions de l'auteur de faire le bilan de l'exemplarisme. Toutefois, il me paraît intéressant de citer ici, en résumé de la théorie qu'il a mise en évidence dans le traîté gnostique une phrase de l'*Asclépius* qui montre à quel point celle-ci a pu être familière aux Égyptiens : (24)" an ignoras, o Asclepi, quod Aegyptus imago sit caeli aut, quod est veritus, translatio et descensio omnium, quae gubernantur atque exercentur in caelo?" (édition des Universités de France, Nock-Festugière, *Corpus Hermeticum*², 326 et note 202, p. 379).   *Ph. Derchain*

72797 ZANDEE, Jan, Sargtexte, Spruch 75. Fortsetzung (Coffin Texts I 348b-372c), *ZÄS* 98,2 (1972), 149-155.

Annotated translation of the second part of *CT* Sp. 75 (continuation of our No. 71641).   *Dieter Mueller*

72798 ZANDEE, Jan, Sargtexte, Spruch 75. Schluß (Coffin Texts I 372d-405c), *ZÄS* 99,1 (1972), 48-63.

Annotated translation of the third and final section of CT Spell 75 (continuation of our Nos 71641 and 72797).   *Dieter Mueller*

72799 ZANDEE, J., A Site of the Conflict between Horus and Seth, *Ex Orbe Religionum* 32-38.

The "unique bush" mentioned in P. Leiden I 348, rt. 4,5-4,9 as the site of a battle between Horus and Seth is to be located on the other side of the Winding Waterway in the eastern part of the sky (*Pyr. Texts* 1377a-c and par.).   *Dieter Mueller*

72800 ZAUZICH, Karl-Theodor, Die Bruchzahlen des Pap. Brit. Mus. 10598, *Enchoria* 2 (1972), 145-147.

Die im W. Erichsen, Demotisches Glossar (unsere Nummer 3305), Seite 706 verzeichnete Bruchzahl 1/64 (Arure) soll vermutlich gestrichen werden und als *ꜣḥ* "Acker" gelesen werden. Es folgen noch weitere Korrekturvorschläge zu demselben Papyrus.   *R. L. Vos*

72801 ZAUZICH, Karl-Theodor, Einige karische Inschriften aus
Ägypten und Kleinasien und ihre Deutung nach der Entzifferung
der karischen Schrift, Wiesbaden, Otto Harrassowitz, 1972
(18 × 25 cm.; 38 p.); rev. *BiOr* 31 (1974), 95-97 (Alfred Heubeck).
Pr. DM 18

The author attempts to improve the decipherment of the Karian
writing with the help of names and some words occurring in
Egyptian-Karian and Greek-Karian bilingual texts. He thus
studies altogether 18 inscriptions found in Egypt and 8 more
from Karia itself and from Athens. The results in regard of the
writing are collected in a table (p. 38).
Zauzich has also been able to add from 8 other texts some
remarks as to the Karian language (p. 30-32). Though many
problems still have to be solved — the 6 different signs for *s*,
e.g., are not yet distinguished in relation to their sounds — he
thinks to have indicated the way to the decipherment of the
writing and the discovery of the language. The latter appears
to be a Greek dialect, though the Karians may originally have
had their own language. The use of the old writing seems to
be due to conservatism, which was particularly found in a
foreign country like Egypt.

72802 ZAUZICH, Karl-Theodor, Korrekturvorschläge zur Publikation des demotischen Archivs von Deir el-Medineh [II],
Enchoria 2 (1972), 85-96.

Verfasser setzt seine Korrekturvorschläge fort zu G. Botti,
L'archivio demotico da Deir el-Medineh (unsere Nummer
67083). Man vergleiche unsere Nummer 71646.   *R. L. Vos*

72803 ZAUZICH, Karl-Theodor, Spätdemotische Papyrusurkunden
II, *Enchoria* 2 (1972), 65-84.

Im Anschluss an einen früheren Artikel (siehe unsere Nr. 71647)
publiziert der Verfasser 3 Urkunden die aus dem Tempelarchiv
von Soknopaiu Nesos (Dime) stammen : Pap. Berlin P 15505
aus dem Jahre 9/10 n. Chr., Pap. Berlin P 15593 aus dem
Jahre 32/33 n. Chr. und Pap. Berlin P 23501 aus dem Jahre
23/24 n. Chr. Alle drei Texte sind Quittungen über Zahlungen.
Besonders erwähnungswert ist die Erklärung wie die ägyptischen
Schreiber die Hälfte bestimmter Geldbeträge berechnet haben.
Den Texten ist ein wertvolles Wörterverzeichnis mit Facsimiles
beigefügt.   *R. L. Vos*

72804 ZAUZICH, Karl-Theodor, Zu einigen Papyri Loeb, *Enchoria* 2
(1972), 149-151.

Die Papyri Loeb 34 und 67 sind Fragmente des gleichen
Textes. Papyrus Loeb 62 und Papyrus Berlin P 15558 sind

Fragmente einer Urkunde. Die Papyri Loeb 40, 53 und 66 sind gleichartige Schriftstücke mit weitgehend identischem Wortlaut. Die Nos 53 und 40 sind anscheinend von der gleichen Hand geschrieben. *R. L. Vos*

72805 ZAWADOWSKI, Youri, A propos de l'"A propos" de M. Galand et suite de ma "Notule" sur l'écriture méroitique, *MNL* No. 9 (June 1972), 9-13.

Antwort auf unsere Nr. 72246. Verfasser versucht mit Hilfe der Phonogrammatologie Ähnlichkeiten zwischen dem Libyschen und dem Meroitischen herauszuarbeiten. Er stellt eine Entwicklung des /r/ im Libyco-Berberischen, Ägyptischen und Meroitischen aus einem kreisförmigen Archetyp fest. *Inge Hofmann*

72806 ZAWADOWSKI, Yuri, Some Considerations on Meroitic Phonology, *MNL* No. 10 (Juillet 1972), 15-31.

In Bezug auf die Transliteration meroitischer Texte schlägt Verfasser vor, Großbuchstaben für die Transliteration und Kleinbuchstaben für die Transkription zu verwenden. Problematisch bleiben die Vokalphoneme und ihre Verbindung mit Konsonantenphonemen. Es wird versucht nachzuweisen, daß sich das Konsonantensystem des Meroitischen in modernen afrikanischen Sprachen, besonders auch dem Sudan-arabischen, erhalten habe. Verfasser stellt ein Konsonantensystem auf, das durch einige palatale oder palatalisierte Konsonanten gekennzeichnet ist. *Inge Hofmann*

72807 ZIBELIUS, Karola, Afrikanische Orts- und Völkernamen in hieroglyphischen und hieratischen Texten, Wiesbaden, Dr. Ludwig Reichert Verlag, 1972 (17 × 24 cm; XXII + 204 p., 1 fig.) = Beihefte zum Tübinger Atlas des Vorderen Orients. Reihe B (Geisteswissenschaften) Nr. 1; rev. *JEA* 60 (1974), 277-278 (C. H. S. Spaull); *Mundus* 10 (1974), 141-142 (Shafik Allam).

Die vorliegende Dissertation ist der erste Band der geisteswissenschaftlichen Reihe, die im Sonderforschungsbereich 19 (Orientalistik) zur Erstellung eines "Tübinger Atlasses des Vorderen Orients" erarbeitet wurde.
Im ersten Teil wird das Quellenmaterial vom Alten Reich bis zur Spätzeit bezüglich afrikanischer Orts- und Völkernamen, nicht nur des sudanischen, sondern auch des libyschen Raumes wie auch der Gebiete von Punt, dargelegt. Im zweiten Teil sind die Namen alphabetisch geordnet, und gelegentlich wird eine Lokalisierung versucht.
Anhang I bietet statistische Bemerkungen zum konsonantischen Aufbau und zur Bildung der behandelten Namen, Anhang II

stellt ein Ostrakon (Stockholm, Medelhavsmuseet MM 14020) mit acht afrikanischen Ländernamen vor (abgebildet S. VII). Abschließend folgen Indices der Orts- und Völkernamen.

Inge Hofmann

72808 ZIVIE, Alain-Pierre, Un fragment inédit de coudée votive, *BIFAO* 71 (1972), 181-188, with 5 fig. and 1 pl.

Publication of a grey-blue basalt votive cubit rod of the Late Period seen with an antiquities dealer in Luxor. The piece appears to join up with another fragment in the Cairo Museum (no. 31.12.22.1.), which may have come from the cachette of Karnak. Together they measure 38.8 cm., i.e. about $^5/_7$ of the complete rod. The author studies the inscriptions, referring to the thesis of Adelheid Schlott (our number 69555).

72809 ZIVIE, Alain-Pierre, Fragments inscrits conservés à Karnak-Nord, *BIFAO* 72 (1972), 71-98, with 30 fig. and 2 pl.

Catalogue describing 32 fragments of statues, stelae, etc., found at Karnak-North and deposited in the storeroom of the Service des Antiquités. The pieces are published because of the occurrence of a name or title. We mention: the names of Hatshepsut (no. 3), Akhnaton (no. 5), Ramses IX (no. 7), Sapair, the son of Ahmosis I (no. 8), Amenirdis [I?] (no. 12), the god Hedjhotep (no. 17), the titles *smdt* (no. 19) and *ḥry sꜣwty sšw* (no. 20). No. 32 + no. 6 appears to be a fragment of the annals of the Amon high priests.

72810 ZIVIE, Alain-Pierre, Hermopolis — El Baqlieh et le nome de l'Ibis, *Annuaire. École Pratique des Hautes Études. Ve section — sciences religieuses*, Paris 79 (1971-1972), 491-494.

Summary of the author's doctoral thesis.
The first part has now been published: Alain-Pierre Zivie, Hermopolis et le nome de l'ibis. I. Introduction et inventaire chronologique des sources, Le Caire, Institut français d'Archéologie orientale du Caire, [1975] = Bibliothèque d'étude 66/1.

72811 ZIVIE, Alain-Pierre, Un monument associant les noms de Ramsès I et du Séthi I, *BIFAO* 72 (1972), 99-114, with 2 fig. and 1 pl.

Publication of a statue base found in Medâmûd in 1925 and preserved in the French Institute in Cairo (inv. no. CAVES IFAO 42), the inscriptions of which mention Ramses I and Sethi I in parallel texts, while in one instance the name of the father seems to have been altered into that of the son.
The author translates the texts, with comments. He also discusses some monuments of both kings in an attempt to define their

"coregency". Sethi has in fact reigned over Egypt without bearing the titles of a pharaoh; the father was Re, the son called a star. The present monument, however, puts both names on the same level.

NECROLOGIES

72812 BRUYÈRE, Bernard : *BSFE* No 63 (Mars 1972), 5 ([J. Leclant]).

72813 HEYLER, André : *BSFE* No 63 (Mars 1972), 6 ([J. Leclant]); *MNL* No 9 (June 1972), 1-3 (B. G. Trigger - J. Leclant).

72814 PIRENNE, Jacques : *BSFE* No 65 (Octobre 1972), 9 (anonymous); *Revue Internationale des Droits de l'Antiquité* 19 (1972), I-XVII, with a portrait (Aristide Théodoridès).